LETTERS
AND
DISPATCHES
1924–1944
CENTENNIAL EDITION

LETTERS
AND
DISPATCHES
1924–1944
CENTENNIAL EDITION

The Man Who Helped Save 100,000 Jews

RAOUL WALLENBERG

TRANSLATED BY KJERSTI BOARD

PUBLISHED IN ASSOCIATION WITH
THE UNITED STATES HOLOCAUST MEMORIAL MUSEUM

ARCADE PUBLISHING • NEW YORK

Arcade Publishing books may be purchased in bulk at special discounts
for sales promotion, corporate gifts, fund-raising, or educational purposes.
Special editions can also be created to specifications. For details, contact the
Special Sales Department, Arcade Publishing, 307 West 36th Street, 11th
Floor, New York, NY 10018 or arcade@skyhorsepublishing.com.

Arcade Publishing® is a registered trademark of Skyhorse Publishing, Inc.®,
a Delaware corporation.

*Portions of this book were published as Älskade farfar! [Dearest Grandfather] by
Bonniers Förlag, Sweden.*

The assertions, arguments, and conclusions are those of the author and other
contributors. They do not necessarily reflect the opinions of the United States
Holocaust Memorial Museum.

Visit our website at www.arcadepub.com.

10 9 8 7 6 5 4 3 2 1

Library of Congress Cataloging-in-Publication Data is available on file.

ISBN: 978-1-61145-181-8

Printed in the United States of America

CONTENTS

Editor's Note   vii

Wallenberg Family Tree   ix

Letters, 1924–1944   1

Introduction to Letters
    by Birgitte Wallenberg and Gustaf Söderlund   3

Letters   9

Dispatches, July 18–December 12, 1944   211

Introduction to Dispatches
    by Per Anger   213

Dispatches   233

Final Letters   271

Afterword
    by Rachel Oestreicher Haspel   279

Selected Bibliography   285

EDITOR'S NOTE

Letters and Dispatches, 1924-1944 combines three sources. The first and by far the largest portion of this book consists of the correspondence between Raoul Wallenberg and his paternal grandfather Gustaf Wallenberg, first published as an independent collection in Sweden in 1987. The letters were discovered by Birgitte Wallenberg and Gustaf Söderlund, RW's cousins, who have written a new introduction for this edition.

The dispatches reproduced here were found in the second source — archival documents reproduced by the Swedish Foreign Ministry, and obtained via The Raoul Wallenberg Committee of the United States in New York, to whom the Ministry had made them available. To introduce them, and to put them into an historical context, the United States Holocaust Memorial Museum, located on Raoul Wallenberg Place in Washington, D.C., has granted us permission to use an excerpt from the Honorable Per Anger's book, *With Raoul Wallenberg in Budapest*. The book was originally published by the Holocaust Library, now the publishing branch of the Museum. I thank Mr. Benton Arnovitz, Director of Academic Publications, for his help. I am also grateful to Mr. Anger for adding a comment intended specifically for this edition.

Nina Lagergren provided the third source, copies of letters in her possession from RW to her and to their mother, the late Maj von Dardel. The latter comprise the final section of this collection. I am very grateful to Ms. Lagergren for her kindness.

The staffs of the Swedish Information Service in New York, The Raoul Wallenberg Committee of the United States — particularly Diane Blake, Elizabeth McGuinness, and its president, Rachel Oestreicher Haspel, who has written an afterword — as well as the Raoul Wallenberg Foundation in Stockholm, and its secretary, Sonja Sonnenfeld, have all been extraordinarily helpful.

Timothy Bent

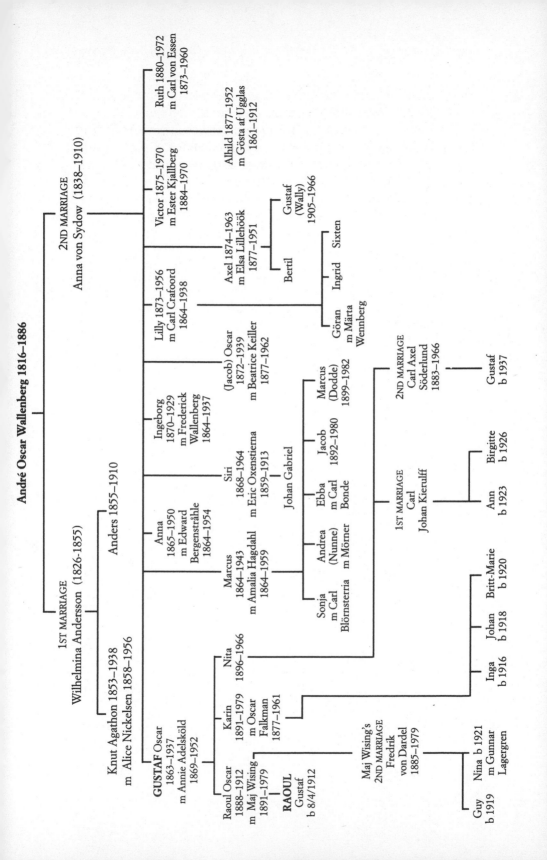

LETTERS

1924–1944

INTRODUCTION

Raoul Wallenberg's story continues to fascinate the whole world, and much has been written about his courage and achievements, though his tragic disappearance — despite all the efforts by so many people for so many years — remains a mystery.

For most, who Raoul Wallenberg was before he went to Budapest in July of 1944 is as mysterious as what happened to him after his arrest by the Soviet army. What drove an anonymous Stockholm businessman to leave his safe, neutral country and embark on one of the most perilous missions ever undertaken — wresting Jews marked for deportation from the clutches of Adolf Eichmann and his henchmen?

A fortuitous discovery made a few years ago sheds some light on the development of Raoul's character: a collection of letters covering his early school years, his university years, and his travels during the first half of the 1930s. The collection consists mainly of correspondence between Raoul and his paternal grandfather, Gustaf Oscar Wallenberg. Raoul's relationship with his grandfather profoundly influenced him. His father, a second lieutenant in the Swedish navy, had died of cancer before he was born. His mother Maj, daughter of a physician, received all conceivable support from both sides of her family. But her father-in-law Gustaf took special interest in Raoul, whose father had been his only son.

Gustaf Wallenberg's father, André Oscar Wallenberg — Raoul's great-grandfather — founded the *Stockholms Enskilda Banken,* sometimes referred to as SEB, the cornerstone of the Wallenberg wealth. The Wallenbergs were extraordinarily successful; indeed, their banking empire has hardly been equaled in Sweden. Like his siblings (he was one of thirteen children) Gustaf was raised to be part of an elite, a member of a family that had contributed more than had any other to transforming his native land from a backward agrarian society into a modern industrialized country. But there was never much outward display of this success. To Be — Not To Be Seen was the motto on the family crest. Among themselves, however, there was an enormous sense of pride. Wallenbergs were brought up to believe that whatever they touched would turn into gold.

Like all the Wallenberg men, Gustaf, the most extroverted of his brothers, was exposed to the banking world but had difficulties adjusting to the sheltered life that accompanied it. Until he settled upon diplomacy as a career, Gustaf was something of a jack-of-all-trades: a naval officer, ship owner, builder of railroads, and politician. One of his first jobs was overseeing the day-to-day operations of the Wallenberg family's Saltsjöbaden railway project. He repeatedly proved his unusual ability to see things in their totality and to remove any obstacle that stood in the way of progress. The Saltsjö railway was completed far ahead of schedule because of the new blasting techniques Gustaf introduced. He even operated the steam engines himself on occasion.

A famous seaside hotel at Saltsjöbaden (which would later play a decisive role in his grandson's destiny) also bears the stamp of Gustaf's energy and character. During the final stages of the hotel's construction, he decided the structure wasn't grand enough and ordered the architect to add another story. This was done. Gustaf's can-do attitude was in part inspired by his experiences in America. He often talked about how much he admired American drive and practicality, which was why he hoped that Raoul would attend school there.

The Wallenbergs were on excellent terms with the Swedish royal family, and during the dissolution of Sweden's political union with Norway, King Oscar sent Gustaf to London to explain the Swedish position to the British, who perceived the Swedish actions as defeatist. So successful was Gustaf that King Oscar immediately offered him the post of Swedish envoy to London. Instead, Gustaf asked to be sent to Asia, a part of the world he had been studying since inaugurating the Swedish Oriental Line. The king granted his request, and Gustaf spent many happy and successful years as Swedish ambassador to Japan and China. In 1920 he was named ambassador to Turkey, where he remained after his retirement.

Gustaf was very much a product of the nationalist bourgeois circles of Sweden of the late nineteenth century. The turn of the century saw rapid industrial and commercial development all over the world. Gustaf believed in looking at the whole picture, and he had a knack for making valuable contacts. He was a tireless correspondent and accomplished at letter writing, a skill upon which he relied heavily and with considerable success. Over the years he built up a worldwide network of friends and contacts. When the time was right he intended to use them to help his grandson make his way in the world.

Gustaf Wallenberg's later letters reflect growing disappointment with the course of events in his country. He composed articles for the Swedish newspapers advocating a more open trade policy, but they were effectively ignored. Gustaf was frustrated with insular, hidebound ways of doing things. He was the impulsive doer of the Wallenbergs, forever advocating reform and change. He found his brothers Knut and Marcus, the family's leading bankers, overly preoccupied with their own projects and worries, and his relationship with them deteriorated. It didn't help matters that on a couple of occasions financial difficulties forced him to seek their help. Their aid was reluctant and coupled with admonitions about how he should conduct himself. By the beginning of the 1930s, Gustaf found himself estranged from his closest family in Sweden and retired, though he was still full of plans. His vision of the world was one of growing markets and steady improvement in the quality of life, a world reflecting the values (for all its flaws) of the Swedish system: relations with countries based on trade relations rather than on military alliances.

Gustaf was a great individualist and completely uninhibited about speaking his mind. This very un-Swedish trait was doubtless a source of irritation to many who could tolerate the Wallenbergs' power and influence so long as it was accompanied by personal modesty. Gustaf Wallenberg, by contrast, was self-confident to the point of being very judgmental of his fellow man. In his opinion, Swedes were more honest, reliable, and capable than citizens of other countries, particularly if the Swedes came from a good family.

His views on women were not nearly as enlightened as his views on trade. They were pleasant company, perhaps, but otherwise calculating and troublesome. Raoul's grandmother Annie, née Adelsköld, occasionally figures in Gustaf's correspondence, but has no active voice in the dialogue between grandfather and grandson. "They just want to display us with the best china in the parlor, where they kill us with their caring," Gustaf wrote in a letter. For her part, Annie created a world of her own by getting out from beneath the shadow of her domineering husband. She eventually moved home to Sweden by herself and devoted her energies to tending the enormous garden of the magnificent villa in Saltsjöbaden. She occasionally went to Istanbul to see her husband, but for the most part lived on memories of her time in Japan and constructed a miniature world around herself with all of the objects she had brought back. When Gustaf visited Sweden, he usually stayed at the Grand Hotel in Stockholm, visiting Saltsjöbaden only on rare occasions. The marriage between Gustaf and Annie was nevertheless regarded as happy by the rest of the family, and they maintained a very tender and loving correspondence.

By the time he was a teenager, Raoul was exhibiting certain of his grandfather's traits: his honesty, his powers of observation, and especially his love of language. Raoul's letters reveal him to be a shrewd and frank judge of human behavior, his own included. Gustaf became increasingly fond of his grandson and increasingly involved in planning a future for him. Typically, he had strong feelings on the subject. He wanted to free Raoul of the comfortable assumptions of the Swedish bourgeois and transform him into a citizen of the world — someone who with the help of training, initiative, and, above all, good contacts would be a leader in a global society. Going to America would be key.

One might have expected differences of opinion between Raoul's mother and Gustaf over Raoul's education after high school, and in particular over Gustaf's plan to send eighteen-year-old Raoul abroad. We know that Maj von Dardel — she had married Fredrik von Dardel in 1918, six years after Raoul's birth — was a strong-willed woman (after Raoul's disappearance, she was the guiding force behind efforts to find him until her death).

But the letters show that Maj concurred with her former father-in-law's thinking. She could even prove less protective than Gustaf. By the summer of 1934, Raoul had been in America for almost three years and Gustaf thought he should return to spend some time in Sweden. But a cable from Maj shows that she gave her consent for Raoul to undertake an adventurous, even slightly reckless, drive through Mexico. Gustaf relented.

The main body of this correspondence begins in 1929, when Raoul's mother and grandfather were busy planning for the boy's future. He was then in his junior year of high school. Along with literature, drawing was his best subject, and he himself had decided to study architecture — as indeed he did — a decision supported by his entire family. These early letters not only testify to the attention lavished on Raoul by his mother and grandfather, as well as illustrating an upbringing both internationalist yet firmly rooted in the family, but reveal Raoul's imaginativeness and self-reliance. He was later to use those qualities to heroic effect.

The correspondence peters out in 1936. Raoul had completed his grandfather's program of study and was anxious to get going in life, helped in part by the contacts in the financial world Gustaf was to give him. Gustaf's death in March 1937 meant that Raoul had to take things into his own hands. These were difficult years. The letters Raoul wrote after Gustaf's death suggest he felt like an outsider among his contemporaries, and that he found Stockholm social life somewhat stultifying. He entered some architectural competitions and eventually became involved in an export business. By the beginning of 1944 he had established contacts in Hungary and visited the country several times, even during the height of the war. Raoul's business activity brought him into contact with Jewish businessmen there, as well as with the ship-owner Sven Salén, and it was through them and his Hungarian business partner Kálmán Lauer that he made contact with a representative of the U.S. War Refugee Board, then returned to Budapest for an altogether different kind of enterprise.

We are extremely pleased that these letters are being published in the United States. The years Raoul spent in America, studying at the University of Michigan and traveling around, were critical to the development of his character, and we believe that the documents will therefore prove of particular interest and value to an American audience. Sending their young men abroad for travel or study had long been a family tradition among the Wallenbergs. It was a way of giving them some measure of the world and of themselves. Nonetheless, no one in this very large family ventured as far, or stayed as long on his own, as Raoul, and the experience had a profound influence.

We are also pleased this correspondence is appearing because it presents such an extraordinary relationship between generations. Until we stumbled on the correspondence — the existence of which we had no clue — we had been unaware of the strength and intimacy of the bond between grandson and grandfather. At a time of crisis in families everywhere, these documents are more than simply poignant mementos of a different age, but testimony to the effect such a relationship can have on both generations. Gustaf Wallenberg, as you shall see, played a major role in who Raoul Wallenberg was to become.

These letters were discovered in collections belonging to Gustaf Wallenberg's daughters, Karin Falkman and Nita Wallenberg, our mother. Those by Raoul are originals; those by Gustaf are copies and generally unsigned.

Gustaf Söderlund
Gitte Wallenberg
Uppsala and Granada, June 1994

BROBY
[DATE UNKOWN] 1924

Dearest Grandfather,

At the moment I am staying with my cousins at Broby. It rains a lot almost every day. A few days ago we went across Kolmården to an ironworks called Näfvekvarn where they make pans, stoves, and all kinds of things. We went swimming there and had lots of fun. We were going to swim out to an island nearby but Uncle Carl said that it was too far. We swam there anyway, and after a while I was going to see how deep it was and put my foot down and scraped it against a rock. I found that the water only came up to my knees. Then I discovered that you could wade from the mainland all the way out to the island. This Saturday we are going down to Lake Vättern, Gränna, and Eksjö in Uncle Carl's car a terrific new Voisin.

Everybody sends their love especially Grandfather's own little Raoul.

[Broby Manor *was located in Södermanland (the southern province of Sweden) and owned by Carl Nisser (*Uncle Carl*) and his wife Anna, the sister of RW's mother, Maj von Dardel. There were four Nisser children, Raoul's cousins, of whom Gösta and Maj — whose married name was von Plauen — will be mentioned subsequently.]*

STOCKHOLM
OCTOBER 11, 1928

Dear Grandfather and Grandmother,

Please forgive these hasty lines. I have a lot of tests coming up soon, but I am expecting to have more time off, and I'll have more time to write then. Last night I went to the golden anniversary celebration at Saltsjöbaden. It was very nice, with beautiful music and singing, which I suppose Mother has written you about. It is too bad that we don't have parties like that more often, for that is actually the only time the whole family is all together. Thank you, Grandfather and Grandmother, for inviting me to the party. I also owe Grandmother thanks for a letter and a postcard. I will write again later.

Raoul

[Knut and Alice Wallenberg— RW's great-aunt and uncle— celebrated their golden wedding anniversary with a family dinner at Hotel Saltsjöbaden. Knut had been Sweden's foreign minister during World War I.]

CONSTANTINOPLE
APRIL 19, 1929

Dear Maj,

My congratulations on Nina's becoming an heiress. I always thought Mrs. Augusta terribly ugly, and because of that assumed she was not particularly nice, but I find that in this case — as in probably many others — I was mistaken. She turned out to have both a good heart and good sense. It was very generous of her to remember little Nina, even though she may not prove desirable on the market. Still — it is rather significant, and will doubtless serve to ease a young girl's anxiety once she is grown and about to choose a husband.

I am pleased that everything is proceeding well with Raoul. We will have to start giving our thoughts to what might most benefit him during the coming summer. If you have any ideas, please let me know. One might be to have him pay another visit to the English clergyman, who seems interested in doing his best by the boy. If you have anything else in mind, however, don't let the idea of the clergyman stand in the way.

It is also time to start talking about his future architecture studies. I assume that Raoul is still interested in it as a profession, and it is one I approve of since it is constructive. The idea behind going to America is that he would learn there, better than here at home, the importance of good organization. I don't mean to say that he should stay there. On the contrary. Just that the experience he acquires in America will give him an edge in the fierce competition that later he will encounter from his colleagues here at home.

I have spoken to Axel about this, and he thinks that I am basically right but that in his opinion a Swedish architecture education is superior to an American one, and that a graduate of the Royal Institute of Technology could easily find employment in the United States. He therefore thinks it would be better to get him trained here and then send him to America to find a job. There may be something to this, but Axel's idea is geared to future employment over there and thus is directly opposed to mine, which is that Raoul would be well prepared for a career here in Sweden. I assume, of course, that you and I see eye-to-eye as to which alternative we prefer, since we would not want to be deprived of the pleasure of having the dear boy around in our old age. I am therefore acting on the assumption that we should investigate the possibilities of an education at an American school. Axel may be right in thinking that the training itself may be better here, and I don't want to underrate the importance of the best possible foundation, but it remains a fact that training is only the beginning. Success depends less on studies than on talent and practical skills. The most studious member of our class at the naval academy, Erik Leijonhufvud, is now a judge somewhere in the provinces, while most of the others have scaled to greater heights.

In the near future we should consider the following questions:

1. whether and to what extent American immigration law presents any obstacles to obtaining an American technical education.
2. whether color-blindness will prevent him from getting a "graduation certificate" from such an institution.

In both of these matters you can get information through Colvin. You could also write Olof Lamm, our consul general in New York, but I think that writing Colvin and talking with someone at the American embassy in Stockholm would be more informative. At least it would reveal whether a general dispensation might be possible.

Later we will have to look into which institution might be suitable and what the costs would be. I want to say right from the start that I am prepared to make any reasonable sacrifice to ensure that Raoul receives good and up-to-date training in a practical field.

My thoughts must not be the deciding factor in these matters, however. They should be taken as a guide. You and Fred are the best judges of Raoul's temperament and talents, and it is up to the two of you to make the final decisions. I have the greatest confidence in Fred's judgment.

Annie and I send our best regards to Fred and Raoul.

Yours affectionately
[GOW]

[This letter is written to Maj von Dardel. Nina is RW's half-sister (today, Nina Lagergren). Mrs. Augusta (Hedenstierna), née von Dardel, was an aunt of Fredrik (Fred) von Dardel, RW's step-father. Axel is GOW's younger brother. As for Colvin, RW's maternal aunt Elsa, née Wising, married the former U.S. military attaché in Stockholm, William Mechtling ("Mech") Colvin. At the time of RW's stay in the United States, the Colvins were living in Greenwich, Connecticut, with their two children, Lucette and Fitz.]

STOCKHOLM
APRIL 21, 1929

Dear Grandparents,

I owe you for quite a number of nice letters and postcards and thank you from the bottom of my heart. Grandfather, it was good of you to answer me so promptly in regard to my suggestions about Nordström's lecture. The tactics you outlined for making N. agree to do it on the whole went along with my own little plan. The executive board of the high school association was naturally most grateful for the suggestion but had already decided to find other speakers for their assemblies in the immediate future. They also thought the fall more suitable, considering the number of examinations and extra work that take up the students' time in the spring.

As you know I've had the rotten luck to get sick again — this time it's the flu. Over Christmas vacation I had made up an even fancier chart plotting my "higher grades," but now all that's a waste because of appendicitis and flu. Three weeks' absence this far into my junior year will have inescapable consequences. If nothing unforeseen happens, I think they may limit themselves to lowering my grade in German, however. Otherwise — as far as I can judge — my grades will be good, maybe even higher in Russian. This year we participated in the graduation tests in Swedish, which was great. The topics were very good this year, as you may have read in the papers. They tried to come up with topics that not only gave the students a chance to shine, showing off knowledge that might be temporary (if they were lucky enough to prepare carefully a special topic and it came up at the examination so that they could get a decent grade even though their knowledge of history might not have been all that good) but also let their skill in language and their feel for logic and intelligent reasoning carry them through. I called mine "The Conditions Facing Swedish Industry and Its Future (Possibly Written as the Inaugural Speech at an Industrial Exhibition)." I started off with a grandiose "Your Majesty, Gentlemen" — and so did all other boys in Sweden writing on the same topic. Since I'm interested in things like that I managed to write a pretty good essay.

[The letter was finished by Maj von Dardel.]

Unhappily, Raoul has caught the flu and is lying here beside me with a temperature of 39 [102°F]. So it is up to me to carry on. The results from his Swedish essay were very gratifying indeed, and I hope a good sign of things to come as far as his work goes this year. He got an A−. The teachers liked what he wrote very much, judging from a comment one of them made to my uncle, Professor Carl Benedicks, without knowing he was related to Raoul. Uncle Carl greeted me one day with "I have to congratulate you on having a son like that." When I looked surprised, he told me that he had run into Dr. Rudberg, who was really very impressed with Raoul's essay! "It won't be long before the boy gives a speech like that in real life." I hope he's right. Raoul is very angry with me for telling you this. He thinks I'm boasting. But I hope that it will please you as much as it pleased me.

We had a lovely supper at Sonja and Carl's. Aunt Amalia had fallen on the stairs and hurt her leg and it was bandaged and propped up on a stool, but she was as lively and cheerful as usual. Otherwise, Stockholm society is beginning to look drained from too many parties.

The crash of the savings bank is the main topic of conversation at the moment, and everyone is talking about Cassel's and Fitger's articles. Why should the state come to the rescue of everyone who put their money in the General Savings Bank? Just before the crash, Mr. Svensson, the director, called up Fred, wanting to buy Kappsta. The Sticklinge proposal for a naval base is probably completely dead now, and Janse's Elfvik would be more suitable.

I have to close now but send you heartfelt greetings from all of us.

Papa's devoted
Maj

[Ludwig Nordström *(1882–1942) was a pro-industry writer and thinker. See letter and note on p. 49.* Sonja *was the eldest daughter of Marcus Wallenberg Sr., and his wife,* Aunt Amalia. *She was married to Carl Blörnsterria. Maj von Dardel's parents had built a summer home on the island of* Kappsta, *located in the archipelago of islands outside Stockholm. RW was born there on August 4, 1912.* Sticklinge *and* Elfvik *are located near Stockholm, the first located on Lidingo Island, and the second a town east of the city.]*

STOCKHOLM RIDDARGATAN 43
APRIL 29, 1929

Dear Papa,

A thousand thanks for your kind letter of April 19, which gave me much food for thought. It was so kind, and contained so many generous offers regarding the completion of Raoul's education, dear Papa, that I want to send you an especially warm thank-you.

First, the summer trip. Raoul has only had a few years of

French, and since it is important not only for his final exam but also later in life, I think a few months in France would be most beneficial. That is not very much time for so difficult a language, but he will learn something, and get a feel for the pronunciation and a sense of the language and the country. He will probably have an opportunity to improve his English later in his education.

And now I come to the very important issue of Raoul's future occupation.

To become an *architect* or a *construction engineer* you have to take four years of course work at the *Institute of Technology*, plus six months of on-the-job experience, plus complete all the requirements for a high school diploma in science. Both professions rely heavily on *drawing, mathematics, physics, and chemistry*. In drawing, he has gotten an A−, and it interests him very much. Math, on the other hand, has never been one of his stronger subjects. His color blindness shouldn't keep him from being admitted to the institute. Whether it might hinder him in his professional life I don't know.

When I studied the curriculum offered at the *School of Economics,* I found that it consisted of precisely the kind of work that interests Raoul more than anything else. The School of Economics takes two years. He might then continue his studies in America, at, e.g., Harvard Business School. I am told that if you have a degree from there your chances of getting a good and well-paying job in the States, and I suppose in Sweden also, are excellent, since he would already have his degree from the School of Economics. The reason I mention Harvard is that it was highly recommended to me by what I heard about Lieutenant Flach. He had been a cavalry officer for four years. In Paris he met Mr. [Pierpont] Morgan and told him about his hope of finding some kind of job in the United States. Mr. Morgan told him that first he ought to attend Harvard. He did, and now has a very good job with Mr. Morgan. I wonder if Bertil Wallenberg may not have also gone to Harvard.

This way, Raoul will have equally good career opportunities in Sweden and in America. Attending the School of Economics in Sweden first has the advantage of making him more mature when he goes to America, and gives him time to do his military service. If everything goes as planned, he will be 20 years old when he finishes.

As I am sure you understand, I have not had time to do any thorough research. This is only a rough sketch.

The family's summer plans have not not yet taken more definite shape, but I suspect that the collective yearning for sun and warmth will propel us toward France. Besides, it is good for all of us to practice that noble tongue. Thank you for sharing our joy over Nina's joining the ranks of the self-supporting.

Well, I have to end now and start hunting down French addresses in preparation for the summer. All these Swedish-run vacation courses are very convenient for the parents, but I still think you do better by going straight to the source.

Bye, dear Papa, and a thousand thanks for all your concern for Raoul. I am sure that he will do you proud.

Your much devoted
Maj von Dardel

I am enclosing catalogs from the School of Economics and the Institute of Technology.

[Bertil Wallenberg was Axel Wallenberg's oldest son.]

STOCKHOLM
APRIL 17, 1929

Dearest Grandfather,

Forgive my not having written a single line to you and Grandmother for so long. In addition to all the interesting letters and postcards from Istanbul, I now have something more to thank you for, namely your offer to contribute to a trip abroad for me again this year. The typewriter does not offer the best means to express my gratitude for offering me the chance to study the languages and manners of foreign countries. As to your suggestion that I do what I did last summer, I think I would find that very useful, but I wonder if a stay in France wouldn't be even more so, since it is a country whose language is relatively unfamiliar to me. If my future studies are to include one or more years in the U.S., I will acquire a thorough enough knowledge of the language and in general build on the substantial foundation of last summer. Consequently, I don't think another summer in England necessary, useful though it would be, and think that I will be able to get by with what I have already learned. The fact that we will have to pass a written examination in French when we graduate also argues for going to France. The requirements for French are as stringent as they are for other languages that we have studied for a much longer time. Since you have already mentioned France on several occasions when discussing the plans for my summer studies, I hope that this suggestion, which Mother already has mentioned in her letters, will win your approval. Except for Uncle Fred, the whole family will be going to France at the beginning of June. I will probably stay in some town in Savoie, at least to begin with.

I have recently begun to get a foretaste of graduation in the form of a sharply increased workload, which is the reason for my lazy letter writing. However, this summer I hope to resume our correspondence. As soon as I have the time I will fire off a more entertaining epistle.

Many greetings from myself and my parents. In haste,

Your Raoul

THONON-LES-BAINS
JUNE 11, 1929

Dearest Grandfather,

I have now settled in with a French family, who seem very decent. It consists of the father, Mr. Bourdillon, a school inspector in the region, his wife, who seems very nice and intelligent, their son, a boy of 16 who will be getting his *baccalauréat* next year, and their nephew, who is about 7. Mr. B. himself is rarely around because he is always out "inspecting." But it's his wife who is in charge of my studies, and you couldn't wish for a more thorough approach than hers, utterly scientific and using terminology that I am used to from school. I think she's trained as a teacher. The son is also very nice and friendly but he's always off at school. His vacation starts in the beginning of July, and we will have more time to see each other then. In addition to the family, there are also four paying guests. First, a boy of about 17 from Paris, second, a young Czech lady of 20 who has been in France a few months and who speaks the language quite well. She is very friendly and nice as well. There are also two Serbian boys, whom I don't like as much. One is 17 but he looks much older, and the other one is older but looks much younger. I don't know anything about the latter because he hasn't uttered a peep since the day I arrived. The other is all the more talkative, however. He's always talking (in excellent French. He has been coming here for three years). What's more, his voice is so loud it would wake the dead. And when he wants to be funny, which is all the time, he raises the noise level to a bellow and from a bellow to a scream, which — at least yesterday — didn't stop until he went to bed about 10:30. He may not have stopped then either for all that I know. Thank God his room is two doors down from mine. I tell you all this with some reservation, since I've only been here one day. It does annoy me, though, to have to listen to the half-baked revolutionary rantings of the Serbian. He goes on and on with great pride and glee about all the strikes and revolts he has seen or been involved with in his orderly Belgrade. When he's not bellowing he is pretty friendly, though.

I left Stockholm on the 4th, the same day classes were over, so I don't know my grades yet. But I'm not expecting any surprises.

The trip went very well and we were lucky to have beautiful weather, except for the morning of the last day. We were joined by a relative, Erik von Dardel. The two of us met lots of people from different countries and had a good time. I'm happy to be able to report that I'm more accustomed to the sea than before. The tendency toward sickness that I always had on voyages before has now completely disappeared.

I'm staying in Thonon-les-Bains, a town situated on the shore of Lake Geneva, on the French side. As you might imagine, the surroundings are magnificent, sort of similar to those of Constantinople, though the mountains farther back from the shoreline are considerably higher and the vegetation is more evenly distributed.

Mother, the children, and I stayed for a few days in a nice little hotel a bit more than 10 kilometers from here. They served the most delicious food, almost as good as the lobsters, melons, and the other delicacies that you treated me to at the legation.

Just like last year, I will attempt to write you in a foreign language, but it may take a while before my French gets going.

They don't have as big a collection of exciting "adventure stories" as Mr. Vigers did, and mostly only boring poetry and stuff. However, there's supposed to be a flourishing library system here so I'll try to find something fun. Mme Bourdillon has found a good translation of Selma Lagerlöf's *The Wonderful Adventures of Nils,* which will keep me busy in the meanwhile.

A thousand heartfelt greetings to Grandfather and Grandmother

from Raoul

[Erik von Dardel *was the son of a cousin of RW's stepfather.* Mr. Vigers *was the English clergyman with whom RW had spent the previous summer.*]

THONON-LES-BAINS
JUNE 22, 1929

Dearest Grandfather,

I got your letter of the 15th a few minutes ago. Thank you for your advice about my studies. I'm happy to report that I followed roughly the same course of action up till now — and with good results.

First, however, I want to give you my grades. I got nothing lower than a B+ except for in German, where I had B−. Too bad, but nothing to worry about. The low grade was the result of my appendicitis. Last term I had a B+, and I'll try to do as well next year. Otherwise my grades were my best ever. I got lower grades in two subjects and higher grades in six.

Religion	B+	(A−)
Swedish	A−	(B+)
German	B−	(B+)
English	A−	(B+)
French	B+	(B)
History	B+	(B+)
Geography	A−	(A−)
Philosophy	B+	(B)
Biology	B+	(B+)
Physics	B+	(B+)
Russian	A−	(B)
Drawing	A	(A−)
Music	A−	(−)

The grades in ( ) are from the preceding term

In my last letter I tried to give you a brief description of the family here. My opinions have changed a little. Now I like the place, my studies, and the people more and more.

My first day here I knew very little French. I had no trouble with the pronunciation, but my vocabulary was in terrible shape. Since I wanted some reading material right away, but would not have understood much of the French books, I chose an excellent translation — as I persuaded myself — of Selma Lagerlöf's *The Wonderful Adventures of Nils.* That way I learned a good number of French words in only a few days. I have bought a book by Maurice Leblanc since (something in the adventure vein) and have taken yet another book out of the library. I have already read several hundred pages. When I read I use a dictionary and write down the words I don't know in a notebook. I also have lessons with Mme Bourdillon in grammar, reading aloud, etc., every day and do a daily translation exercise. I will eventually start writing essays in French. My spare time is divided between conversations with Mme B., the young people of the house, and their classmates. I am also taking the opportunity to do some sports. I didn't do any sports all winter, and next winter I'll probably have even less time because of graduation. There are excellent opportunities for swimming and rowing here (in very nice little canoes), so I take long walks, and best of all have done some mountain climbing.

Thonon is pretty flat but surrounded by high mountains. Just 10 kilometers into the country and you find yourself in the middle of an Alpine world. One of the closest of the mountains is Dent d'Oche (2,300 meters). From Thonon it looks like a tall rocky point sticking up over a strange rock formation, which in turn appears to be the continuation of some smaller and closer mountains. Actually Dent d'Oche is freestanding, surrounded on all sides by valleys, the bottoms of which are only occasionally higher than Thonon. So you can reach the foot of the mountain walking or driving. The little Alpine village of Bernex is the starting point. Our trip took two days and began on Wednesday afternoon at four, when we got into the car that was to take us to Bernex. The group consisted of the son of the house, the Parisian, two of the Serbs (yet another has arrived), the Czech mademoiselle, and myself.

From Bernex the road goes through a narrow valley, one side of which is a steep rock about 300 meters high. A small path snakes its way up the slope. From time to time little log bridges cross over babbling mountain streams. Nature looks like something of an eighteenth-century pastoral. However, after no more than a few hundred meters' "ascension" you find yourself at the entrance to a side valley, rising up steeply toward the foot of the peak of Dent d'Oche. The entire valley and of course the 1,000-meter-high peak is treeless, with only a sparse covering of grass and a variety of different flowers. Down below, you have a wonderful view of the main valley, with its tiny villages, forests, and steep crags — everything forming a frame for Lake Geneva, which you can just make out way down. The last part was by far the hardest. To begin with, there is an extraordinarily steep grassy slope up which you climb by following a meandering path, barely 30 centimeters in width. This comparatively easy stretch only takes you halfway there, however, ending just below the so-called Stovepipe, a crevice filled with loose stones that are a danger for those behind you. Actually, one of our group injured his finger from a falling stone. The Stovepipe takes about a quarter of an hour and ends on a little plateau about 6 meters wide. On it sits a little hut, the mountain climber's shelter against the cold night, fog, and storms.

Here, we took off our huge rucksacks filled with food, clothing, and all the firewood that we'd gathered in the valley below for cooking. The ascent from Bernex to the hut had taken 3½ hours.

After supper we continued the climb to the actual peak, another hundred meters farther up. This stretch is less steep but no breeze because of the sharpness of the peak. It's shaped like a narrow ridge, so narrow that there's barely enough room for one person. On either side of the path was a drop of almost a thousand meters.

When we got to the very top, we found ourselves on a plateau only a few square meters wide. From here we had the most magnificent view imaginable. On one side, Lake Geneva, visible in its whole length from Lausanne to Geneva, on the other, the Alps, culminating in Mont Blanc, covered in snow.

The descent to the hut in the dark posed some problems, in spite of a flashlight, and was not particularly pleasant.

We spent the night, a sleepless one for everyone except me, on the wooden bunks in the hut. At 3 A.M. the sun rose, and so did we. Between 3 and 11 we had lots of fun climbing around on the slopes, eating, drinking, and talking.

Next on the program was the descent, kind of risky but a lot of fun. We did it sitting down like the alpinists do and sliding, rather than by following the paths. This was naturally only possible on the grassy slopes, but the first ravines we climbed down were even worse because of falling rocks and slippery sand.

I had intended to write another couple of pages but have to stop now, since I haven't started today's assignment yet.

Before I close, I wanted to express my gratitude to you for contributing financially for yet another summer of travel. I can already tell that this vacation will be pretty inexpensive, and I think that it will not exceed a total of 700 Skr [Swedish kronor], at most.

My fondest greetings to you and Grandmother,

Raoul

THONON-LES-BAINS
JULY 5, 1929

Dear Grandfather,

Many thanks for your letter, which I received a few days ago. I will find those expensive books you ordered very interesting. I would be very grateful if you would tell me some stories about conditions in the Balkans sometime.

Now that I am completely surrounded by representatives from those countries, I feel pretty ignorant about them, since our schools don't treat them as important. I have therefore begun to study a Larousse, as well as all the geography books I can get my hands on, and a French book on Yugoslavia (industry, customs, etc.). But this only gives me the outlines of a foundation, hardly more.

A few days ago we were joined by a Serb of about 23 who appears to have embarked on some kind of diplomatic career. I've tried to get him to talk about his native country, but he doesn't appear particularly eager to. Maybe he's afraid that by giving out information about conditions in his country he'll divulge state secrets.

A while ago I promised to keep you informed of any improvements in my French.

Comme les étés précédents je vais avoir le plaisir de correspondre avec vous dans la langue du pays que j'habite en ce moment. Il est certain que pour commencer mes lettres ne seront sans doute, ni très longues ni très interessants. Ils seront plutot des moyens de vous montrer mes progres en francais. Vous m'avez donné le conseil de prendre des leçons aussi d'un pretre d'ici. Je ne crois pas que cela soit possible parceque les cures ne donnent pas de leçons. Ils sont comme nos pasteurs, pris par leurs fonctions. Cependant, j'ai commencé à travailler beaucoup plus, dirigé par Mme Bourdillon.

C'est dommage que mes vacances sont seulement deux mois. Je crois qu'il faut au moins quatre ou six mois pour apprendre une langue si difficile comme le francais. Je sens que, bien que j'ai fait des progrès considerables, je n'ai pas encore ce sentiment de la valeur de la langue qui est si important. Cependant je crois que "l'oreille" a commencée a fonctionner. Mais encore je ne suis pas maitre de subtilités comme le subjonctif etc.

Je commencerai dans quelques jours avec Victor Hugo. J'ai trouvé quelques livres de cet grand écrivain: *Notre-Dame de Paris, Les Burgraves, Han d'Islande*. Aussi j'ai trove un livre: *Cent dessins extraits des Oeuvres de Victor Hugo*. Ils sont excessivement jolis. Un de Messonier est un chef d'oeuvre. Je ne suis pas expert de la peinture mais il me semble que la style de Messonier ressemble a celui de Rembrandt.

J'ai acheté un carnet pour faire des esquisses de cette petite ville, qui est très pittoresque. Aussi sont les environs vraiment jolis. Malheureusement je n'ai pas eu un carnet a l'ascension de Dent d'Oche. Mais nous ferons une autre ascension en peu de temps est alors je vais faire des dessins.

Il y a ici (dans cette ville) un monsieur suédois mais ni lui ni moi n'avons pas essayé de nous rencontrer.

Voila ma premiere lettre francaise. Je l'ai fait sans l'aide de quelqu'un. La fois prochaine j'espere que je la peut faire plus longue et mieux.

[This letter is reproduced uncorrected. English translation as follows: "As in summers past I will have the pleasure of corresponding with you in the language of the country in which I am living at the time. There is no doubt that to begin with my letters will be neither very long nor very interesting. Rather, they will be ways of showing you my progress in French. You advised me to take lessons from a local priest. I do not think that will be possible because the curates don't give lessons. Like our pastors they are busy with their duties. Nonetheless, I started to work much harder, guided by Mme Bourdillon.

It's too bad that my vacation is only two months long. I think you need at least four or six months to learn a language as difficult as French. I feel that even though I have made considerable progress, I don't yet have the sense of the value of the language. Still, I believe that the "ear" has started to work. But I have not yet mastered the subtleties, such as the subjunctive, etc.

I will start with Victor Hugo in several days. I found several books by this great writer: Notre-Dame de Paris, Les Burgraves, Han d'Islande. *I also found a book:* One Hundred Drawings Taken from the Works of Victor Hugo. *They are amazingly beautiful. The one by Messonier is a masterpiece. I am not an expert in painting, but it seems to me that Messonier's style resembles that of Rembrandt.*

I bought a notebook to do sketches of this little village, which is very picturesque. The surrounding countryside is also really beautiful. Unfortunately, I didn't have a notebook for the climb up Dent d'Oche. But we will do another climb in a little while and so I will do some sketches. There is here (in this town) a Swedish man, but neither he nor I have tried to meet.

That's my first French letter. I did it without anyone's help. Next time, I hope I can make it longer and better."]

You see my French vocabulary could hardly be characterized as enormous. I've only mastered ordinary words, but then I will have about another month's practice to draw on.

I'll say again that I find my family here excellent. I like the lady of the house more with every passing day. The cost of staying here is well worth it. I'm working with a serious will to learn something. I'm not expecting any miracles when it comes to getting higher grades, which primarily reflect the written tests you take during the semester. How well you do depends on a thorough knowledge of grammar, and it isn't possible — at least in my opinion — to master French grammar in only two months. On the other hand, I should be able to conduct a passable conversation in French, write a letter, and have no difficulty reading a book.

I am sorry to hear that you are bedridden. Grandmother did write to say that you were feeling better, however, and I hope this letter finds you completely recovered.

A thousand greetings to you both,
Raoul

CONSTANTINOPLE
JULY 12, 1929

My dear boy in Thonon-les-Bains,

Your letter of the 5th pleased me very much, and I am pleasantly surprised by your progress in French. It proves that you have made good use of your studies in Thonon-les-Bains, and that you have pumped your friends for useful idiomatic phrases. My opinion is that the most important thing is to get the sound of the language in your ear. That happens through constant conversation; something is bound to stick.

I asked to have the Hagberg books sent because I found them to be extremely interesting reading. You must not take it as an attempt on my part to pass off the remarkable statesmen that populate his books as some kind of ideal to model yourself on. No, I assure you that I have no such false hopes. I want to shape my dear boy into a useful member of society, someone, first of all, who knows how to stand on his own two feet. A child starts out wanting to play drums because it appeals to his rudimentary sense of things. Then he moves on to shiny buttons, etc. For my part, I have become convinced that young men should not or ought not decide on their path in life until they are in their thirties. Exceptions obviously need to be made for those who enroll in the military or civil service, and whose careers will be guided exclusively by the principle of seniority. Instead, I would love to train you to take care of yourself and to become an independent man, so that as you mature and begin to be able to appreciate the experiences of others, you will be able to tackle such problems as prove to be compatible with your temperament —

Yours affectionately,
[GOW]

*[*The Hagberg books *probably refer to the Swedish writer Knut Hagberg's biographical collections of essays* Children of the World *and* Fellow-Beings.*]*

THONON-LES-BAINS
JULY 23, 1929

Dearest Grandfather,

Thank you very much for your kind and interesting letter. I've now read Hagberg's books. They are wonderfully written.

The reason I'm not writing in French this time is that I have an awful lot to do. The final spurt before my return trip home in three weeks has now begun. I am returning early to do some reviewing of other subjects before school starts. I think this is a good idea, and I don't think my French will suffer. Mme Bourdillon has been kind enough to give me two lessons a day, in addition to which I've got plenty of homework.

I heard from Mother that deliberations concerning my education are now underway. I am more grateful than I can say that you are making it possible — both economically and in other ways — for me to contribute to society by having the best preparation possible.

The intent of your American plan is to give me a trump card vis-à-vis my Swedish peers. I agree that going to an American university, possibly combined with a few years of practical experience, would be close to invaluable.

If I don't fail my exams next May, I'll leave school at only 17. It might be a bad investment to have me go to America *right away*, since I would be less mature than my American classmates and thus have difficulties with the harder courses.

Graduating so young, as you know, gives me an extra year "free." It might be better if I did my military service before going to America, in part to arrive there more mature, and in part to avoid the danger that my memory will weaken and the value of my American experiences become diluted by having to load manure and such after I get back home.

You wrote in your last letter that your intention is that my education be designed to afford me the chance, right from the start, to earn my living in a practical job, so that later, when I'm older, I can take on whatever I feel most attracted to and best suited for. Everything points to my final career beginning when I'm 30 or older.

It isn't very likely I'll pursue a civil service career. I expect a business career to be my final goal.

To make my transformation from "architectural animal" into commercial creature as painless as possible, some training will be called for.

I don't know if you intended me to get this training in America. Having studied the program of the School of Economics last spring, I got the impression that it has roughly what I need. You get a far-reaching general education in practical matters, but they also have excellent language courses (like the one in English), which might be very useful to my subsequent American studies.

One of the School of Economics's biggest advantages is that the program is short. If I graduate from high school at 17, I could be on my way to America at 19. Because (unless I'm mistaken) it's possible to do military service during the summer and the School of Economics during the winter. I've already spoken of the advantages of doing my military service and the School of Economics before and not after I go to America. To do my military service before and the School of Economics after would be the least efficient way, since that way I lose the chance to gain time by combining them.

You've never spoken to me in detail about your plan, and therefore I don't know if you think the School of E. at all necessary, or whether an American program would do as well. It is probably not possible to replace the program of the School of Economics, which is designed for Swedish conditions, with a similar program geared to American conditions.* Another thing is that in terms of technology, the Americans probably are ahead of us. Finally, if I go to an American equivalent to our School of E., I would have to stay home for my military service and thus lose time.

When I went to see Uncle Knut a year ago he inquired about my studies. He approved of the American plan but thought going to the School of Economics necessary first in order not to arrive too young and unprepared for independent study.

A thousand fond greetings to you and Grandmother from your grateful and affectionate

Raoul

---

* This assumes that my career will be in Sweden and not in America. I am absolutely determined to return to Sweden after my studies in America.

[P.S.] I would be grateful if you'd take all this under consideration. I don't know whether Mother sent you a catalog from the School of Economics last spring. If not, I will get some when I get home and send them to you, so that you can get an idea about the school and its usefulness in my education. As to costs, I know nothing about that. One thing is absolutely certain and that is that it would be less expensive than an *equivalent* American school. The issue is therefore whether an education of this kind is necessary at all.

Mme Boudillon has asked my permission to write you a few words when I'm finished. I am in no way responsible for anything she might write.

Your Raoul

CONSTANTINOPLE
JULY 28, 1929

My dear boy,

I've just received your long letter and the enclosure from Mme Bourdillon.

Summarizing the issue of your education for the immediate future is no simple task. Nevertheless, I do want to touch on the reasoning behind my wish that you be educated in America. First, let me make it clear that I know that a Swedish book education is as good as an American. My reasons for wanting to send you there are based on something completely different. In Sweden, young men are still brought up to adhere to military principles so far as their schooling and social position go, and then throughout their lives they are taught to march to a regular beat and always to keep in step.

Even though my father was an unusual person for his time, it was decided sometime in the mid 1870s that we would all join the navy, and then the subject was closed. This held for all of my able-bodied brothers — Axel and Victor could not take the entrance test because they suffered from albuminuria, a very common disease at that time. Given my father's broad-mindedness, one might have expected him to educate his boys to take on the great problems facing their country, problems of which he as the fore-most pioneer of his time was more aware than others. But as I said, that was out of the question; the boys were put in the compartment labeled "navy," a comfortable way of dismissing the question of upbringing that was understandable during a time when the field was less crowded and the competition for daily bread less fierce. Our book education was as flawed as our practical education. Neither was truly effective. Worst of all there was no one to train us to become men of firm character and to have the indomitable will to succeed. Such training was viewed with suspicion. No one was permitted to march out of step! Even so, in his day, my father was unusually independent, because in his twenties he had gone to America with two navy friends and served in the merchant marine. He stayed for three years, right after the 1838 crisis. America was in her infancy then — I am firmly convinced that Father's financial acumen developed dur-ing the time he spent in America, and I am also persuaded that my own ambition grew out of my having spent rather long periods working in America forty-two years ago. The common prejudice was that only criminals and losers went to America. My brothers teased me plenty for what they saw as my perverse inclinations. None of them went there until twenty or thirty years later. But one thing is certain, and that is that neither Saltsjöbaden nor any undertaking requiring initiative other than the usual homegrown variety would have seen the light of day had it not been for my stay in America. It put me ahead of my time and contributed to the feeling — which must not be taken as smug self-sufficiency but rather as a firm sense of purpose — that I could accomplish whatever I had undertaken. Do you think that anyone taught to keep "in step" could have carried off as enormous a project as Saltsjöbaden at the age of 30, and practically single-handedly? This fall I will go over all of the background to this project with you.

It is because of what both my father and I found in America that makes me so eager for you to get your *direction in life* there. No one has ever understood as well as I have, because I saw it in my youth, how decisive his time there was for my father. . . . I use the expression *direction in life* and not "education" on purpose. And that is what I think you are failing to take into consideration when you make your calculations for your schooling. The curriculum offered by an American school is in no way superior or even equal to that offered in Sweden. No, what I am trying to give you is completely different: insight into the American frame of mind, the kind of upbringing aimed at teaching men to be self-reliant, even to feel that they are better than others, which may just be the basis and the source of America's position of leadership today. This is something very different from "keeping in step" here at home. That frame of mind struck me so forcefully when I first went to America that I never even talked about it with my brothers when I came home: I listened, smiling secretly and silently, from an American point of view, to all the naive viewpoints prevalent at that time, because I knew they came from a different perspective. Maybe now you can begin to see that what I want you to get there is not schooling but life, contact with young Americans, so that you can learn how to develop into a well-organized fighter ready to make his way in the world. Allow me to point out a few Swedes who have made more of a mark in life than others: Edström, head of ASEA; Lundqvist, head of Stora Kopparbergs Bergslag; Prytz, SKF; and finally Ivar Kreuger, who has done better than the whole pack of them, including the Wallenbergs. Where did they get their direction? Where did they learn how to run an organization? In America!

And then there are those who kept "in step," who arranged their "paths in life" by squeaking by on their exams to become officers or lawyers, started a career, got engaged, etc., then before the age of 30 realized that everything was wrong, that they had failed, and now that they were burdened with a family that realized more and more with every passing day that they were not up to the task. This is the fate of most people, and it is nothing to be coveted.

When one comes from a family in which several generations have managed to acquire a certain reputation for competence and skill, it is more important than ever that you understand how unacceptable failure is as a legacy. The fact that one generation has succeeded financially makes it almost harder for those who follow —

Now, I don't want you to take all this to mean that I am opposed to our School of Economics. What worries me is that the ideas you might acquire there would take you in a different direction than going to America would give you, and that is my basic point. We will talk about this when next we see each other. I am ready to yield to persuasive arguments. Actually, I would be less opposed to your attending the School of Economics after your return from America, so that you might be able to judge with fresh eyes the caliber of our boys. But this might just be complicating matters. We will see when we talk with your mother and Uncle Fred about this. I am better, but still in bed. Grandmother has decided to go home to Saltsjöbaden. My going depends first and foremost on when I can get up and second on the progress of the negotiations over our new treaty in Ankara.

Your affectionate
[GOW]

[The Crisis of 1838. *Growing tensions between England and Russia caused both countries to fortify their positions, leaving Sweden in the uncomfortable position of being caught in the middle. War never broke out, and a visit to Sweden by the Russian czar calmed fears.* ASEA *refers to Asea Brown Boveri, a manufacturer of electrical generators.* Stora Kopparbergs Bergslag, *which started as a mining concern, is one of the world's oldest incorporated businesses, founded in the fifteenth century.* SKF *stands for Swenska Kullager Fabriken, still the world's largest maker of ball bearings.]*

THONON-LES-BAINS
AUGUST 7, 1929

Dearest Grandfather and Grandmother,

Received Grandfather's letters of July 28 and 30 as well as the card and the check for 100 kronor. Thank you very much for the birthday wishes. The check, too, makes for extremely interesting reading of which I heartily approve. I'm happy that Grandmother is going to be able to come home so that we can see each other.

As for the first of Grandfather's letters, I have nothing to add.

We should probably postpone discussions until you get home. I hope you won't be too delayed by the treaty negotiations, because by then my term will have begun and work will have started in earnest. It would be hard to see you with any frequency.

I'll go back to Sweden in a few days, having spent a most beneficial and very enjoyable summer in Thonon. I won't forget that all of this, and more besides, was made possible because of your generosity, Grandfather.

As far as my studies and my progress are concerned, I think I can state that my time has been well spent.

The books by Hagberg that you sent have also proved useful to my French studies. Each day I translate one of the essays. So far, I've done Gladstone, Edward VII, and Deschanel, and today we are going to do Lord Fisher. Kind of a curious selection, I admit, but it can be explained by the length of the chapters and by Hagberg's style, which at first may seem clear and straightforward in Swedish, but the deeper you go, such as when you do a translation, the more complicated it turns out to be. He excels in the use of unusual words with novel meanings, and there are lots of abbreviated phrases. I wanted to translate him because unlike what we find in our final exams he is witty and gives you food for thought. Mme Bourdillon also enjoys his writing. I translate orally, which is of course quicker than doing it in writing. I suffer horribly from the fact that my Swedish-French dictionary is 35 years old and lousy. In just six lines in *Children of the World,* I found three words that were not listed in my dictionary, words that were difficult to find synonyms for. They were: ruthlessness, fumbling, and true-hearted. You can only figure out their equivalents by dint of great cleverness and ingenuity. When you look up the word "oaf" you get "maladroit." The minute I get home I'm going to buy another dictionary so that never again will I find myself in the situation of being unable to locate "honorable," a pretty common word after all.

I still have a few days left, as I told you, and intend to devote one of them to going to Chamonix and take a look at Mont Blanc and Mer de Glace. I hope you don't mind this extra expense, but since I'm so close it would be a shame not to take advantage of the opportunity.

AUGUST 8, 1929

The excursion was canceled today and will probably have to be postponed for a few years since the weather insists on presenting obstacles.

I feel real sadness at having to leave this kind family. I am especially fond of Mme B., so will write her this winter.

A thousand greetings to Grandfather and Grandmother,

Raoul

[P.S.] Forgive me for not writing more but I have lots of letters to answer, in addition to translating all of Lloyd George (45 pp), half the grammar, as well as packing suitcases, going for a fitting at the tailor, and getting information from the travel bureau, etc.

[Paul-Eugène-Louis Deschanel (1855–1922) served as president of France in 1920. Lord Fisher (1841–1920) was an admiral in the British navy.]

STOCKHOLM
DECEMBER 21, 1929

Dearest Grandfather and Grandmother,

Miss Wernberger called me up two days ago and told me to come down to pick up my Christmas gift. It was even more generous than usual. The money is burning a hole in my inside pocket, but I guess I'll hand it over to Uncle Marcus and Uncle Jacob's care. Thank you very much, Grandfather and Grandmother.

The term ended yesterday and I got my grades. This letter should reach you a little after Christmas, but I waited in order to be able to include the results of my work this term.

this last term

Religion	B+	(B+)	
Swedish	A−	(A−)	
German	B+	(B−)	
English	a	(A−)	
French	A−	(B+)	The grades in ( ) refer to preceding
History	B+	(B+)	term

Geography	a	(A−)
Philosophy	B+	(B+)
Biology	B+	(B+)
Physics	B+	(B+)
Russian	B	(A−)
Drawing	A−	(a)
Music	A−	(A−)

A is the top grade and then a, A−, B+, B, B−, and C. B is "pass," B− and C are "poor" and "failed," respectively.

To show you the value of the above grades, I made up a table showing the grade distribution among the nineteen students in my class.

A	1%
a	8%
A−	15.8%
B+	32.9%
B	36.5%
B−	5.4%
C	0.4%

I'm especially pleased I was able to keep my A− in Swedish, for my class's grades in that subject have generally dropped and now I'm up among the top three.

I'll be staying in Stockholm during the Christmas vacation, except for maybe a week or so in early January, when I'll go down to Broby. In Stockholm I will devote my time to a much-needed review of history, religion, Swedish, and Russian, among other things, since we probably won't be able to cover all the course material in those subjects before graduation.

When I went to see Uncle Marcus a few weeks ago, he loaned me a book in Danish by Gustav Cassel called *Progress or Socialism*, which was very interesting. I have also acquired a passion for economics and even started to read your *National System of Political Economics [Das nationale System der Politischen Ökonomie.]*

I have read all the novels you left behind at the Grand Hotel, except for Hagberg's book, because Aunt Nita borrowed that one.

Anwers to the questions of how, when, and where I will do my

military service have now been been found, happily. At one of
our dinner parties recently was among others a colonel or something, whose acquaintance Mother had made. She asked him if he
knew how someone could get placed in the branch of service of
his choice. She was surprised to hear him reply that he could take
care of it since he was the head of the authority in charge of the
matter. All I have to do is to go and see him later in January and
tell him of my preference and he'll take care of it.

The watch that you gave me is running very well. It was
probably wise to take an unpolished one, for it still looks pretty
new.

As usual, Aunt Amalia was kind enough to send me a little card
asking what I wanted for Christmas, and soon after I wrote back I
got a large package, which naturally I opened on the sly and
which turned out to contain a book by Catherine Mayo, *Mother
India,* and a gift certificate at Fritze's bookstore. Catherine Mayo's
book is supposed to be excellent, all about the social problems of
India and the position of the British vis-à-vis the same.

Mother, Uncle Fred, and I wish you both a Merry Christmas.

Raoul

*[Miss Wernberger refers to Hanna Wernberger, who for many
years was GOW's trusted private secretary. Uncle Marcus and
Uncle Jacob are Marcus ("Dodde") and Jacob Wallenberg, sons
of GOW's younger brother Marcus, and the directors of SEB.
Jacob was RW's godfather. Aunt Nita is GOW's youngest daughter,
whose second marriage was to Carl Axel Söderlund, an engineer
working for AGA, the well-known gas company, in Mexico City.
RW would later visit them there.]*

ISTANBUL
FEBRUARY 1, 1930

My dear boy,

Thank you for your letter informing me of your final grades. I am
satisfied with them, and was interested to see the statistical account or rather overview you did to figure out your rank relative

to your classmates. I observe with satisfaction the effect of your stay in France last summer as well as your progress in English.

I have no objections regarding the proposed minor changes in the plan for the next two years. It is up to Mother and Uncle Fred to decide. I would prefer that you got away from Stockholm — and I say this without wanting in any way to cast aspersions on anyone — and away from your cousins and other young people there. I got justification for my worries when I learned that one of my brother Axel's sons has become a jazz dancer, I think in Paris. Probably the result of associating with and being surrounded by people who are accustomed to taking life too easy. Even so, we must bear in mind that youthful folly can be found in everyone, to a greater or lesser degree of course, and that each one of us is primarily responsible for combatting it. This is best accomplished by developing an interest in something. I am therefore very pleased with your growing interest in the field of economics —

I gave your grandmother a "bon" for a trip to Egypt and Palestine. She's been wanting to travel there and last week she set out. She will be arriving in Alexandria today. As for me, I am busy with a question I want to pursue, and about which I will tell you later. Facing retirement is like having one foot in the grave when you feel a certain urge to fight to stay alive. I don't want to give up being active. My fondest greetings to Mother and Uncle Fred.

Your affectionate
[GOW]

[*"One of my brother Axel's sons" refers to Gustaf Wallenberg (stage name, Gustave Wally), actor and cabaret artist, the son of Axel Wallenberg. He eventually settled in California.*]

ANN ARBOR, MICHIGAN
NOVEMBER 7, 1931

Dearest Grandfather,

I'm sorry I haven't written in several weeks, but I've had lots to do and not too many free moments.

I've been meaning to write and give you my impressions of

America, since I expect you want to hear about them to see if they tally with yours.

As a matter of fact, I've been a little upset that I haven't experienced the powerful impressions of America of which you spoke and to which you attributed both your own and your father's later development. But I think I've found a natural explanation for the disparity. I assume that when you first came here America did not enjoy a particularly high reputation in Sweden, and that what you found made all that much more powerful an impression because it was new and surprising. Secondly, I assume that American inventions and experiments had not yet reached Sweden, which primarily happened during your generation, and that consequently what appeared like a huge gap between America and Sweden was not a difference in degree so much as in principle. Thirdly, you spent your time in large cities, where the American spirit finds its most overwhelming material expression.

Things are different for me. Swedish newspapers and opinion makers no longer presume a lack of education and culture in America, any more than they talk about English conservatism or German boorishness, for example. Secondly, returning emigrants or letters from them have done a great deal to keep us up-to-date about America. Slowly but surely Sweden has come around to assimilating all the technical innovations America has produced.

But I think what you intended by sending me here was not so much to acquire the skill to build skyscrapers and movie houses as to acquire a desire to build them! In other words: to catch some of the American spirit that lies behind their technological and economic progress.

That brings me to my third point: Americanism is not actively taught at American universities. Educators seem to think that young Americans get enough of that in high school and that it's better to give them a classical education and European polish once they get to college. Here there is marked prejudice for European ideas or at least for an awareness of them. This, combined with the fact that competition is designed to be less fierce than at European universities (in order to foster team spirit and "social-mindedness" among the students), makes American colleges less typically American than they might be.

I write this that you might understand and forgive me if my

"development as a person" — the expression you used in your letter to Milles — is less speedy than your own was.

As I wrote you, they keep us very busy. The work in and of itself is not particularly difficult or demanding but it is very time-consuming.

As for my rank in my class, what I told you before still stands. I'm pleased that up to now I've had the highest grade in my class on all of our take-home English essays. I was less successful on an in-class test, on which I got an average grade. Math is going better, and my status in the other subjects remains unchanged.

I am convinced that it was a smart decision to join a debating society within the College of Engineering and Architecture. Each week we have a long and thoroughly prepared debate, which is good practice for my English, extemporaneous speaking, and public debating skills.

Mother sent me a copy of your pro memoria and I've read it several times, liking it more and more with each reading. I'm glad you've taken a public stand on the issue, because in doing so you've washed your hands of any responsibility for the conse-quences of the current lack of initiative. If people are afraid to depart from their usual way of thinking, even though the situation calls for it, that isn't your fault.

I believe that England's departure from the gold standard and the ensuing loss of purchasing power and the Tory elections and the prospect of import duties are almost better as *arguments* than the five-year plan, since it's still unclear whether the five-year plan is realizable — at least, that's the viewpoint of those who for some reason don't want to lend their support to the plan — while the consequences of the English crisis is a harsh reality no one can doubt or dispute.

I assume, however, that the five-year plan has gained wider "acceptance" since I left home.

It gets colder every day here, but the climate is excellent in that there isn't much rain.

I still have about $105 left from what you gave me, apart from the letter of credit. The largest expenses so far have been: registra-tion $163, train fare $38, rent until beginning of December $28, school supplies $50, and somewhere under $1 per day for food.

Except for movies there have been no unforeseen expenses. I have not yet put my money in a bank since I'm not familiar with the banks yet and there have been lots of failures. Enskilda Banken lists a bank in Detroit, but I haven't had time to go there yet. One thing that I'm not sure about. Do the withdrawals that I make now from my credit account suffer from the current poor rate of exchange, or is a draft governed by the exchange rate of the day it was deposited into the credit account?

A thousand greetings to both of you from

Raoul

[RW matriculated at the University of Michigan in the fall of 1931. GOW had selected Michigan on the recommendation of Carl Milles, a friend and sculptor who was teaching at the Cranbrook Art Academy in Michigan. In addition to its solid academic reputation, the university had the advantage of being located in Ann Arbor, fairly distant from any large urban center — and its temptations.]

ANN ARBOR
NOVEMBER 21, 1931

Dearest Grandfather,

A thousand thanks for your letter and the two articles. I never cease to admire your style.

Midterm is now over and I thought I would get grades, but it turned out that only those who are failing get them. Since I wrote you last my average has improved somewhat. I'm especially pleased to report I'm slightly above the class average in geometry. This is all the more pleasing since during a conversation with my teacher I admitted I'd never taken solid geometry in Sweden, only plane geometry, which should have made it very difficult to follow the course. I suspected this would be the case at the beginning of the term, so I wisely avoided mentioning this gap in my previous education.

I managed to recapture my position in English class, lost for a week, at the top of the heap with an essay entitled "The Magic Mirror of Statistics," which my professor really liked. I will soon lose it again because my last essay was poor, partly because I had no time to develop it properly.

I read the *New York Times* every day, and find that it covers all of my interests. It's the best paper I've ever read and considered the best in the country. The *Christian Science Monitor* is the next best, but its high tone is based on negative qualities: it will not publish scandals and it will not publish rumors, etc. I have read about the copper conference, but Sweden was not mentioned by the countries involved.

I've started to give some thought to next summer and come up with three possibilities. The first is to go to one of the large cities, the second to take part in a so-called military camp with my R.O.T.C. for six weeks, and the third to go to summer school at another university. I myself am most interested in the latter project. The reason for going to another place would be to see another part of the country and to get to know people elsewhere. These summer schools are usually pretty demanding, and the courses are twice as long as the corresponding course during the winter term. What I would study obviously depends on what the rest of the winter courses tell me I need. English, writing, and some business subject would seem likely subjects. If I went to one of the large cities I might find something to do in an architecture firm. I'll look into the possibilities for this.

Yesterday was so-called "black Friday," the day when all new freshmen and the upperclassmen go out into the streets yelling and fighting. The freshmen are the butts of all kinds of ridiculous jokes. It doesn't seem too fashionable at the moment, though: I was left alone, in any case.

My closest friend here is a boy by the name of Wehausen. He's very talented in languages, and very nice and intelligent. He's also one of few I've met with outside interests. We eat together at a cheap little place the others don't want to go to as a rule.

One thing that has struck me is that all the offices and work-places are filled with very stern-looking older and younger women. As a rule they are nice and quite knowledgeable. They also have more backbone than most of the men. I have noticed the same thing in school: the female students are much better prepared and less conservative than the boys. I'm almost beginning to understand why American women's organizations are so powerful. Two out of eight candidates from both parties in our elections are female students, i.e., a much higher proportion than one might expect from their number in the class.

As for my matriculation here, about which you asked, it worked this way. There are certain minimum requirements for each applicant. If he exceeds these requirements but is deficient in one or more special subjects, he must continue his studies in that special subject while completing his ordinary course work. When judging a student's standing — at least when it comes to foreigners — they seem to pay far closer attention to the number of hours he has studied in a given subject in high school than to what he actually knows, or has acquired on his own outside his regular course of study. So they paid no attention to my final grades but had me draw up a list indicating how many years and how many hours a week I had studied each subject. Even with these limitations, my background seemed to be sufficient, except for in certain subjects, such as mathematics and chemistry. As for the entrance exam mentioned in the catalog, it's a psychological profile used for statistical purposes. It was not hard at all. I didn't use the letter from the admiral, since mostly I was dealing with underlings and since I became convinced from the very first day that I'd have no difficulty; and being a foreigner made the formalities all that much easier.

Apart from the letter that Milles wrote to the head of my department, he has not had to do anything on my behalf.

> A thousand greetings and kisses to both of you,
> Raoul

[P.S.] I am getting *Business World* [Affärsvärlden] regularly.

GREENWICH, CONNECTICUT
DECEMBER 25, 1931

Dearest Grandfather,

The Colvins have been nice enough to invite me for Christmas. I traveled the entire distance between Ann Arbor and Greenwich, near New York, by bus, and the trip took almost twenty-seven hours. It was pretty tiring, but far more interesting than going by train. A round-trip ticket only cost $14.85, compared to the $37 that I paid for the one-way train ride New York/Ann Arbor last fall!

I'm having a good time here, and the parties and dances I've been attending are a pleasant change from my somewhat monotonous life in Ann Arbor. The other day my cousin Lucette and I went to Philadelphia, about 150 miles from here. She drove me there in her own car. We stayed with a wealthy family, and in the evening went to a dance at the Cricket Club, which is supposed to boast the cream of American society. What struck me was that the boys were the worst dressed and seemingly most stupid that I have seen here.

On the way down we drove along the most magnificent roads and also crossed the George Washington Bridge, the longest bridge in the world, considerably longer than the Brooklyn Bridge. Roads and bridges are what impress me the most here. When it comes to private homes and small houses they are probably behind Sweden, at least in terms of aesthetics. A truth that had not dawned on me until now is when it comes to architecture generally, we are America's equal. Of course they are much further ahead when it comes to construction methods and in building skyscrapers, but the Swedes are not as far behind as I had thought.

I've now had the opportunity to form an opinion about New York, having strolled around it for a few days. Several of the skyscraper districts, especially the ones around Grand Central Station, i.e., from 41st to 52nd Streets, are magnificent. The new Empire State Building and Chrysler Building, among others, with their 107 and 72 floors respectively, far surpass the Woolworth Building. Down in the Wall Street area several new 40-story buildings have been constructed. These new skyscrapers are very beautiful, and their appearance is light and graceful. In general neither the horizontal nor the vertical line has been exaggerated, and all the ornaments and classical columns have disappeared. They are usually covered in marble, in the lightest of colors. Cornices and complex systems of little turrets have disappeared, and my impression of them is unconditionally favorable.

I went down to the Aquarium to look at the fish, which I enjoyed very much. The big movie houses are fascinating. The largest ones hold over 6,000 people.

Consul General Lamm lives in Greenwich, not far from the Colvins, and I paid him a visit the other day. He's eight feet tall and incredibly fat. I don't think that he shares your conviction that something positive should be done to improve our export organization. He did talk about his difficulties persuading Swedish businessmen to centralize their export methods, "but I have stopped preaching," he added. Since he's lived in America for so long and has such great faith in this market, he obviously wants America to have most-favored nation treatment ahead of more exotic trade fronts. But in one respect he and you are in the same boat, namely in that he didn't meet with much sympathy at home.

I like this big city atmosphere very much, and I'm not particularly looking forward to going back to my little Ann Arbor. The Colvins are very pro-American, and I have learned more about the real America in my two weeks here than during the whole term in Ann Arbor, where there is never any serious discussion.

Good of you to send me the book on criminal law.

A thousand greetings to Grandmother and your warm climate from

                                                                 Raoul

---

ISTANBUL
MARCH 21, 1932

My dear boy,

It has been a while since I heard from you, so I must confess to being eager for news. I hope to have some eventually, but you have probably sent me a letter by way of your mother.

The event filling everybody's minds with speculation and, naturally, sadness is the Kreuger affair. All the newspapers are crowded with articles, and you will be aware of most of it through DN [Dagens Nyheter]. That newspaper has been somewhat more levelheaded, so to speak, than most, and has openly avoided turning Kreuger into a national hero. He was actually nothing more than a self-centered, large-scale speculator with some attractive qualities, first and foremost his great modesty and wonderful organizational ability. But much of what he did must in all honesty be described as lacking in judgment. The German loan, now generally recognized as the straw that broke the camel's back, proved that he was not familiar with the political situation there. He didn't grasp what was happening in Germany, and forgot that the Germans already tricked the world once by foisting their ever more worthless money onto a lot of naive foreign buyers, thus getting out from under almost their entire national debt. It is a serious deficiency in a man in charge of such enormous capital not to be more aware of the political situation —

The first lesson to be learned from the Kreuger affair is that it is not good for a small country to get too involved in speculation on a worldwide scale. Nor is it a good idea to start up subsidiary companies abroad for industrial activity — a practice that has increased in recent years — which never actually works to our advantage. It provides food for workers in other countries but not for ours. If you consider that wages account for 80 percent of the costs incurred in industrial production and that the raw material seldom accounts for more than 10 or 15, you are better able to judge the value of foreign enterprise. What provides full value for our own people is a well-organized market for what we are able to produce here at home. To live well, we have to have a vital foreign trade.

As you see, I never lose an opportunity to propound my pet ideas. At the moment, my prospects for convincing those at home seem rather minimal. They have so many other things on their minds, poor things. Before leaving the subject, I would like to indulge in talk about some of the leading figures in our financial circles and what I think of them in light of the Kreuger disaster. Marcus, our leading banker, gets high marks. You must understand his position. As I understand it, SEB is not involved in the Kreuger affair in any way. In that respect, it now appears that Marcus showed foresight. His position was that he simply did not want to engage in any business dealings with Kreuger because if they were to become too extensive one day, it would be hard to say no to him. . . . Another banker who has not earned such high marks is Rydbeck. He joined the Kreuger concern four years ago. From the point of view of his bank, he misjudged the situation. From the point of view of the general public, he assumed tremendous responsibility by his statements and by lending his name to

Kreuger's deals. And since in addition he acted arrogantly, the public has a right to draw its own conclusions. It has the right and ought to do so, for it is dangerous to turn the big financiers into some sort of gods. There is a tendency to do just that, and it is obviously the result of a lack of judgment.

I want you to know that none of this has affected me, however. I owned quite a lot of Grängesberg and LM Ericsson stock, but sold it all off a year and a half ago because Kreuger was meddling in the cellulose business.

We are well. Winter is over but spring has not yet arrived. It is usually late. Grandmother has not yet talked of going home, and I would like her to stay here. I myself am happy not to be home right now. It is good not to have to listen to all the well- or ill-founded comments and epithets regarding K., whom when all is said and done I did like. As a person he was a charmer. I'd known him since 1919 and corresponded with him off and on.

I'm looking forward to a letter telling me what you are up to. I am terribly glad you are far from Sweden under the present circumstances. Learning to be a pessimist is as bad as learning to be an optimist. And they have now started down that path. Everything will go downhill: enterprise, zest for life, and opportunities for work. It is good to be away. Sometimes there is a hiatus in life; it can't be helped. We are now going into a long hiatus. How we will survive it I do not know, but somehow we will.

Greetings! Your affectionate
[GOW]

[The Swedish financier Ivar Kreuger committed suicide in Paris on March 12, 1931.]

ANN ARBOR
APRIL 9, 1932

Dear Grandfather,

A thousand thanks for your last letter, which made me very happy. I'm sorry to have been so negligent in my letter writing, but I have actually not had much to write about.

We are now at the beginning of what is referred to as Spring Vacation. I got an invitation from the Colvins to come to New York again but decided not to, in part because it's pretty expensive and in part because I've been lazy about some of my courses, especially chemistry and mathematics, and have to pick up my pace a little. Architecture is beginning to be considerably more interesting now that we're getting further into it. For the past month we've been immersing ourselves in Greek civilization, partly because we've been dealing with the history of Greek architecture and partly because we've been concentrating on Greek designs in drawing and freehand. I now know the Parthenon and all the other temples inside out. Architectural history is a fascinating subject. The school has a large auditorium with two big projectors, which makes the whole thing come alive. We take notes and make sketches of everything said or shown.

In freehand drawing I will only get a B (the second highest grade) no matter how hard I try. Nobody else has a higher grade, however, so I'm not worried. I did very poorly in architectural drawing last term even though my grade was good. I feel more secure in that subject now, but I don't think my grade will improve. In wood construction, a new subject, I started off poorly at the beginning of the term but am beginning to pick up now. On the chemistry and math front there is, as I told you, a real disaster brewing. Since this is mostly due to laziness I'm not worried.

You asked about my daily life in your last letter. I must confess that I hardly have one. I get up around 7. If I have time, I eat breakfast at the Michigan Union. It often includes grapefruit, which has become my favorite fruit. Two days a week my classes start at 8 and the other days at 9. I have a full schedule, and classes go until 5. Many of my friends have now joined these so-called fraternities, so I don't see as much of them at mealtimes as I used to. My best friend is a red-haired engineering student who is lame in one leg. He has no special extracurricular gifts, but he is very clever. Last term he was first in his school, which has around seven hundred students. His name was in all the papers, and I basked in his reflected glory.

Getting in the paper is otherwise not particularly noteworthy here, because they print long stories about anybody and anything. If a few students go to a factory to flirt and pass their time, a couple of columns immediately appear about how a "student group investigated social conditions of working class," with pictures of all the participants and their comments reproduced in full. The other day I saw in large letters on the front page of a paper

847 School Kids Enter Spelling Contest
Nation's Best Speller at Lansing, Mich.

All this hoopla about students is part of their student government policy, which is that the students should — not govern themselves — but act as if they governed themselves. Lots of associations and clubs are being organized and overorganized. I admit that they are more parliamentarian than Swedish students and argue much less at their meetings than we do. But I suspect this is because they are actually not the least bit interested in arguing and possess very little common sense. As far as I am able to tell, they have an easier time subordinating themselves to and acknowledging the skill of a leader, or the advantage of having a leader, or the superiority of an established organization. Their faith in authority, or whatever you want to call it, is part of a very real effort you find here to foster tradition and continuity. This is especially apparent when you compare it to Sweden, where there are so many traditions and rules and regulations that the response of the students is not one of faith but of opposition.

I encounter one example after another of how relative truth is. Almost all the educated people that I know here, especially those studying architecture, are appalled by skyscrapers and standardization and straight roads, which they find ugly, and the factories, which lack poetry, and jazz music, which they hate. Their counterparts in crooked, classical Stockholm, where there are no skyscrapers, want nothing more than jazz symphonies at the opera and to build a suspension bridge across Riddarfjärden. I have also noticed that here they will do anything to latch on to historical continuity, and to feel that they are part of progress. (I have a feeling that this movement sprang up after your time, probably as a reaction to the pioneering stage.) Sweden and all of Europe have done much to foster the feeling of being a new world, reborn and guiltfree. Here we find copies of the Pantheon and the Parthenon everywhere, which would be unthinkable at home. But all this is nothing but ripples on the surface, noisy and demonstrative reactions to the real development that naturally will take them in a direction totally different from that of Europe.

It's easy to find examples of this difference by looking at European and American film. European film, especially Russian and sometimes French, likes to dwell on life in the factory, the rhythm of machines and all that. I have actually never seen an interior shot of a factory in an American film. The obvious explanation is that the Americans are so used to that environment, having grown up with it, that they shy away from the mere thought of idealizing or symbolizing industrialism in any way. In Europe, this school has no trouble finding followers because it is new (relatively speaking at least). That is why Theodore Dreiser's books on contemporary social life are so tragic and why Ludvig Nordström's are so forward-looking and upbeat. It also explains why Ford is such a romantic figure in Sweden while people here don't as much admire as envy him.

It would be a shame were this true, for not only would it mean that we possess a lesser degree of large-scale industrialism, rationalization, and organization than America, but that we're not even working in the same spirit. That we had no use for the American ideal other than as fodder for novels and as a disturbing and thank-God-we-are-not-there-yet backdrop in films.

A thousand kisses and my special love to Grandmother, whom I have owed a letter for quite a long time,

Raoul

[As much a mystic as a writer, Nordström *placed industrial expansion and entrepreneurship at the center of his world view, which he called "totalism."]*

Dearest Grandfather,

Thank you very much for your last long letter.

I have a confession to make. I'm ashamed I didn't make it the last time I wrote. Namely that I lost $175 of your money in Kreuger shares.

I had basically decided to put half of the sum from my travel credit in a bank and invest the other half in the best American shares not international in character, since this country will probably recover from the crisis first even though everyone is pessimistic. When Kreuger committed suicide, I had only withdrawn my operating expenses from my letter of credit. Before March 13 the shares were at about 5½ dollars. Right afterward they were at 1½. I bought a hundred when they were at 1⅜ a piece. It was mostly just speculation, and that's why I'm so embarrassed, for I bought them, aware that the New York Stock Exchange always reacts the most sharply to both good and bad news. I thought that the value of the share would climb back as soon as the first scare was over. The actual value of the shares, as gleaned from the latest annual report, was quite a bit higher than 1⅜. In addition, only six months ago, Kreuger had declared that the earnings of the first six months of 1931 had only been insignificantly worse than they were for the corresponding period in 1930. If any such earnings actually took place, that alone would have been enough to justify a value of approximately what I paid per share. Maybe I should have become suspicious and wondered about the reason behind that big a decrease in the value of a share on the market, and whether persons with more sense and acumen than I "knew something" about the company and were selling when I was buying. On the other hand, I also knew that incredibly safe stock such as those in banks headed by National City, the Steel Trust, and General Motors also were decreasing in value — not as much as in the case of Kreuger and Toll, but in any case enough so that those who bought in 1929 now have lost about 9/10 of their fortune.

However, I don't want to excuse what I did, for I know that what you will reproach me for is not so much the loss of $175 as the fact that I bought stock on speculation, taking advantage of what I thought to be only a temporary fluctuation in value.

This might be a good time to ask you if you think it wise to buy American stock with half of my credit account this summer. Even though I'm convinced that the Ann Arbor banks are fairly safe, primarily because this is a student town with very little industrial activity, there are bank failures everywhere and the banks offer no absolute guarantee against the speculative nature of buying shares.

Spring has now arrived in earnest and it's getting pretty warm. I'm going to get another room for the summer because the one I have now is in an attic and I'm sure it will be insufferable.

I'm seriously considering going home in the middle of July, making sure that I return here by September 28, which is when school begins. The reason is the following. A Practice Office School that is to last for four weeks has been arranged for us in order to fulfill the practical requirement for graduation.

Taking this course means I can't really benefit from any of the summer courses, as summer school is harder than the regular terms, and an absence of four weeks right at the beginning would make it difficult to keep up with any of the ordinary subjects and absolutely impossible in an architectural subject. I had planned to go to Chicago, where there is a university based on the European system of independent study. But as I said, I don't think it would pay off. On the other hand, if I go home now, I would have a whole uninterrupted summer the next time, during which I could probably do a full term's work. If I do this again next year, I may gain a maximum of one year (although I honestly don't think I could, because it's hard to get grades transferred from one university to another), and then I might either leave for home or start post-graduate studies, or begin to work in the fall of 1934. I want to know your thoughts on this since it's your wallet that's being hit. I assume you don't like my flitting back and forth between continents, but on the other hand it makes little difference if I go home for a visit now or next year. I feel no special need to go home, except I half promised Mother that I would come and see her once during my four years away. As for the risk of returning home and learning to become a pessimist, I don't think it is particularly great. Although people back home may be gloomier than they are here, at least (judging from the newspapers) the depression has at least not yet turned into the preaching and spiritual plague that it is here.

However, there is a plan that is almost better yet, and that is not to worry about summer school etc., to go home next summer, and in general to take what comes along. There is so much to see here, and it might even be possible to get a job of some kind or other.

Ticket prices to Europe are pretty inexpensive at the moment. I saw a round trip advertised for $108.

I haven't been particularly successful in school this term, nor am I making too many frantic attempts to reach Olympian heights. I have a lot to do periodically and I think that my grades, although mediocre, will be as good as circumstances allow.

My friend the English astronomer and his Swedish fiancée are leaving in a few weeks and I feel pretty sad about that.

A thousand greetings to the two of you from

Raoul

ISTANBUL
MAY 18, 1932

My dear boy,

In my last letter of April 23, I asked about your plans for the summer. Ever since the question has been raised I have been thinking continuously about what would be best for you. Two alternatives seem to me worth pursuing during the summers you will spend in America. One is to find work, to get an idea of what it means to earn a living. However, I think that this should wait for another year, since I am aware of the tremendous unemployment in the States and hence the difficulty of finding anything, especially on a temporary basis.

The other is a trip to California to meet people and to establish contact with "personnes de valeur." I think it useful that your book education be supplemented by knowledge of human nature: a study of the character, customs, and ideas of mature people. Overaccumulation of theoretical knowledge can easily lead to a sense of self-satisfaction, a kind of arrogance —

I have already related my observation that in Sweden we are much too prone to force young people into a niche, expecting them to await developments without a fuss, and to accept whatever circumstances warrant. You are in America precisely because I do not want you assigned to a niche. Where you will stand out when you return to Sweden is in your knowledge of human nature and experience with life. During your studies in Ann Arbor, you have already had the opportunity to exchange ideas with people who live and think differently from us. I don't mean that the American way of thinking is superior to ours. *But it is different.* So you are already ahead of the game through your contact with young people in Ann Arbor. My plan now is to place you even further ahead by putting you in touch with the right people during a vacation trip to California, so that you might profit by their experience and their views on life.

A project like this is much easier to carry out than you think. Nearly every door is open to a young man with your name and your qualifications. Americans are exceedingly hospitable and accommodating toward Europeans and especially toward Swedes. They like to discuss things with them. They are delighted to have a chance to talk of their accomplishments. Maybe more so now than before the crisis, if you know how to provide them with the right cues. They share their experiences openly and love to meet anyone versed enough in the art of discussion that it's worth their while persuading them the American way of life is best. You should turn it into a challenge to provoke a discussion in the course of which you might learn what they think of the future and how they think the great problems facing mankind should be solved. Begin by inquiring about conditions in America, always with the idea of extracting their thoughts about the future prospects for the various European countries. That is of great interest, because Americans have a practical streak and are quicker to perceive possibilities than we are. If you manage to get your foot in the door, people will be lining up to welcome you. The decision of whom to contact should be made from the point of view of how best to accomplish what you set out to do.

I used to have an old friend living in California by the name of Lindström. The consulate will give you his address — if he is still alive. I last saw him in 1919, on my way back from Japan. He was the brother of one of my friends in the navy, Carl L., now deceased, and of Axel L., who applied to the Naval Academy the same time I did. This was in 1876. He was involved in physical education and ran a store that sold Jaeger undergarments, knew the whole world, and was well off. We never spent much time together, but no matter; when you have known someone for fifty years or more you always feel that you are "old friends."

The consul in San Francisco is C. E. Wallerstedt, b. 1882; the vice consul is C. F. Hellström, b. 1890, and the first secretary is Carl Otto von Essen, b. 1897 (of the noble Skåne branch).

But you should not just look up Swedes. They will act as intermediaries to the Americans, men as well as women, and provide you with the opportunity for these beneficial conversations. I assure you, once again, that older people enjoy meeting with young people of intelligence. More so in America than here. If you succeed here and there, word will spread about what a pleasure it was to meet that intelligent young Swede. Everybody already knows our name. It will be easy to arouse people's interest. You have seen a great deal, and you have a knack for conversation. Use it for the purpose I have outlined and you will find your summer was well spent. The climate in California is excellent, not too hot. Behave simply and unpretentiously. Seek out the company of young people. Don't stay in a luxury hotel but in a simple place. This will seem perfectly natural. It isn't the address of the hotel that is supposed to attract attention but your talents. If those don't prove sufficient for the proposed program, you'll have to give up and go back to Ann Arbor. I want for you to enjoy yourself, but without incurring too many expenses and only on the condition that you reap the benefits I have listed above. Travel around freely in California, but you must get in touch with people of substance wherever you go.

If we are lucky and Lindström is still alive, speak with him openly of my wishes. Tell him you would like to make the right contacts. He knows everyone. Should he not be alive, the people at the consulate will point you in the right direction. You must not lend anyone money, this I must emphasize, for it may be that California Swedes have the same tendency as those at home and times are bad. But if this is the case you are required to say no.

California has a very large Swedish population. Around 40,000 strong, I think. Old Matson, who was our consul general for many years, is dead. He went out there at the age of six and became a very important figure in shipping, sugar, and oil. He went into partnership with an American named Spreckles. They started a large sugar business in Hawaii, and Matson owned the steamship line there. America had two sugar barons in the eighties. One was S. and the other was Havemeyer. I knew the latter as well. He lived in N.Y. and was part of my company.

If you make it to Vancouver and San Diego, follow the same plan of action. In my youth I had sailing ships that sometimes visited those places. There is much to see and even more to experience.

I am sending you a copy of a letter to Sahlin. It should be self-explanatory. Also an introduction to Consul Wallerstedt. I am looking forward to hearing your impressions. Take your Corona along and make copies of your letters, so that you have them in your file as a diary detailing your experiences.

I think that you will find this trip very useful, and am therefore happy to defray the costs, but be careful because times are tight. I am well pleased with your regimen so far and therefore have complete confidence in how you go about accomplishing the purpose that I have outlined for the trip. Of course, you should feel free to stop on the way out to California. Take buses every now and then. It is worth it, especially when you go through the mountains.

See that letters addressed to the Swedish consulate in San Francisco get forwarded no matter where you go, and read an appropriate book about how California was first Spanish and then American.

Grandmother sends her greetings. She is well, and still here, and seems to like it. However, I expect she'll be going home soon. The garden at Saltsjöbaden beckons.

Your affectionate
[GOW]

ANN ARBOR
JUNE 4, 1932

Dearest Grandfather,

Thanks for your long and informative letter, which I just received.
I was ashamed when I read "I am well pleased with your regimen
so far," as you will have had a chance to change your opinion
now that you've read my confession in my last letter about buying
Kreuger stock.

Since I wrote you I've learned that summer school doesn't end
until July 27. This means that going home this summer will be
impossible; instead I'll have just enough time for your trip out
west. I want to express my deep gratitude, which I owe you not
only for the financial responsibilities you undertake for my sake,
but because I know that I am the constant object of your concern
and love.

I really have no idea of what such a trip would cost. You often
hear about boys here who have bummed a ride from coast to
coast. That is, they got free rides along the roads. This practice has
become more common during the present crisis, and lots of car
owners have even put little signs on their windshields with the
words "Let's Go, America — Ask for a Ride." As I said, I've no
idea how much you save traveling this way, but it's worth a try not
only because it's cheaper but also because it's a lot more fun. It's
as American as hiking is in Germany. If I undertake this trip I will
try to fulfill your wishes as closely as possible. I'm completely
with you on this, and had come up with similar ideas of my own
when I learned that summer school had been moved up, making
a trip home out of the question. Actually it was mostly for
Mother's sake that I'd thought about going home at all, and I don't
want you to think that I have an uncontainable urge to spend
money.

I have an incredible amount of work at the moment, and the
tests are coming fast and furious. Today I will turn in a "final
plate," a restaurant, which I finally finished after many long nights
of work. My last trial will be over on the 13th, then I'll head to
Chicago, where I've been invited by one of my friends to stay in
the bosom of his family until summer school starts on the 27th. I
think I've mentioned him before. He's the best student in the

Engineering School, which has 1,500 students. His father is an "efficiency expert" at a large electricity company. Summer school will go until the end of July, as I've said, and then I have a choice between a trip to San Francisco or summer school in Chicago. The decision depends on what information Chicago sends me about their requirements.

I just got a letter from Mother in which while writing about the Kreuger crash and Uncle Marcus's relationship to him, she quotes Nunne as having said that "Uncle Marcus was so affected by Kreuger's death that he became an insomniac afterward." Whether this is due to fear and panic or to overwork I don't know, but I mention it to do my small part in forewarning you of the reaction you may expect from Uncle Marcus.

I've been following the political development inside and outside the country with interest. The revelation that New York's lord mayor, Jimmy Walker, has been taking bribes on the side doesn't appear to have excited anyone, since no one seems to have expected otherwise. Americans generally feel hearty contempt for their politicians. You often find cynical articles in the paper saying that America is not a true democracy, because if the people had a real say there would be neither a president nor a congress. Hoover's popularity, which last fall had become pretty feeble, has increased some because of all his savings proposals, and perhaps even more because Congress has routinely voted them down, thereby putting him in favorable light.

In half an hour I'll take my final in my military course. It has surprised me very much that, so far as I can tell, the organization of the lower units of the American infantry isn't much better than the Swedish. Every "squad" has eight men and a corporal, rather than eleven men and a corporal, as in Sweden. That, combined with the fact that in addition to the commanders an American platoon has six officers as opposed to two, as in Sweden, makes the fighting ability of American infantry greater than the Swedish. But in almost every other respect, such as in the regulations governing attack and defense, the Swedish army is as good. In one respect, i.e., the lack of highly complex Prussian parade maneuvers, the Swedes are even considerably ahead.

It is now the morning after my R.O.T.C. exam. I passed, and probably did pretty well on it, but I am totally exhausted, because a couple of friends and I stayed up all night studying chemistry, in which we all are rather weak and need to review. These late nights have gone on for a few weeks now and I'll be glad when it's all over. I've also just been told that I am exempt from the final in architectural history as I already have an A average. That will be one of few courses in which I'll get a good grade this term. But I have a considerably heavier course load than most of my friends, so I may be excused.

Looking back on the academic year I find that I've had just a wonderful time. The climate has been considerably better than its rainy reputation, actually better than at home. I have lots of friends whom I like very much. People have been very nice and treat me well. My schoolwork has, on the whole, paid off not only when it comes to grades, because that isn't too important, but because I really feel that I've learned something. You remember that before I came here, I argued that our institutions were better than American schools. But now I find that apart from the intended benefit, which was that I come to America to catch its spirit, I've also been getting a technical education that isn't inferior to what I would have gotten in Sweden. And at least it isn't marred by laziness.

A thousand greetings until next time, which will be after the exams.

Raoul

[P.S.] Letters arriving here after the 27th should be addressed: "Kappa Delta Rho," Ann Arbor, Michigan. This is a "fraternity" where I have a very inexpensive room for the duration of summer school.

[Nunne *was the family nickname of Andrea Mörner, daughter of Marcus Wallenberg Sr.]*

Istanbul

June 20, 1932

My dear boy,

Thank you for your letters of May 15 and June 4. My last one was written May 18 and contained an outline of a summer trip to California and the western states. I see from your last letter that you have grasped the thoughts behind my plan for the journey. My letter didn't address the issue of your returning home, but now I can say that it would have been completely inopportune. It smacked too much of pleasure, which is unsuitable, especially given the current economic conditions, and would have demonstrated that you do not take the whole purpose behind your stay in America *au sérieux*. It is true you do say — and I noted it carefully — that you yourself had no desire to go home but that it was the thought of pleasing your mother that gave you the idea. I should mention for reasons of consolation and explanation that I sent your mother a copy of my letter to you and explained my reasons. I've received an answer from which I see that she wholeheartedly approves of my plan and expresses her pleasure with it. So now we have to make the most of the venture.

Mr. Gillespie, who just returned from a six months' stay in the States, was very interested to hear my account of how the plans, which he helped me formulate a year ago, have worked out. He especially liked the rationale behind this summer and recommended you should learn as much as you can about the outstanding organization of the fruit-growing industry in California, which is supposed to be centered in Fresno, and about an irrigation project called Imperial Valley. He will also recommend you study the Ford factory in Detroit, as well as General Motors. They are probably the two most fascinating organizations in the world. I will be seeing him in a few days and will talk more with him about this. It is of less importance to marvel at the machinery. All workshops are basically the same. What is interesting is to get in touch with those who are able to keep operations of this magnitude running and to understand how. It will be useful to have a good recommendation. I will write you as soon as I have seen G——.

I noted your speculation in Kreuger stock, and I disapprove.

You will have to pay for half of the loss out of your inheritance. I am glad, however, that you made no money on the deal, since it would have led you to believe that speculation is easy. It is a game to everyone except those whose profession it is to do it, and should never involve more than a small part of your earnings.

Grandmother writes that her trip home went well, and that she enjoys being at Saltsjöbaden. I am well and as ever follow your doings with the greatest of interest.

Affectionately,
[GOW]

[Mr. Gillespie was probably an American diplomat GOW knew in Istanbul.]

ANN ARBOR
JULY 12, 1932

Dear Grandfather,

I'm back from Chicago, where I had a wonderful time. As I think I told you, I got there by hitchhiking and found a ride all the way to Chicago, right to the very door of the place I was staying. My friend and I spent most of our days walking around the city or going out to one of the long beaches that surround Chicago. One day we took a long hike through a forest preserve, and it felt good after all that sitting around in Ann Arbor. I didn't attend any of the large political conventions, because the only one in progress while I was there was the Republican and I'd been wrong about when the Democratic convention was starting, otherwise it would have been very interesting to attend. The Democratic conventions have always been more popular than those of the Republicans, who are too well behaved to be much fun. I have, however, listened night and day to the Democratic proceedings on the radio. Roosevelt's victory was always taken for granted, but [Al] Smith is much more popular, especially among the "people." They thought that if Smith managed to keep his forces consolidated through a sufficient number of roll call votes, Roosevelt's forces might tire and cross over to him, but I just heard on the radio that it didn't work. Generally speaking, I liked Chicago more and more the longer I stayed. The city has probably changed more than most since you were here, for it has grown, not only on the outskirts in the form of private houses, but also along huge stretches of the Lake Michigan shore, where the large Century of Progress Exposition, popularly referred to as "The Fair," will take place. Many of the buildings are already finished and needless to say very impressive. One of my friend's friends took me down to Donnelly's printing company, which was very interesting. They're by far the largest printing company in the world, and have enormous capacity. Among other things they're capable of delivering several hundred thousand telephone directories a *day* without any difficulty. One day I went to a dinner at the Swedish Club. Sven Hedin was the guest of honor. I've never been much of an admirer of Sven Hedin. His books always seemed strained, and his style reminded me somewhat of Selma Lagerlöf's. But having listened to him, I can now understand why he manages to persuade American millionaires to defray the costs of his expeditions, even in these hard times. He's a wonderful speaker and talked for almost two hours without the aid of written notes of any kind and without losing any of the thread or thrust of the presentation.

Among those present was District Attorney Johnsson, the man who spent four years preparing a case against Al Capone, the smuggler king and mass murderer. Capone was convicted on a count of income tax evasion over a period of years and sentenced to prison for eleven years. It was the only thing that would stick. Johnsson was surrounded by his bodyguards, burly men with bulging pockets. The danger of gangsters in Chicago doesn't appear to be as imaginary. At the printing plant I mentioned above, an old Englishman who was their special expert on handmade, beautiful covers of sharkskin, tigerskin, and other rarities said that he never got over his surprise and his pity whenever a customer would bring him a book worth fifty thousand dollars — they exist — accompanied by a whole line of policemen armed with submachine guns. The young woman who gave us a ride back to Ann Arbor told us also that gangsters had raided her house during the night and after puncturing the tires of the two family cars, proudly made off with — the backseats. Her father had been attacked not long before and beaten bloody and had his watch and his wallet stolen. But I had no firsthand experiences with gangster activity and indeed was pleasantly surprised by everybody's kindness and helpfulness in this Babylon, so famous for cheating the unwary. One night, returning to Oak Park, where I was staying, I had to use the Elevated, and since the trip itself took around three hours I slept soundly between the changes. I was awakened punctually every time by the conductor whom I had asked to wake me. I was also surprised by Chicago's many parks; I had always imagined the city as a veritable stone desert.

I've just read in the papers that Carl Bonde is one of the leaders of the Olympic team Sweden has sent to Los Angeles. I hope I'll get there in time for the Games. He may also be able to do something for me.

Summer school has been great so far. The boys who will be graduating next year or have finished their studies, and who only need to put in their required practical time, are working as architects in a make-believe architectural firm set up by the school. The professors are their bosses, presenting them with rough ideas to flesh out. We underlings do all the detail work. This is much more fun than ordinary school, because this way everyone is a little cog responsible for an area of his own. We work eight hours a day but have no homework, which is nice. I'm in a good mood today, for I was complimented by a professor yesterday on a rather difficult construction I had made for a bathroom. I am sending you a blueprint of a "final plate" that I made in my wood construction class. I have no idea what grade I got on it. Probably not too good, but it doesn't matter. In any case, it was one of the hardest tasks we have had up to now. We had to draw a house with a ground-floor space of 550 square feet and with a certain number of rooms prescribed for each floor. In other respects we were given a degree of freedom. We were not permitted to simplify the task as much as many of us would have wanted, however. For example, we couldn't use flat roofs. It was not an architectural task in the true sense, because the quality of the drawing and the completeness of the notes were as important as aesthetic and practical considerations.

My grades were an A in freehand, R.O.T.C. (the military course), and in architectural history, Bs in two architectural subjects and math, and a C in chemistry. As I told you, C is "fair" and D "passing." These are the same grades as last term, and so my fears were unfounded.

A thousand greetings from your
Raoul

*[*Century of Progress Exposition *refers to the Chicago World's Fair.* Carl Bonde *was married to Ebba Wallenberg, the daughter of Marcus Wallenberg Sr.* Sven Hedin *was a Swedish explorer and writer whose travels through Asia made him a celebrity. As concerns units of measurements in this correspondence, RW's habit was to employ the system of the country from which he was writing. Conversion to imperial measurement is therefore not provided.]*

ISTANBUL
JULY 22, 1932

My dear boy,

Many thanks for your letter of July 12. I was interested to hear about your trip to Chicago and your meeting with Dr. Sven Hedin. He is, as you say, a wonderful lecturer. Let me tell you about the time I met him. It will not hurt to have on record Hedin's first step on the path to becoming a world celebrity.

It was late in the fall of 1907. I had gone to Japan at the very end of 1906, and after being there for four months suggested to then foreign minister Trolle that I come home to consult with him about a possible plan for our commercial expansion in the Far East. I went home but I got nowhere, except they did go along with my suggestion for setting up a shipping line to the East, and I was present at a celebration given on August 20, 1907, on the occasion of the departure of the first boat from Gothenburg. Her name was the *Canton* and she measured about 5,000 d.m. tons. Upon returning to the East that fall, I went to Peking to present my credentials to the emperor of China. There I met with the German minister, Count von Rex, formerly in Teheran. He told me he'd

just had a letter from Sven Hedin, whose acquaintance he had
made in Teheran some years earlier. In it, Hedin described the
difficulties he was experiencing because the Chinese authorities
had refused to issue him a visa to travel to Tibet. Hedin had been
away several years and obviously knew nothing about the creation of a Swedish diplomatic mission in Japan and China.

"This will be an excellent thing for you to handle," said Count
Rex to me. "There is no chance of my being able to do anything
for Hedin, since I'm on rather shaky terms with the Chinese
government, having failed last year to procure a visa for a German explorer" — whose name I have forgotten — "to travel to
exactly the same area. And," he added, "it might just be that as a
newcomer you will be treated better." I protested that since I was
new to the profession and had no experience with or knowledge
of those in charge at Wei Wubu (China's Ministry for Foreign
Affairs) it might be better, after all, if R. helped Hedin with his
request, not least because — since I was more likely to fail than
R. — Hedin might blame me for the change of dispositions. I got
nowhere in my attempt to persuade R., however. He told me he
intended to write Hedin that he had handed the matter over to his
Swedish colleague but that this colleague was unwilling to deal
with it. I had no choice but to give it my best shot. Before ending
the conversation, I managed to extract a fair amount of information from Rex. Among other things, it turned out that he had
forced the issue of the passport for his countryman with the result
that Peking had issued a prohibition against the German scientist's going to Tibet. I therefore decided to make certain this
would not be the case with Hedin, and during my negotiations
with the Chinese foreign minister, Na Tung, actually managed to
accomplish that, although he denied my request for a passport for
H. Under no conditions did the Chinese want explorers traveling
in Tibet — all this was shortly after the then quite famous English
colonel Younghusband's raid on Lhasa, very reminiscent of that
of Dr. Jameson's 1888 raid on the northern parts of the Boer
Republic, which resulted in the Boer War — but somehow, I
managed to assuage them. In my letter to Hedin, I pointed out
that though no prohibition had been issued, it was up to him to
weigh the possible risks. These were small for an experienced
traveler like Hedin, and he complimented me on my achievement.

After this digression let me resume my account of the events in Japan and Hedin's part in them. The Japanese-Russian War had ended in 1905, and the question of what direction the country would take was uppermost on the agenda. The government was in strong hands. The emperor had created a new Japan. He had been alive during the Restoration in 1868, the Chinese War of 1895, and now the one with Russia. England, which had concluded a controversial alliance with Japan in 1902, had provided them with economic support during the war. The Japanese were obviously very grateful for this, but when in return the English wanted to influence the direction of the country, the Japanese objected. Japan was for the Japanese. The result was a huge outcry from the English press in the East and in London. Japan was accused of being the Prussia of the East, a danger to humanity, interested only in war and naval victory. Their rearmament (which was intended only to replace matériel destroyed during the war) was seen as a threat to all foreign powers in the Far East.

I got fairly close to Baron Makino, then minister of communications. This was natural. Issues involving communication had been my hobby for some time, and I had developed something of a following after giving a lecture on the organization of international communications before a large gathering of the top people within the Japanese communications industry. The lecture was published and the following year led to the establishment of a communications network among the different countries in the East and centered in Japan.

During one of my visits with him, Makino told me of the government's worries about the tensions with England. "We're currently paying 6 percent for our loans," he said. "The time is right for a conversion. We would probably be repaying the loan at an interest rate of 4.5 percent or maybe 4 if this trouble hadn't started. And all because England began telling the world out of spite that we were the Prussia of the East and interested only in arming ourselves. A sad state of affairs," said M. "What should we do? You are good at finding practical solutions. Can you not do something in this case?"

I had felt very cut off from things after my return from Sweden. No one out there was familiar with Sweden, and I had yet to come up with a way of changing that. One boat had been launched, but the impression I had gotten during my trip home was that no one was ready to make a serious effort. Interest in foreign trade was particularly slight at that time. We were inexperienced and unambitious. Everything necessary for starting new steamship lines to the Far East and to South America was not in place yet. Our leaders at home felt no urge to venture into uncharted waters. Night and day I racked my brain to come up with something that would put us on the map, but jealousy between the various players within the commercial area meant that every attempt was nipped in the bud because it provoked the kind of hostility that the acquisition of money is capable of provoking among ill-mannered colonials. My situation was rather hopeless. I hadn't found a way of breaking through either the heavily fortified positions of my competitors out there or the indifference at home.

All this flashed through my mind while Makino recounted the worries of the Japanese government. I said to Makino: "If the English have persuaded the rest of the world that Japan is interested only in war, you will have to find a way to convince everyone of your interest in cultural matters and science and their practitioners. They can provide good publicity if you give them any reason to." "What do you mean?" interjected Makino, seeing the glint in my eye. "Well," said I, "it seems fairly likely that Dr. Sven Hedin, who is in Tibet at the moment and who I know is about to go home, could be persuaded to pass through Japan and give some lectures here. Properly staged, they might afford you an excellent opportunity to demonstrate to the world Japanese interest in scientific questions and thus refute the English accusations." "An excellent idea," replied Makino. "I will speak to the prime minister [Prince Ito] right away."

M. came back the following day to tell me that the government was delighted with my idea, and asked me to implement it. I asked if this meant I could wire Hedin on behalf of the Japanese government and invite him to come. "Yes, of course." I sent a wire and immediately received the answer that Hedin would come.

Soon after, a delegation led by the former minister of education, who had become president of the university in Kyoto, appeared at the legation to inform me that they had been appointed as a reception committee. They declared that they had been instructed to present Hedin with a check in the amount of 3,000 yen. There were no conditions, though they wished to express their hope that H. would give one lecture at the university in Tokyo and another in Kyoto. I immediately realized that refusing this magificent offer would deepen the obligation on the part of the Japanese (which later won the wholehearted approval of Hedin), and so I replied on behalf of Hedin and myself that while we were very honored, we were unable to accept the check. If my famous countryman Dr. Sven Hedin had decided to come to Japan, I continued, it was because of his interest in the ancient culture of this country and his sympathies for its courageous and industrious people. This had an enormous effect. A delegation was sent to meet Hedin, who was in Shanghai by this point. When he got to Tokyo he was received in the most glorious fashion. At an audience before the emperor he was given his first great order, and instead of staying for only one week, he extended his stay to 64 days, during which 63 parties were given in his honor. Hedin gave a lecture at every one of those parties. I have never encountered his equal as a lecturer. All this happened twenty-five years ago, when he was in his prime and his handsome face much admired, especially by the ladies. Everybody wanted to hear him. I remember that once, after a dinner at the British embassy given by Sir Claude MacDonald, at which, as usual, H. was to speak, the blackboard on which he had sketched the sub-Himalayan mountains was varnished and preserved as a family treasure. I later saw it many times in the hallway of the British embassy, but expect that it was burned during the world war, after Hedin did his ill-advised propaganda work for Wilhelm II.

Hedin was a hit in Tokyo. The Japanese got what they wanted, namely to persuade the world that they had wide-ranging cultural interests. I also got what I wanted. Sweden became famous overnight in Japan, and was held in higher esteem than other countries. We had thus made a good beginning, and results eventually followed. Four years later, we were third behind England and Germany in terms of imports.

There you have something about Sven Hedin. Since then I've rarely seen him, the last time being at a meeting of the China Society last fall. He is still full of energy, in spite of his years, but in these depressed times has a hard time raising the large sums to continue his exploration around Asia.

There's too much about Hedin in this letter, but I got started on the subject and old memories came to life. Actually I decided to write to offer my congratulations on turning 20. You have covered a good deal of ground for someone your age. You have also given me great pleasure, and are the dearest thing I have on this earth. This is why I am trying with such anxious care to shape your character. . . .

We are having a rather hot summer, 34 to 36 degrees Celsius [93 to 97°F] in the shade. The nights are pleasant, however. I still have no thoughts of going home. I find the thought of seeing Knut and Marcus repugnant under the present circumstances. I am very fond of my brothers, but their idea of what needs to be done to save our country during these difficult times is very different from mine. I think they're on the wrong track, as you know, but for the sake of family unity I haven't wanted to provoke an open fight. I've been hoping, and I continue to hope, that eventually we will see eye to eye. It would have been better had we been able to do so two years ago. Now it will probably be necessary. But I will also do everything in my power to avoid their interpreting any change of position as capitulation. This is best accomplished by letting some time pass, and by staying off the battlefield. At least that is what I think.

Adios, my dear boy, and all good wishes for the coming years.

Your affectionate
[GOW]

Los Angeles
August 8, 1932

Dearest Grandfather,

I've seen and done quite a few things since I last wrote. I left Michigan the very minute school was over. First, I'd like to explain why I chose to hitchhike. To begin with, I hate the train and dislike bus trips even more after that trip to New York last Christmas. The bus did offer plenty of adventures involving delays and luggage trouble, and although I liked it — maybe precisely for that reason — I wouldn't want to sit on a bus for an entire week. When you travel like a hobo, everything's different.

You take it for granted that you'll have to be on the alert the whole time, and if it turns out to be a relatively easy trip, so much the better. You're in close contact with new people each and every day. Hitchhiking gives you training in diplomacy and tact. It's also inexpensive; transportation costs for a distance of 2,000 miles were fifty cents. As for the risks, they're probably exaggerated. During the last few years, a reaction against hitchhiking has sprung up in America, and several states have outlawed it because of the number of robberies attributed to hitchhikers. Hitchhikers have also been attacked and robbed of their extremely meager means. But common sense tells you that it is the hitchhiker who runs the smaller risk, and I think that risk is pretty minimal. In any case, I haven't had a single unpleasant experience of this kind. And even if I had been held up, the loss would have been small because I only carried $25 in bills the day I started, and this sum got smaller with every day. The rest was in traveler's checks. I'd also sent $100 ahead to a bank in California. But as I said, these safety measures proved unnecessary and nothing happened. There's a general tendency to exaggerate unknown dangers. Just imagine the enormous risks you expose yourself to every time you cross the street. Yet it would never occur to anyone not to cross the street. And when they counter this by saying that everyone knows how to avoid risks when crossing the street, I say that the same is true of hitchhiking. You don't have to accept a ride from everyone who offers one. Personally, I find all the arguments against using this mode of transportation very weak given all its advantages.

I started out on Saturday the 23rd at one in the afternoon and by that very evening found myself about 100 miles east of Chicago. I'd actually hoped to get there that evening, but couldn't manage it. The next morning I continued on through Gary, the steel town named for one of the former directors of the Steel Trust. This was the first time I'd ever seen Chicago on a Sunday, and it seemed almost as empty and deserted as Stockholm. I went up to the offices of the *Tribune,* and asked if they wanted to buy some articles that I proposed to write, but they seemed fairly reluctant. I finally did manage to convince them to consider the articles when they eventually arrived, but I didn't leave their skyscraper, which reminds you of a Gothic cathedral, filled with hope. I actually haven't sent them any articles as yet mainly because I haven't had time. I took the Elevated out to Oak Park, where my friends the

Wehausens live. The father was not at home, however, so there went my hope of getting a ride out of the city. I did have something to eat there, though, and got a letter of introduction to a lady in Hollywood. After that I got luckier, because an older couple only out for a spin took me twenty-five miles farther than they had intended to go. Like the princess in *Arabian Nights,* I kept their attention riveted by telling stories and talking, especially at those spots where they had the best chance of turning around. I continued traveling late into the night, and even walked a few miles. I met a poor starving ex-student on his way to Denver, where he had managed to find a job. He was very well educated but seemed totally helpless when it came to practical matters. I treated him to dinner, and I've never made anyone as happy as that, except possibly the same man when I gave him an opportunity to talk about Russian writers, whom I naturally hadn't read. This kind of thing is not unusual here now. After a good night's sleep in a guesthouse, I pushed on toward St. Louis on foot. I'd made up my mind to see it even though it was considerably out of my way. Eventually I got a ride, and before long was in the city. It seemed in some way less orderly than the northern cities I'd become accustomed to. The architecture of the skyscrapers struck me as more honest and less theatrical than what you find in Chicago and Detroit. Toward evening I reached St. Charles, situated on a branch of the Mississippi, and which, at first sight, reminds you of Tours in France. A young man stopped and picked me up, then gave me a tour of the city. Since I'd lost time in St. Louis and made such poor time the previous day I decided to press on through the night, but to target trucks rather than passenger cars. People are usually not eager to pick up strange men on the road in the middle of the night. I managed to become buddies with a trucker driving one of the enormous eight-wheelers that you often see here in America, on the way to a little town called St. Joseph, north of Kansas City. Those trucks are impressively elegant. They usually drive at night in order not to compete with normal daytime traffic. A backup driver always sleeps on a cot behind the driver's seat while the other one drives. I sat next to the driver and slept as best I could. Shortly after we'd passed Hannibal, the birthplace of Mark Twain, a storm broke out that was so violent we couldn't see more than a couple of meters in front of us and soon had to stop and wait for it to clear. Unfortunately, it turned out that the motor had gotten wet.

We then had to wait for an hour before another truck came and helped us out. During the morning hours I lay half-naked on the roof sunbathing. It was incredible. In St. Joseph, I met the Swedish-American owner of a gas station. With almost Spanish hospitality, he put his house at my disposal, and I shaved and had a thorough wash. When I was cleaned up, I learned to my surprise that he had arranged a ride for me that would take me 30 miles south, i.e., halfway to Kansas City. I got there in the afternoon, and immediately sent my clothes to be washed and ironed, for they had become thoroughly soaked, and were dirty and wrinkled, and I knew from experience that it pays to look clean and respectable. While my uniform was being spruced up, I made the rounds of the various hotels and tried to strike up an acquaintance with someone who might be heading west, for I was beginning to move into areas that were pretty sparsely populated and where the prospect of being stranded out on the plain was in no way appealing. My rounds turned up nothing, even though I'd become fairly experienced in the art of approaching doormen. So I had to try my luck hitching. My first goal was Topeka, and I got there after a trip that included a long hike by foot pretty late at night. Again, I decided to go all night to make up for lost time. A little exhausting, but that's part of the appeal. At a local truck depot, I found a man who said he'd be happy to help me because, as he said, "I've been in the army myself." (Did I tell you that I was wearing my R.O.T.C. uniform? Reserve Officer's Training Corps.) He gave me the address of a gas station outside the city limits where the big long-distance trucks usually stop and then he wrote the mysterious words "O.K." (approval) on a scrap of paper and handed it to me with a smile. I'm beginning to learn that people really are quite nice. At least those in the trucking business. I immediately headed off to the address listed and arrived there at midnight, having passed and watched a lively Negro party in a park. When I got there, I sat in a chair to get some sleep and was awakened an hour later by a truck pulling in with its horn blaring. Unfortunately it wasn't going as far as Denver, only to the little town of Salina out on the plain. I accepted gratefully, especially since the truck was almost empty and had a magnificent cargo of sacks in the storage space. I slept until morning, when I was

awakened by the truck jerking to a stop. We'd reached the home
of the trucker, and he evidently was as tired as I had been and
went to bed. I took the opportunity to shave and clean myself up.
When I'd finished, the trucker's wife came out with breakfast.
Kind soul, she probably thought I was starving. Afterward we
continued on to Salina, where I immediately got a ride with a
pistol-toting traveling salesman in a magnificent Oldsmobile.
Here the real West began, and I saw more and more cowboys in
wide-brimmed hats riding on the plains watching over giant
herds of cattle. The day passed without any noteworthy experiences, except that it got noticeably hotter the closer we got to the
great deserts. At night I slept in a tourist place of the usual kind.
The next morning I was lucky enough to get a ride in a fast car
that took me almost three hundred miles west through the blazing
heat to the relative relief of the large valley that runs south, and in
which Denver, Colorado Springs, and Pueblo are situated. I was
just north of Colorado Springs and immediately faced with the
decision of whether to go on through Denver and Salt Lake City
and then down to Los Angeles, or to take the southern route
through Pueblo, Santa Fe, and then west to Los Angeles. I let fate
choose by hailing cars going both north and south and taking the
first one to stop. Pueblo won. A quick trip on wonderful roads
took me through Colorado Springs, "the garden of the gods," as
it's called. These regions are very enterprising and still not fully
exploited, and you find ads offering this or that property everywhere, unfailingly pointing out that in all likelihood lots of gold
and oil wait just beneath the sand. I wonder what people here
were like when times were good, given how optimistic they are
now. I vowed I would stay in Pueblo until I found someone going
all the way to Los Angeles, still over a thousand miles away, for
west of Pueblo the terrain consists of terrible deserts and mountain areas, and I didn't intend to take any risks. I started "canvass-
ing" the hotels the same way I had in Kansas City, but without
success. When I got up next morning, I caught sight of a young
man in a car from Minnesota, and after striking up a conversation
with him I learned he was leaving for Los Angeles. He offered to
take me along if I could set out right away. I'd left my few
valuables locked up in the hotel safe, and the man who had the
key was off having breakfast somewhere. I tried to get a Negro at
the hotel to run and find him, but could only prevail on his

laziness after an argument that almost ended in blows. Finally I was ready and began the final stage of my trip.

I'll send you an account of it before long. I'm having a very nice time here, and have visited the Swedes several times with Uncle Carl and Johan Gabriel, who are here for the Games. Tuesday, I'm going to Boulder Dam in a truck I have ferreted out. I'll be in San Francisco in three/four days and will stay there as long as I find things to do. My birthday passed quietly because I'd asked the city authorities not to make any special fuss.

1,000 kisses,
Raoul

[Johan Gabriel (Oxenstierna), the son of GOW's sister Siri, won a gold medal in the pentathlon at the 1932 Olympic Games in Los Angeles.]

SAN FRANCISCO
AUGUST 16, 1932

Dearest Grandfather,

My new travel companion had been by himself the whole long trip down from Minnesota, and now that he had an opportunity to vent his talkativeness it came out in a torrent. I'm afraid I have to report that many of his jokes were aimed at the Swedish race. This is, unhappily, hard to escape here. Swedes are known for their honesty and stupidity. Americans are famous for their contempt of foreigners, however, and that probably explains it. In most other countries, those foreigners whom the natives get to know are fairly high-class tourists — students, lecturers, and others who don't disguise the fact that they're foreigners and who therefore make a good impression. Representatives of foreign nationalities such as these are almost entirely absent in the United States, except for some from Asian nations. The foreign element in this country consists of people who intend to settle here. They can see that it's to their distinct advantage to become Americanized as rapidly as possible. The most intelligent ones are the most successful. Their transformation from immigrants to true Americans sometimes extends to a change of name. Therefore the brightest immigrants disappear into the mass of Americans and will never help them change their impression of foreigners, who are represented mainly by their least desirable elements. What has struck me is that this must be why Swedes, who nowhere in Europe have a reputation for low intelligence — not even in Germany, despite the expression "die dumme Schweden" — seem to enjoy that reputation here.

As I said, we started out from Pueblo early in the morning and got to Santa Fe at lunchtime, having passed over some high mountain ridges from which we could peer down on the yellowish-brown sand and grassy desert land that we knew would stay with us all the way to just outside Los Angeles, almost 1,000 miles farther west. Santa Fe turned out to be a city almost European in appearance, with narrow winding streets and an old and at first glance fairly ugly cathedral. It actually has the honor of being the oldest church of its size in the United States, just as Santa Fe is the oldest state capital. The area is still Spanish or Spanish-American, and the Spanishness here is genuine, i.e., inherited from their ancestors, and not a false veneer the way it is in California. There is a primitive, un-American quality to this area, with its peculiar road surfaces and semiwild population. Not far from Santa Fe we passed through one of the major Indian reservations and made a long detour to come into closer contact with the natives. These southern Indian tribes are supposed to have kept their civilization fairly unspoiled by outside influences. Their facial features are not at all what we have been taught to expect from the northern, warlike tribes celebrated by [James Fenimore] Cooper. Mexican Indians are supposed to be related to the now-extinct Aztecs. They farm the land, make rugs of exceptional quality, and have maintained the same pottery designs for the past five hundred years. They've also developed a distinct urban architecture. In Acoma, New Mexico, for instance, the population lives in an old city whose history is virtually unknown. It is called "the city in the sky" because like many other Indian cities it is located high up on a rocky plateau. In this case the plateau can only be reached by means of a long, well-constructed flight of steps. At the top of these you're surprised to find large buildings, including a church that is among the largest in the United States.

After an hour or two playing at archeologists, we relaxed by taking a long hike that included mountain climbing and a walk in the desert. Since no one was around, we took our clothes off and ran around naked in the sand. The air is incredibly clear in this region, and we kept misjudging distances. So it took us two hours to reach an interesting rock formation called "the magic city," and it had only looked as though it were 200 meters away. We asked an old Indian guarding a herd of cattle where it got its name, and he said that since time immemorial the top of the rock had been inhabited by a now-extinct race. One day, when all the inhabitants of the city, with the exception of three women, were down working in the fertile fields, a terrible rockslide sealed off the only exit. The distraught women roamed the edges of the rock screaming until their food supply ran out and their voices grew silent. No one had ever managed to scale the sheer cliffs again.

Our trip from Santa Fe to Los Angeles took four whole days, instead of two or three, as we'd planned. This was actually my fault. From the very beginning, and with diabolical cunning, I concentrated on describing the attractions of the area we were passing through. I told my traveling companion about the splendid petrified forests that could be reached only thirty miles from the main road; about multicolored deserts, stretching endlessly on both sides of the road, which saved their greatest views only for those who ventured off on the small bumpy backroads; and finally about the Grand Canyon, which meant a detour of one 150 miles. He had hardly given a thought to the fact that his route to California happened to take him through some of the world's promised lands. All it took was to tell him this, and he would enthusiastically veer off so that we could visit these places.

We started with the multicolored deserts. They consist of deserts within the desert that because of the abundance of fossils from different periods offer a range of colors, surpassing that of any rainbow. In the middle of the yellow, parched desert there is a craterlike chasm, probably a mile wide and apparently an old riverbed. The sides and bottom of this valley are made up of sand striped in the most brilliant shades. In the rather subdued light of the moment, red seemed to predominate, but a little later, when we got out of the car and went closer to the rim, the sun came out from behind the clouds, sending a dazzling swath of light over the desert. The scenery changed: yellow, blue, and green and their combinations overpowered the red, and along the edge itself there was a dazzling white streak. We stood in silent admiration for quite a long time, more out of amazement at finding such a spectacle out here in the desert than from the beauty of the thing itself. We hurried on, however, to reach the one and only petrified forest before evening. The petrified tree trunks that one often finds in this region of America seldom or never grew where they're found. They have usually first been transported a considerable distance by rivers before finally becoming embedded in clay or some other material acting as a preservative, whose silicate and other chemical components slowly became pressed into the fibers or cells of the tree trunk and which, long after the wood itself has decomposed, leave behind an absolutely faithful impression of every minute detail. As if that isn't enough, the reproduction is done in a range of colors any tree would envy. The most beautiful example of a petrified tree is the so-called agate bridge, a tree trunk lying across a chasm, looking perfectly natural except for its bluish hue and shiny crystalline surface. If you polish these rocks, you get a rare, colorful, and probably very decorative material but far too costly to use as a building material.

After spending the night in the little town of Flagstaff, surprising mainly because all its banks have collapsed, leaving its economic system in a state of hopeless confusion, we went to the Grand Canyon. Like the petrified forest, much of its charm lies in the suddenness with which this wonder reveals itself. There you are, traveling through huge pine forests and marshlands, when all of a sudden you find yourself on the edge of the canyon itself. It comes as a shock. Far away, sometimes in sharp outline, sometimes shrouded by a blue mist, you can see a sharply illuminated black plateau stretching across the bottom of the valley, cut down in the middle by the present river canyon, the black mouth of which gives you the feeling you're staring into the yawning jaws of hell. Standing on the edge, you face a dizzying abyss, a terraced pit that you're sure must defy any human attempts at scaling. Nevertheless, we could see a ribbon of trail laboriously winding its way down, down, bracing itself against every precipice, seeking shelter under every jutting edge, finally landing safely at the lighter plateau bottom. We realized that this is the way to ford the Colorado, a path long sought and the final discovery of which took so many lives. Since a mule ride along the path to the river and back takes as long as two days, we declined the pleasure and turned to the task of crossing the desert instead. We soon found that the last stretch is the worst, as well as the hottest. Here we are only a hundred miles from Death Valley, the hottest place on earth, located about 880 feet below sea level, covered by a forbidding layer of mineral salts and completely devoid of life. We sat naked in the car, sweating as the car glowed and the motor groaned strenuously. What the temperature was in the shade I do not know. There was no shade with which to measure! However, I later did find my broken fever thermometer, which had done its duty to the last drop of quicksilver. We continued this way, hour after hour, stopping from time to time to keep the motor from overheating. The worst crisis came as we were making our way across the steep mountains surrounding the Colorado River, which has turned to the south at this point and therefore has to be crossed. Halfway up, we met a poor old Ford that had given up and was being turned around on the narrow road winding along the edge of an abyss by a couple of stout men. The car had apparently not been able to handle the steep incline, and so they had to back it down and wait for help at the bottom of the hill. Eventually, we reached the summit, and then slowly slid back down into the furnace again. From here the trip was relatively easy. In the evening we went to sleep only 150 miles from our goal, Los Angeles. I couldn't get there in time for the opening of the Games, as I'd hoped. The last day, my friend woke me at 4 in the morning, and we set off. Before long, we smelled the salty breezes and palm trees and flower beds that began to appear along the side of the road. The houses became Spanish, down to the last detail, the billboards assumed a sophisticated air, and you felt that you were approaching that earthly paradise, Southern California. We drove quickly through several miles of snobbish suburbs, and at exactly 9:30 pulled up in front of a large hotel in the center of the city, and I had traveled 3,000 miles for free without coming to any harm.

Spent a week in Los Angeles, where I had a good time. Then went to Boulder City and had a look at Hoover Dam. It was very impressive. The trip from Hoover Dam was pretty strenuous, and included an almost 20-mile hike through an awful desert without a drop of water or a single shade tree. I spent one night on the roof of a truck, and since we were going through the mountains north of Los Angeles, I half froze to death. But I have had lots of fun. Uncle Carl Bonde is here in Los Angeles. I haven't been able to reach Consul Wallerstedt, since he hasn't been at his office. Will stay here a little over a week. People here are fairly optimistic about the prospects for next year.

A thousand greetings and thanks for the interesting letter about Japan.

R.W.

ISTANBUL
SEPTEMBER 8, 1932

My dear boy,

Thank you for your last letter, which I got via your mother. It was dated San Francisco, August 16. I very much enjoyed your account of your free ride through the various states. I assume that you took the train back. Traveling the way you did is in the end the most interesting way imaginable of seeing the country from below, so to speak. The conversations that I hope you have had with various people in San Francisco and other cities will round out the picture. I shall therefore be very interested to hear about your contact with people in the western states, as it will give me the chance to learn your impressions. Your letters are always read by highly qualified people, and it is therefore of the greatest importance that they be written to make a good impression. Remember what I've told you, that your fiercest competitors are the young people in our own family. The real value of your trip consequently resides in your account of it. The fact that you've had a good time is of secondary importance and should be downplayed. One should not seek enjoyment in these serious times, and if one does one should not talk about it. My own conviction is that this trip has been of great educational value to you. What I hint at above constitutes a reminder that it might also be extremely useful to you in other respects.

Some time ago, I received a blueprint of one of your designs for a small private home. I studied it with great interest and found it well thought out. To prove that I have some knowledge in such matters, I scrutinized it to see if I could find any fault. My critical scrutiny has only yielded one point. It concerns the kitchen. You have included all sorts of modern conveniences, garbage chute, icebox, sinks, etc., and I deduce that the stove is either gas or electrical and that there is thus no need for a stovepipe. But it does seem to me that some kind of ventilation is imperative, either through a duct in the wall, which would have to be modified in such case, or through an exhaust fan. This was all I could find, and I will enjoy hearing your justification. The heating in the dining room and the bedroom above it may also be on the weak side.

I wrote to Miss Wernberger to send you another letter of credit, as the one you have expires in September, if I remember correctly. I told her to ask your mother for your address, for I am not absolutely certain that the one I had is the right one, since you have not acknowledged my letter of July 22, addressed to "Kappa Delta Rho, Ann Arbor."

I note the rising stock market in the U.S., but find it difficult to believe in its solidity so long as reports still reveal a decline in steel production. It may be because investors are tired of being pessimistic. A rise like this often happens on the stock exchanges during a crisis, and carries some people away with it, but it is nothing to build on. I am fit, in other respects, and am tolerating the heat well. The summer has been excellent.

Your affectionate
[GOW]

ANN ARBOR
OCTOBER 22

[Written in English]

Dear Grandfather,

I thank you very much for your last letter dated the 8th of September. The reason that I am writing you in English is that my little typewriter is sent for repair and I have borrowed one from a friend that has no Swedish letters. I am sorry that I have neglected letter writing but my time has been terribly taken up since the start of the semester.

Having given you little information about my trip westwards, I will tell you more about it now. Just as you expected, the west coast proved to be the most interesting part of the voyage, which I believe to have told you in my last letter. Some of the pioneer spirit is still left and people's opinions are less standardized than in the East. On the other hand this freedom of thought is now partially hidden by the fact that political feelings are running high. Since none of the major parties, except the socialists, have any outstanding differences in their platforms, the question becomes very much influenced by personal feelings. It impresses a foreigner favorably to hear the different candidates being assailed as crooks and imbeciles by their respective foes. It seems that parties should represent different sets of ideas and ideals but here they seem to represent only different sets of personnel with the openly avowed object of aiming at power for power's own sake. Maybe it appeals more to practical-minded Americans to treat the whole thing as a business proposition where more depends on the man who does it than on the principles according to which it is done. However, everybody seems to be very tired of politics as a whole, and Norman Thomas, the socialist candidate, is expected to draw a large number of votes not only from the unemployed and the radical elements but also from those who think that both parties show a record of graft and inefficiency. That prediction will not mean that he will come anywhere near to any of the other two large parties, for naturally, everyone knows that a vote for Thomas will bring no positive results. It is whispered that Norman Thomas is supported by the Republican Party in order to take the radical votes that Roosevelt otherwise would get. But this also seems improbable in view of Mr. Thomas' record of honesty. He has published a list of his campaign expenses from which it becomes apparent that he has spent only eight thousand dollars during his trip through thirty-eight states. It would not seem probable that a man who knows to get along on that small a sum would have to take recourse to bribes as a source of income. Since the Democrats are sure of their victory, every step taken by the president has been watched with great care, and all his speeches give rise to hopeful predictions in his favor. I happened to be in California — his own home state — when he gave his speech of acceptance, which was very impressive. It was delivered in measured and forceful sentences which must have appealed to the sturdy westerners. As a whole I had the impression that the Republicans although less numerous were more enthusiastic and energetic in their outlook on the political future.

I made a point of interviewing all representatives of Swedish trade that my limited time permitted me to see on the west coast. They were all very optimistic about the future, particularly so about the strength and inherent soundness of Swedish enterprises here. Transatlantic's line from the north to the East Indies, however, seems to have been a disappointment. I also inquired about the prospect for an expansion of Swedish trade in the west.

I found two groups with different opinions. One was represented by the shipping people. They thought that Swedish exportation to the west coast ought to consist primarily of heavy products and that one should not bother about small articles. Naturally their point of view is narrowed by the fact that their biggest gain comes from the heavier trade. They didn't believe very much could be done in the way of improving sales organization to promote trade, but told me that the most important factors were the prices we put on our articles and the tariffs that this country would impose on them. However they believed that credit institutions of the kind you've proposed would be of some help. I spoke to Mr. Snowbohm, a representative of the Johnson Line in San Francisco, Mr. Doelker of Grace & Co. in S.F. Grace & Co. are a shipping line and they represent the Johnson interests. Mr. Snowbohm sits in their office. Mr. Doelker told me a peculiar story that goes to show that business doesn't always mean buying where one can buy cheapest. Some twenty thousand tons of newspaper is apparently carried by their line every year to a San Francisco newspaper. This paper seems to have bought its supplies from American enterprises before Mr. Hearst, the American newspaper king, meanwhile secretly got control of these newsprint companies and one day the S.F. newspaper was surprised to receive a letter from their newsprint company informing them that their orders wouldn't be honored. The paper, which needed its supplies very badly, was in an awkward position and swore never to buy from an American firm again. And that's how the Swedes received these orders instead.

The other group consisted of members of the foreign representation, representatives of the Swedish American Line and businessmen of Swedish descent in less important trades. Their view
was that Swedish commercial organization on the west coast was
scandalously neglected. Mr. Lundequist, Swedish vice consul in
Seattle, Wash., charged that representative Swedish businessmen
who had traveled three thousand miles across the continent to
inspect the market and to conclude new deals would stop over
only for a day and spend an hour or so talking generalities with
some American businessmen. He gave me some examples, such
as how a good-intentioned and energetic man would come over,
go out to the saw mills (if he happened to sell Sandviken blades),
look things over, talk to everybody, inquire about conditions,
show interest, and in the end only sell a hundred blades. Mr.
Lundequist stated that nothing hurt our trade in this part of the
States more than the behavior of our representatives. This is
further complicated by the fact that such a large percentage of the
population here are Swedes or Swedish descendants. As a whole
I think that one will find more outstanding Swedes here than
anywhere else. The Swedes in Minnesota are the ones who have
acquired a reputation of stupidity for their countrymen, but the
Swedes in Washington and Oregon have no such reputation. As
far as I can see, these two states are two of the most popular of the
whole forty-eight. Anybody who's been there likes them and they
know it. For a Swede from the old country to come there and not
show any enthusiasm is a slap in the face. It's all the more
deplorable that we have no consistent organization of any kind in
that part of the country, as these Swedes and descendants of
Swedes show wholehearted enthusiasm for things Swedish and
want this enthusiasm returned in kind. The Swedes that have
come here during the last year, even if they bear some grudge
against the old country, are very willing to promote Swedish
interests. But they're not only willing; they're also more qualified,
for they know our language and they have confidence in both our
ability to pay and our reliability. They're easy to flatter and the
finest flattery you can give them is to tell them that they've built a
fine country. If that ritual is observed, they're more than willing to
buy and to *sell Swedish* things, all else being equal. They often felt
that not enough economic and moral support is given their loyalty. I frequently heard complaints that small Swedish-American

firms selling Swedish goods on the American market failed in their efforts because of the difficulty they had obtaining credit from the banks to finance these deals. There's a tendency for this business to fall into the hands of larger American enterprises. Earlier efforts were made to create Swedish-American banking institutions on the west coast, but these companies have disappeared in this and previous crises. However, these banks seem to have been institutions of essentially local character, and based on the supposition that feelings of national solidarity could be commercialized and that the Swedish population on the west coast would rise as one around them, preferring them to the older and more solid American institutions. Their failure was obviously due to the fallacy behind this theory, rather than to any losses caused by the promotion of Swedish trade. Another frequent complaint was that Swedish exporters didn't understand the mentality of the foreign markets. They were said to insist on selling the things they knew were technically perfect rather than those that the customer for some reason preferred. I saw to my pleasure and surprise that Gahn & Co., soap manufacturers, sold very exclusive soap of the highest quality in drug stores throughout S.F. This latter group hadn't taken any particular stand on the tariffs and their influence on Swedish imports, probably because they didn't have either a broad outlook or the same kind of precise information the shippers had.

In Vancouver, Canada, Swedish motors were sold for smaller craft but I don't know the figures. It's too bad that Canada should be so much more closely tied to England through the Ottawa Agreement, for I have a strong feeling that regardless of the technicalities of the question the Canadians would be very good customers, for they resemble us rather closely and do not recoil at Swedish "respectability" in the way some Americans do.

Contrary to what you seem to have expected, I went home the same way as I came, "hitchhiking," that is.

As I said, school has started and there's lots to do. Maybe I have taken on too heavy a schedule, because I really don't have the time to do everything I should. However, so far, major disasters have been avoided. I don't know whether this is the character of an adventurer shining through, but I take a particular pride-pleasure in relaxing for a week or two, to get time to do what I like, and then suddenly pulling myself together and working through the night, which gives me a little more of a thrill than plodding along with the everyday tasks.

So far I haven't been out dancing once this semester but that doesn't seem to have given me any more time.

I'm taking physics and two courses of mathematics, all three very hard subjects and far removed from what I call a pleasant time.

Many thanks for all your fond letters. I have also received the new letter of credit from Miss Wernberger. It's far more than I will spend. A peculiar thing happened and that is that the Kreuger shares, which had been declared worthless by the Swedish investigation committee, rose from $\frac{1}{32}$ to $\frac{3}{8}$ on the Stock Exchange.

I'm going to try to get what they term "advanced credit" on the French and Swedish I know. That way I'll be a "junior" next February.

Kindest regards,
Raoul

ANN ARBOR
DECEMBER 24, 1932

Dearest Grandfather,

Just got a letter from Aunt Karin with a copy of that letter from Mustapha Kemal to you on the occasion of the fiftieth anniversary of your joining the navy. I imagine you were very pleased. I felt as proud as if I'd been the one to receive it.

This is to wish you a happy New Year and to send you my best wishes on your name day. I hope you're as fit as when last we saw each other.

It's been raining here nonstop for the entirety of the Christmas vacation. Most of my friends have gone home, and the town is deserted. I'm spending almost all my time sleeping, which feels good after such an exhausting term, and writing to my family, which I didn't have time for during the term. My plans for the vacation call for studying hard, but so far I've been too lazy to get started. I'm going to tackle it though — tomorrow, or maybe next week. Never postpone until tomorrow what you can postpone until the day after! Now there's a good vacation philosophy.

I just saw in a technical journal that the French are building a hospital in Paris patterned on the American model. There's a general desire for an exchange of know-how between the old world and the new at the moment. The same issue carried a speech by some American architecture bigwig who said that the French should pray to God to be spared the skyscraper epidemic, "for if you allow one person to build high you have to allow everyone," he said. I wonder whether he's right. It seems to me to be a question of city planning. A city can be divided into zones, and each zone could limit building height. If a city is very sensitive about its architecture, as is the case with Stockholm, the zones could be very small, and the building height carefully gauged so as to correspond with necessity. We should not build skyscrapers for the same reasons the Americans do, however. Here, we're always told that their existence has to do with economic necessity. The great Finnish-born architect Saarinen, one of the most prominent here, has started a campaign against the construction of skyscrapers, stating that they're prompted primarily by snobbism. He cited as proof that most big skyscrapers in New York are empty or half-empty and usually bankrupt; furthermore, that if skyscrapers actually were financially necessary, you would see a clear gradation of height from the outskirts toward the center, but that that isn't the case, and instead there's an abrupt shift between low buildings and tall ones: that as you increase the height of a building the price of the surrounding property also increases, in turn leading to more tall buildings, by which he means that tall buildings rest on artificial economic foundations.

On the other hand, it's hard to escape the notion that if billions of dollars are invested in the building of skyscrapers over a period of thirty years, and if this investment continues during a crisis such as the current one, it must be based on a true economic necessity, not simply snobbism. To counter this you could argue that an individual entepreneur's optimism may be based on his confidence that his special skyscraper will be able to draw customers from *already existing skyscrapers*. The construction of new skyscrapers need not therefore indicate greater need.

All this partly proves that skyscraper construction in the U.S.

isn't quite as natural as we might think. So you might expect their status in Europe's large cities to be even lower. I think the opposite is true.

American cities are constructed on the gridiron principle. This means that transportation between different parts of the city can move along parallel streets, that the traffic lights that regulate the traffic may be coordinated without difficulty, and that an even traffic flow may be established. Because of this, American cities have an enormous capacity for traffic. Even though this country has such a large number of cars in active use, traffic never reaches the chaotic state that you find in many places on the Continent.

In Europe, on the other hand, cities are built according to this principle or at best according to this. A quick glance is enough to convince you that this kind of a system necessarily means uneven utilization of various streets and makes any coordination of traffic impossible. Traffic bunches up and chaos ensues. In American cities, the location of the center with the most valuable land seems arbitrary. First come, first served. In Europe, on the other hand, you can point out the most desirable locations on a map with some degree of certainty. As if that weren't enough, there are also innumerable buildings within any city that we would like to preserve in their original state and at their original location for historical or aesthetic reasons. This makes any comprehensive widening of a street or other attempts at organization absolutely impossible. You're forced to choose the one or two streets in which historical monuments aren't crammed too closely together, widen them as much as you can, and then try to direct traffic through them.

But in order to compensate for that expense, concentrated to certain places, and also to take full advantage of the locations along these streets, resorting to skyscrapers should be a rather natural thing.

You shouldn't have to hesitate for aesthetic reasons, for aren't some of Europe's most beautiful buildings tall towers? The tower of the cathedral at Ulm is 525 feet high, and you probably wouldn't have to build a skyscraper that high to compensate for the increased land cost. Even ancient Rome had nine-story houses. A common European argument against skyscrapers is the ugliness of American skyscraper cities. But if this argument had any validity you wouldn't be able to build two- or three-story houses either, for if there is anything less attractive than an American skyscraper it is an American two-story house. And there are plenty of examples in America of how beautiful skyscrapers can be and *how they may be incorporated in the city landscape.* (I would be grateful if you would return the postcards or ask mother to return them in case you pass on this letter to her.)

A thousand greetings to both you and Grandmother and best wishes on your seventieth birthday.

Affectionately,
Raoul

[Aunt Karin refers to GOW's elder daughter, married to Oscar Falkman. Mustapha Kemal Atatürk (1881–1938) was the founder of modern Turkey.]

Ann Arbor
[NO DATE], 1933

Dearest Mother,

Since I couldn't find any other kind of paper I tore this one off a sketch pad. . . . As for my work habits and the poor grade in mathematics, I want to tell you that the reason is that I intend to go back to "architecture" once this term is over. Since this math course isn't required for "arch." but only for "arch. engineering," there is no need to study math.

[Continued in English] I have ample proof both now and before that — while I am quite good in architectural subjects and not at all bad in speech and related courses — I am far from proficient in mathematics and physics. I am not only following the road of least resistance when I choose not to study hard in those subjects but rather deliberately giving more and more time to things that agree with my nature.

I have written a carefully planned letter to the Swedish Exposition at the World's Fair in Chicago offering my services without any remuneration (salary). With the usual Swedish tact those people have *not even answered me*. They couldn't know that I was only a little Swedish student. For all they knew I might just as well be an important man.

[Continued in Swedish] I wonder if anything strengthens your love for your native country more than a lengthy stay abroad. From time to time I feel kind of hopeless when I think of how small and contained Sweden is, especially when compared to America. As I see it, three things have contributed to make America what it is. Size and population, natural resources, and finally the fact that its population is so mobile and free of the constraints of tradition. Americans view their future in terms of achieving a certain result — in contrast to the Swedes, who perceive theirs in terms of attaining a certain position in society. Average Americans are no more intelligent than Swedes, but they have the ability to simplify things, and find it easy to change their position and talk things over. They aren't intellectual snobs.

If it were worthwhile creating the same conditions in Sweden that exist in the U.S., the only way would be to form a trade union and open borders between the three Scandinavian countries. This would result in exactly those three factors. I have thought about this all year, and sometimes resorted to statistical studies to try and find some economic basis for a union. Unfortunately there is none. But since industry will become increasingly important every year, what now only appears desirable will soon become necessary because of the importance of mass production to industry. It would be politically advantageous to fuse Scandinavia together, for the more unsettled Europe becomes, the more critical it is to make production more efficient, apart from purely technical defense considerations.

This is one of the issues that has interested me the most during my years abroad. Years during which I have not seen my mother.

The other issue is contemporary architecture. But on that subject, my views are far too impassioned to commit to paper. The Chicago Fair opened today and looks rather unattractive (in photographs). I will be seeing it this summer.

I don't think that I'll go as far south as Mexico City. Communications are probably pretty inferior down there.

You complain in your letter about all the things under my bed. You should have seen all the stuff I had piled up *behind* the camera.

> A thousand greetings from your affectionate
> Raoul

ANN ARBOR
ALPHA RHO CHI
JUNE 27, 1933

Dearest Mother,

I just received your letter from Germany.

I've been to Chicago. Mr. Sjunnesson, administrative head of the Swedish exhibition, finally wrote me back after almost three weeks to say that I could come for the period during which I had offered my services, i.e., between June 6 and 25. School ended on the 6th and started up again on the 26th.

I packed my stuff as quickly as I could and happily left Ann Arbor. Miss Ringman, the girl I've been seeing off and on this winter, took me to Ypsilanti, on the "Federal Highway" to Chicago.

There it didn't take long before I was picked up by a truck.

I arrived in Chicago the next morning, and found a room at the YMCA, an enormous establishment of 2,000 rooms. My room was on the nineteenth floor and so I slept well in spite of the heat. The heat the first day set a new record. It was 100 degrees, i.e., 38 degrees Celsius. It has never been that hot in Chicago in June according to records. But it was even hotter in Needles, Arizona, where I was last summer. I looked up Mr. Sjunnesson and he took me to the exhibition pavilion. He also gave me a pass for the Fair.

In addition to Mr. Sjunnesson, Miss Peyron, the daughter of the naval commander, also worked in the building. And Miss Barbro

Gyllenkrok, who is terribly pretty. Also a Mrs. Sabelfeldt, without husband. Best of the females however was Miss Virdö from Småland. She's an older lady, incredibly nice and friendly, a friend of the kind Milles, and has been working at Cranbrook, teaching spinning to Americans. Among the gentlemen was Tage Palm, an energetic and kind man. He owns Swedish Arts and Crafts, a store in Chicago. And a certain Alvar Hermanson, a Swedish gymnast and trainer in Chicago. As visitors and supervisors we sometimes had the bureaucratic consul Lundqvist, the dictatorial commander Peyron, Axel Johnsson the steady and imperturbable, and the royal emissary Folke Bernadotte the polite and decent, and his good-looking Estelle.

I was used for all kinds of odd jobs. I guided, washed windows, sold glassware, china, furniture, books etc., i.e., everything the others did. My last week there Thiule paid me $3 a day to distribute fliers.

We had incredible visitors' figures and the pavilion was very popular, except among some Swedish-Americans, who called it a box.

One day I went uninvited to the enormous administration building and managed to see one of the top dogs, whom I succeeded in persuading of the necessity of pointing a big spotlight down from the top of one of the 600-foot Skyride towers to illuminate Milles's statues in our courtyard.

After yet another visit to the representative of the giant Skyride organization, I got their permission and now our courtyard is bathed in soft light every night for free.

When it was time to head home, I packed my stuff into two large suitcases, which were so heavy that I felt pretty athletic carrying one on my shoulder and one under my arm. It got very hot again, but it felt good to work up a real sweat. I was carrying my pay, and what was left of my money, and that meant that for the first time since I took up hitchhiking I was carrying cash rather than travelers' checks.

A short ways outside Chicago I was picked up by a gentleman in a nice car. He was very interesting, and among other things he told me he had run away from home in his youth and been gone for three years, during which time he suffered many hardships. We made good time on the excellent roads outside Chicago and were going along at 70 miles/hour when we suddenly saw a train hurtling across the road 500 feet ahead. We saw the danger too late and with a terrible crash ran our right front fender straight into the car ahead of us, which had braked. Slowly and inexorably we spun around and slid across the right-hand edge of the road toward a fence. We were incredibly lucky, for although the front end of the car was pretty badly crushed, we emerged without so much as a scratch. No one in the other car was hurt either, except an old lady who had been thrown onto the floor.

Now it was a matter of finding a tow truck. I unloaded my luggage, and the owner of the car got in the car with the shaken old lady and drove off. So I was left alone in the middle of the road, and it was starting to get dark. I tried very hard to hitch a ride and was delighted when a car with four people in it stopped and picked me up. They had Iowa license plates and, since that's 60 miles east of Chicago, I was surprised they had no luggage. They were in their mid-twenties and looked a bit suspicious.

One of them asked me, "How much would it be worth to you if we took you all the way to Ann Arbor?" "Nothing," I replied, "because in that case I would have taken the bus." Suddenly we heard a noise from the back of the car, and the driver stopped to see what it was. It surprised me that they all had to get out of the car for this. Suddenly another car passed us, and the four of them got back in.

By now I had become very suspicious because of their questions about money, their lack of luggage, and the sudden stop. I started to work my poverty into the conversation. Suddenly the car turned onto a country lane so abruptly that it almost turned over. Fearing the worst, I tried to keep a cool head so as not to make things worse. After another couple of miles through a dark forest they stopped after a rather clumsy and theatrical bluff: "Get out and see what's the matter with the gas tank, Joe."

They got out one after the other and then I was asked to get out "so that they could take a look at me." One of them had a large revolver in his hand. It might not have been loaded.

They demanded my money, and I gave them what I had in my breast-pocket and said I had more in my suitcase. They opened it and took out an envelope that in addition to money contained some papers and the key to my safety deposit box. The latter items I managed to retrieve by bluffing. "Sentimental value to me, no value to you." I didn't tell them it was the key to my bank deposit.

Maybe it was stupid of me to volunteer where I kept my money, but I'd heard so many stories about people being searched and occasionally left without any clothes at all. I did forget to tell them that I had three dollars in another pocket, however. When they thought they had all my money, I decided it was their turn to show some goodwill, so I asked them to drive me back to the highway, since it was late and my suitcases were heavy. They let me sit next to the driver and then put the luggage up on top to keep me from jumping. By this time, they were the ones who were frightened, maybe because I was so calm. I really didn't feel scared; I found the whole thing sort of interesting. Maybe they thought I was planning to lure them into a trap. The result was that all of a sudden they threw me into a ditch and then tossed my luggage after. I immediately flattened myself under a bush, for fear that they might fire a farewell shot from the revolver. Later, I managed to stop a suburban train that took me to South Bend, 200 miles from Ann Arbor, where I reported the incident to the police.

This will not make me give up hitchhiking. I'll just carry less money on me, and try to become more devious. I think it was bad psychology to hand over the money. They were amateurish enough to have let me go with the money from my breastpocket as their only booty.

Summer school has just started.

A thousand greetings from your unharmed
Raoul

[To Marcus Wallenberg Jr.]

ERIE
DECEMBER 17, 1933

Dear Dodde,

I am currently paying a visit to Ernest Behrend, who it would seem once had the pleasure of being your guest in Stockholm. I met him in Chicago during the World Expo and have been here twice since then. They often talk with pleasure of their visit to Stockholm. I also met a boy named McDonald who accompanied them. Everyone sends their regards. I'm now on my way to Greenwich, Connecticut, where I intend to spend Christmas with my relatives, the Colvins.

I am very impressed by America. The people are natural and good-natured, hospitable and easy to get along with. I've seen quite a lot of the country during my two summers here and made some friends. If you are in a position to widen my circle of acquaintances by sending me some addresses, I would naturally be very grateful.

It's been very interesting to observe the immediate effects of the NRA [National Recovery Administration] movement. The enthusiasm was incredible at first, but has now cooled down considerably. However, I think that this change has been exaggerated by the European press. Roosevelt's personal popularity is still enormous, and he's obviously able to count on the support of all those who have been put out of work since March 4.

At first glance it looks as if quite a bit of the money now being lavished on the country by the government to increase purchasing power has instead served to increase the amount of inert capital, in the form of buildings, etc., which future generations of taxpayers will have to pay for. In Detroit, for instance, the Civil Works Administration will use $153 million to build 2 square miles of workers' housing. The population that will fill these houses, however, will move out of, empty, and ruin the other housing surrounding the new construction. And the impoverished slum dwellers now living there will be forced out into so-called "Blighted areas," i.e., slums, which are so run down they are uninhabitable. The net gain will therefore be small, for all it means is that a certain class of workers will get housing at a somewhat lower rent than before, and will have work for a year during the construction of these houses. Any gain is probably outweighed by the damage caused by not improving conditions for the poorest segment of the slum population, which is responsible for 90 percent of all murders and major crimes in Detroit; by making conditions worse for the landlords, who formerly rented out housing to those workers who will move there after the project has been finished; and finally, by increasing the burden of debt of the government and hence of the taxpayers.

Regards to your wife. Wishing you a Merry Christmas,

Your devoted
Raoul Wallenberg

1021 Hill Street
Ann Arbor, Michigan

GREENWICH
DECEMBER 25, 1933

Dearest Grandfather,

Since I last wrote, I've spent Christmas with the Colvins here in Greenwich, Connecticut. They lead a very ordinary life but are very interesting people. Uncle Mech, who was the American military attaché in Stockholm just before the war and after America entered the war, and who has also served as the commander of forts in the Philippines and in the Panama area, has a very nationalistic and militaristic outlook on things. He's always defending lynching, which annoys me, as well as autocracy, which annoys me somewhat less. He's an imperialist and argues seriously that America must be prepared to expand its territory. He is, I think, friendly toward Sweden, admiring many things and ridiculing and despising relatively few. Aunt Elsa, on the other hand, finds Sweden and things Swedish ineffectually petty and narrow. I think that she takes this somewhat extreme position for my personal edification, however.

Bibi is in New York at the moment and I've seen her only once, when she came out here to have dinner. She is selling a tapestry and some paintings, and while I am sure she's a very smart and efficient woman, her business is based on her ability to meet people and to win their confidence.

The more I think about the trip to South America, the more I think I ought to wait until after school is over in order to take full advantage of my stay out there. There's no point just going as a

Gustaf Oscar Wallenberg in full-dress uniform, about 1910. *(Courtesy of The Raoul Wallenberg Committee of the United States)*

Portrait of Raoul Oscar Wallenberg, senior, GOW's eldest son and RW's father, taken in 1911, a year before his death. *(Courtesy of The Raoul Wallenberg Committee of the United States)*

Grandfather and grandson in 1915. *(Courtesy of Birgitte Wallenberg)*

Sophie Wising, RW's maternal grandmother, standing in front of the house on the island of Kappsta located outside Stockholm, where RW was born and where he spent his first year. The photo was taken about the time of RW's birth in 1912. *(Courtesy of Birgitte Wallenberg)*

Mother and son in 1915. *(Courtesy of The Raoul Wallenberg Committee of the United States)*

RW and his half brother, Guy von Dardel, in 1920. *(Courtesy of The Raoul Wallenberg Committee of the United States)*

RW at the University of
Michigan. *(Courtesy of The
Raoul Wallenberg Committee of
the United States)*

One of RW's assignments at
Michigan, dated October 21,
1932. He got a B. *(Courtesy of
The Raoul Wallenberg
Committee of the United States)*

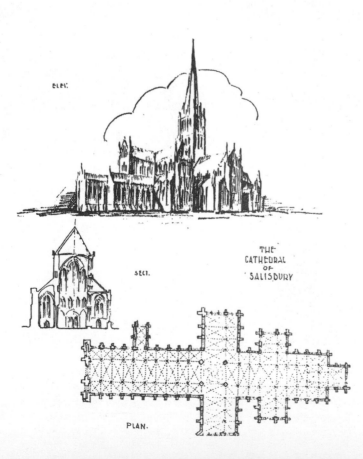

ELEV.

SECT.

THE
CATHEDRAL
OF
SALISBURY

PLAN.

RW's freshman registration photo for the University of Michigan, September 1931. *(Photograph used by permission of the College of Architecture and Urban Planning, University of Michigan, Ann Arbor)*

RW, in his R.O.T.C. uniform, standing on the Golden Gate Bridge during his hitchhiking trip to California in August 1932. *(Courtesy of The Raoul Wallenberg Committee of the United States)*

RW in Ann Arbor, 1933. *(Courtesy of The Raoul Wallenberg Committee of the United States)*

ABOVE LEFT RW in Mexico City. Pictured in foreground is Birgitte Wallenberg, RW's cousin. *(Courtesy of Birgitte Wallenberg)*

ABOVE RIGHT RW in Mexico City with friend Woodard in August 1934. *(Courtesy of Birgitte Wallenberg)*

LEFT Cape Town, South Africa, 1935. Pictured at far right is Björn Burchardt. Man in center is not identified. *(Courtesy of The Raoul Wallenberg Committee of the United States)*

One of RW's drawings for the Riddarholm pool project. *(Courtesy of the Raoul Wallenberg Foundation, Stockholm)*

tourist, taking a quick look at the region, and then going home. I should go there to learn more about the countries and at the same time about how to make a living. I also should stay here long enough to learn something about certain American things. I've made up the following list of things to study, things that are better here than anywhere else:

air-conditioning, restaurants, hotdog stands, drugstores, hotels, kitchen-installments, small newsreel-theaters, cleaning and laundry-service and advertising and newspaper techniques.

If I knew something about these areas I would be of greater use both on the frontier and in Sweden than I would be if I only came home with theoretical experience. I therefore emphatically suggest, since I have thought the matter over, that I wait to go to South America until early in 1935, having gone back to Sweden before then, so that I can seize whatever opportunities I find once I get there without having to worry about going home. I also think that Mother's loyalty should be rewarded by my showing her this consideration. She never complains about my having been gone for so long, yet I know from relatives passing through that she would love to see her firstborn.

I would like to see my parents and my beloved grandfather before I become too much of a foreigner.

School continues as usual, though this term I'm taking a number of technical courses in which I have not been too outstanding. Nor have I celebrated any great triumphs in architecture, but I have high hopes that a dairy farm I turned in before Christmas will raise my average.

I've helped the Colvins by coming up with some suggestions about the use of a building in their backyard. I took a couple of days to really give it some thought. The Behrends in Erie are building a large house and they, too, had me look through the building plans to see if they might be improved upon.

Having my tonsils removed last summer made me gain weight, and I now weigh 152 lbs.

Many heartfelt greetings to both of you from your devoted

Raoul

[Bibi, Aslög Adelsköld, was GOW's wife Annie's younger sister.]

ANN ARBOR
JANUARY 2, 1934

Dearest Grandfather,

I'm writing you mainly as an excuse to send you the two pictures that Gösta Nisser took of me during his two-day visit to Ann Arbor.

He was very pleased with his visit and, I hope, suitably impressed by America.

My Christmas vacation was wonderful. I went to the Colvins after spending two nights with my friends the Behrends in Erie, Pennsylvania, and one night at my architecture professor's in Jamestown, NY.

For the first time I've had a taste of the society life that you always warned me about. Probably because my cousin Lucette is a little older now and because of that or some other reason I no longer found an imbalance in maturity between ladies and men the way I always had in the East.

This time I found the dances very pleasant and you had the time to get acquainted before someone cut in. "Cutting in" — which means that anyone has the right to go up to a couple dancing and ask the man to step aside and hand the lady over to him — is a custom in the East. At the dances I went to before, you didn't have more than a few seconds to dance with a popular girl.

I stayed with the Colvins for about a week and a half. Then, after spending half a day in New York, I went to Washington. In Washington I saw Admiral Bristol, who was very kind and took me on a "round" of the city, which in addition to sightseeing included five teas and one dance. I also had lunch with Minister Boström, who was very nice to talk to. He doesn't believe in Roosevelt's methods or in American "drive" in general. I had a chance to talk to Bristol for half an hour, during which he expressed your motto, although in slightly different words, about learning "to stand on one's own two feet and develop one's own abilities."

Uncle Axel left behind a very good impression, at least in society — which seems to be very important in Washington — for everyone lit up when Mrs. Bristol informed them that I was a relative. Some of them knew you from Constantinople or Japan.

I hope that one of the letters I sent during my Christmas vacation got there around the 6th.

School is now back in session, and I've made up for my somewhat battered record by getting an "excellent" on my last assignment, which involved a dairy farm. My grades as a whole aren't by any stretch as good as they were before. I've started preparing for my thesis, which will be about Swedish architecture. I wanted to write about something American, but thesis topics are chosen by the head of our school and the topic he assigned me was Swedish architecture.

I saw Bibi Adelsköld twice during Christmas and she asked me to send you her respects.

Heartfelt greetings to both of you from
Raoul

[Minister Boström *refers to Wollmar Boström, the Swedish minister in Washington at this time. Axel Wallenberg had been a Swedish envoy to Washington.*]

ANN ARBOR
FEBRUARY 24, 1934

Dearest Grandfather,

I hope you have had a pleasant winter in Constantinople and on the Riviera. February has brought nothing but snowstorms and cold spells, and I envy you. I'm now studying Spanish to be somewhat better prepared should I go to South America.

We are two weeks into the spring term, and I don't have very much to do, which is fine, because last term I was under a lot of stress. My grades last term were about the same as before, except that I improved considerably in architecture and was somewhat worse in drawing. I may not have to go to summer school and still be able to graduate in February, 1935. That would mean I would have the summer off and be able to do something else. It would be a good chance to go home for a visit, especially if I were to stay on here after school ends a year from now.

My Christmas vacation was very nice. I spent a few days in Washington with Admiral Bristol, who was *very* good to me and whom I liked a lot. The Bristols seemed to know everybody and took me to a lot of teas and to a dance. I also paid a visit to Minister Boström, who was kind enough to treat me to lunch. The first time I went to see the Bristols he told me very interesting things about his experiences in China, and how the various great powers were jockeying to get on the best terms with the Chinese.

I was also in New York, having driven there from Ann Arbor with one of my architecture professors. I stopped at the Behrends in Erie on the way and at the professor's house in Jamestown.

The Colvins are very nice and the colonel is a nationalist of the same stripe as Randolph Hearst (the newspaper mogul). He's a realist and fun to talk to.

A friend and I have planned a trip to Mexico this summer, possibly all the way to Mexico City. This would be an alternative to going home to Sweden. It is my friend Woodard, whose father is a furniture manufacturer in Owosso, Mich. He has finished school and is now working for his father. I'm not taking our plans too seriously, however, for we have planned trips like this before and he's backed out at the last minute. We would use one of his parents' cars. If Woodard lets me down and if you don't want me to go to Sweden this summer I can always attend summer school or maybe work at the World's Fair in Chicago again, if they'll take me.

There's been a lot of grumbling and gnashing of teeth among the students because money that was to have gone for enormous construction projects in Detroit under Roosevelt's program has now suddenly been withdrawn and their hopes for finding employment faded again. Many of my friends have found work in private industry, however, so it may just be that things are picking up.

Heartfelt greetings to both of you from your
Raoul

ANN ARBOR
FEBRUARY 9 AND APRIL 10, 1934

Dearest Grandfather,

My friend Woodard just flew down from Owosso. He "dropped in" for ten minutes to tell me that his family's old Ford truck has been placed at his disposal for this summer's escapade to Mexico, if we are going. I told him I was delighted to hear this but didn't commit myself definitely, since I have not yet heard what you think I should do this summer. In order that you might get a better view of the situation, I have drawn you the following table:

JUNE 1934	JULY	AUGUST	SEPTEMBER	FEBRUARY 1935	JUNE 1935
School	Mexico w. Woodard		Fall term	Graduate Go to Sweden	South America
School	Summer School	Work in Chicago or go to New York	Fall term	Graduate Go to Sweden	South America
School	Go to South America		Fall term	Graduate Go to Sweden	
School	Go to Sweden		Fall term	Graduate Go to Sweden	

So there are lots of possibilities to choose from.

I haven't heard from you since just before Christmas.

I've been leading a very pleasant life this term. My friends and I have gone for long Sunday walks, Swedish style. The last few weeks, and especially now during the vacation, I have amused myself by painting murals on heavy paper and putting them around the walls of my room.

On two walls is a picture of paradise, with Adam and Eve, an elephant, a pig, a giraffe, a polyp, a peacock, and lots of trees and hills. On the other two walls is an allegory showing the (Stockholm) City Hall, a white transatlantic steamship, and New York harbor. I use ordinary pastel chalk, and of course none of this is great art.

I've also gone to the library a lot during the vacation, and read about England and Germany, and also — although less often — about Sweden.

I've been reading a new book by Churchill called *Amid These Storms*, which is a collection of his reminiscences of various events in his life. It is very well written and his use of the language is beautiful.

My Swedish is getting worse and worse, and I no longer have even a written command of it. When my cousin Gösta Nisser was here during the fall term he told me that I spoke with a pronounced American accent.

The weather has been strange and annoying, and today we had another snowstorm even though it's Friday, April 13, and we had had wonderful spring weather for several weeks.

The depression is either definitely over or at least interrupted. You can find proof of this not only in statistics in the newspapers and announcements of sales figures from various companies, but also from talking with various people whose lifestyle has changed. Many of my friends who graduated in February have found employment, and others who had had to lead a very frugal life up to now because their parents were so poor have suddenly received large checks from home. The NRA codes have affected prices so much that the man in the street can see a clear difference. It costs more to have your clothes and suits washed and ironed and to get a haircut than it did before. Most of the banks that had closed down have opened again, and you find an enormous number of new cars on the streets. The newspapers have become considerably fatter because of increased advertising. Magazines have also gotten heavier, due largely to increased advertising by manufacturers of alcoholic beverages. Ann Arbor, which is very Republican, is dry again, and no beer is served after midnight. Nor are you allowed to dance and drink beer at the same time. But the state has opened a store where you can buy what you want during daylight hours. You see very little drinking.

The other day a friend took me out to play golf for the first time in my life. It was kind of fun, and I think I'll try to keep it up.

I feel so at home in my little Ann Arbor that I'm beginning to sink down roots here and have a hard time imagining my leaving it. But I am not doing anything very useful here.

Every now and then I feel strange when I think about how tiny my own country is and how large and wonderful America is. The best thing about America is that people here are not envious and they are not petty. Just imagine how much energy we waste at home by being suspicious of everything and everyone! Just think how unpleasant we make it for ourselves and everybody else by being pessimists instead of optimists! On the other hand, no one can deny that Swedes are incredibly clever at whatever they undertake. They seldom make a mistake. But just think of all the things they don't do. Nevertheless it is a wonderful country. I had some proof of this recently from Mother, who wrote to tell me that my cousin Lucette, who is now in Stockholm, likes Sweden very much indeed. That really makes my soul rest easy, because she comes from the best and wealthiest and most upper-class circles in the East and those circles are extremely *wide*.

I really can't wait to see her and to hear her impressions. I'm impatiently awaiting another one of your letters, which I look forward to so much. I always reread them several times, and keep them out on my desk long after I open them.

A thousand kisses and greetings from your devoted
Raoul

ISTANBUL
MAY 11, 1934

My dear boy,

There are periods when one loses the urge to write. I have found myself in such a period during my stay in Nice. There were so many distractions. I am sorry that you haven't heard from me. Your letter of April 10 came as a reminder. Your proposed modification of my plan for a trip to South America got me moving. As you suggest, it would be better to make the trip after your studies in Ann Arbor are completely finished. It pleases me, however, that we agree that studying trade frontiers is worthwhile. I am convinced of that, now more than ever. The political situation in Europe is going from bad to worse. The one in America appears to be turning out well, as I have long thought that it would. Your comments confirm my opinion. These two facts combined lead me to conclude that your stay in America, particularly during this initial phase of an upward trend, will be useful, and that now is not a good time to come home. In other words, you have nothing to lose by extending your stay abroad.

I am thus in complete agreement with you that excursions to the trade frontiers should be postponed until the beginning of 1935. Under such conditions, a visit to your native country during the coming vacation would be possible. I am certain that it would give your mother great happiness. You may therefore make the necessary preparations for a trip home. Get the sailing schedule from the New York agency of the Swedish Line. I think the director is still a man named Lundbeck. Ask for the same conditions you got on the trip out. You don't have to do it ahead of time as there is plenty of space on board the boats. You can see to the matter when you get to New York.

Behind my wish that you stay away as long as possible is, as I am sure you understand, my fear that until you have acquired a sufficiently strong and markedly global (not mundane) perspective you will be unprotected against the frivolity and pleasures to be found at home, and which unfortunately, because life is cheap, also prevail here in Istanbul. It looks as if the Swedes have learned nothing from the great world depression. It is hard of course to generalize, but when you see two of our royal princes and one of the young men in our own family display such a lack of self-control that without considering the consequences they rush off and bind themselves to persons completely different from themselves, it does call for caution. It destroys the resistance of your own race and class from the galloping attacks from below on what has taken so many centuries of work to build within a culture. All it takes is a moment's mistake under the spell of unchecked natural urges. A young man is helpless against this danger unless he has acquired an outlook on life sufficiently wide that he doesn't get lost. Whenever you find yourself in such a situation, I'd prefer you to be cynical rather than show any evidence of being naive. When you find yourself tempted by the charms of young girls, I want you to remember that a woman's beauty is nothing more or less than well-situated fat beneath the skin. Her inner worth depends on breeding, character, and talent. Those sorts of qualities are not flaunted, only those that tempt the eye and addle the mind. Nowadays, the battle for existence is so keen that a young man must not limit his mobility by entering into marriage too young, lest he lose the chance to become independent. The opportunities accorded you by your global education must not go to waste. They are to be used to make you independent before you assume such responsibilities. I have observed that the lack of mobility of our pioneers is often due to the fact that their wives want them home to be active in society, which often is nothing more than an exhibition of *toilettes* and provocative curves. When you come home, you should not forget to look hard at older women, and not just at what you find in the dance halls, so that you can see what they will look like twenty years from now. In this respect, our families have set a proud example. No one has gotten there by displaying legs and uncovering bosoms, and everyone frowns on painted lips and cheeks.

You know, of course, that you will be well received everywhere you go. I want you to value that. Everyone is pleased that you have conducted yourself so well, and they will show you kindness. In return, offer your attentiveness and don't leave behind the impression that they were mistaken. Among our elders you will find very strong family pride. They frown on frivolous and impulsive things. Diligence reigns supreme. Be sparing with your wisdom, for it is likely to pale by comparison with that of those who have led an active life. The older generation has a full measure of what the young lack — experience. Seek to take advantage of that through polite questions. This will be interpreted as interest, and they will be happy to share what they know with you if they believe that the questions stem from a desire to learn and not just from curiosity. Joking is fine among the young, but not among persons of advanced years.

Your letter reveals a certain admiration of the progress that America is *beginning* to make in overcoming the ill effects of the economic world revolution. You should not engage in comparisons with what you may find at home. It is true that in some respects we are behind, but that is not for you to judge or comment on. You may be certain that the same observations have been made by many here, but you must not forget that Sweden is part of Europe, and that our country is bound to follow certain patterns in its development, patterns that are difficult to escape. Hard work is called for, something that they seem to have realized in America. I am glad that you have made that very observation, for I think it is the crux of the matter.

I am sending a copy of this letter to your mother, so if you are in agreement you can make the arrangements for a visit to your native country during your vacation. Stay well, and let me know the dates of your departure from New York and arrival in Gothenburg.

Your grandmother, who is here now and who is well, sends her fondest greetings.

Your devoted
[GOW]

ISTANBUL
JUNE 6, 1934

Dear Maj,

Your telegram of June 6 — "Would it upset your plans and disappoint you if Raoul went Sweden February. Has fine opportunity to go to Mexico. Answer Dardels" — was answered that same evening "Approve. Please advise Raoul." I want to reply right away, without knowing your reasons, as I must say that I was a trifle hesitant because I would have preferred for Raoul to come home for a brief visit during the summer rather than during the height of the season. My hesitation was based on the very thoughts that I gave in my letter to R. of May 11, of which you have a copy. I decided to throw my doubts overboard, however. One should never believe that one is always in the right, and it might even be better if his visit to Sweden is postponed a bit longer. Furthermore, having given the matter some thought, I have realized that the revised plan involves his car-owning friend Woodard, and it could be rather instructive for the two boys to drive over the mountainous Mexican landscape in an old Ford truck. I immediately put together a complete list of all the Swedish consulates in Mexico with names and addresses and will send it to Mexico to Söderlund's address — and a copy to Ann Arbor, in case the boys are still there, which I doubt, however.

The reason for my adding in the telegram that you should advise Raoul was that I wasn't quite sure whether a telegram would reach him at his old address, since you mentioned that he would be out at the beginning of this month. We can only hope that everything works out. Once he gets to Mexico, I am certain that Carl Axel, who everyone says is a clever man, will give him good guidance. I have met his superior, engineer Dalén, several times, and he has said good things about C.A. My brothers have the same impression.

Fondest greetings to Fred and the children from us both.

Your devoted
(GOW)

HOUSTON, TEXAS
JULY 14, 1934

Dearest Grandfather,

Just a few lines while my traveling companion has his shoes shined.

We've had a very pleasant trip. We stayed with relatives in St. Louis for a few days, and then continued on to New Orleans, pitching a tent every night along the way, which worked out fine. Every afternoon we did a sketch and sold it. Excellent salesmanship training. I have now earned $8.25, and I know that if worse came to worst, I could earn my keep doing this. We had a lot of fun in New Orleans and stayed for three days. On the way to Texas, we stayed with a "southern" family and sketched their house. They treated us to a wonderful crab dinner.

We're now only two days away from the border and wilderness, so it may not be such smooth sailing from here on.

Fond regards,
Raoul

SAN LUIS POTOSI
[UNDATED]

Dear Mother,

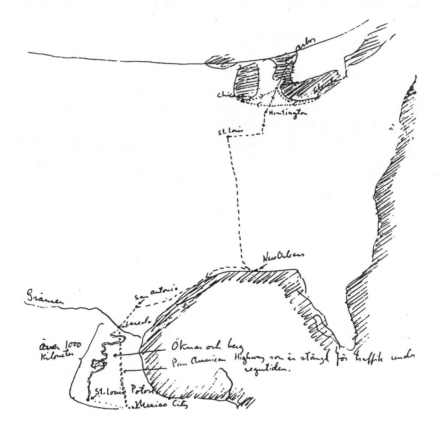

We've now almost reached Mexico City. Only 300 miles left to go, but it will probably take a couple of days because of bad roads and the downpour.

In Laredo we picked up a Mexican boy who had been deported from America because of an invalid passport. He's been serving as our interpreter. There are only two roads between Laredo and Mexico City. One is the famous "Pan-American Highway," which will be finished in a year but which is already relatively passable. During the rainy season it's muddy and dangerous, however, because it goes through high mountains. Therefore it has been officially closed, and we had to take the other road, which goes via Saltillo and St. Luis Potosi. This road consists of cattle and donkey paths, and right now, during the rainy season, travel is extremely difficult. We've been on the road for four whole days, and still not gone more than ⅔ of the way.

To be on the safe side, we joined up with two newlywed couples going down to Mexico City in their Ford. We are very well equipped with shovels, chains, rope, ax, tent, blankets, water-skins, clothes, kitchen utensils, and medicine, and prepared for any danger. Sometimes this has turned out to be a good thing, as we have both gotten stuck at least twenty times, but we haven't had more than five or six flat tires and the cars have given us very little trouble. During the whole trip from Monterrey to St. Luis Potosi, where we are now, we only met *three* automobiles, except in a town, Vanegas, where there were some local cars. We bought some very inexpensive but beautiful pottery there. Oddly enough, we haven't seen any rattlesnakes, except for a dead one. The flora has consisted of nothing but cacti and desert vegetation the entire week. We are filthy from the mud and the dust and wading in dirty water, and I have let my beard grow, just for fun. So far, I've had a great time, and I'm in excellent health.

More later,
Raoul

General Delivery
Mexico City
Mexico

[P.S.] I don't get many opportunities to write so please forward this to Grandfather.

MEXICO D.F.
AUGUST 5, 1934

Dear Grandfather,

I have arrived and been here for some time. Didn't feel well
because of some food but am now right as rain. The trip was
exciting and fun. From Monterrey to Saltillo was uphill for most of
the way. We made good time. Our group consisted of us and two
Jewish couples in a Ford sedan. The idea was that we could help
each other if and when one of us got stuck. We spent two nights in
Saltillo, admiring all the cars that had been abandoned there by
previous tourists conquered by the rigors of the trip through the
desert, and who had preferred to take the train to Mexico City and
leave the car behind in Saltillo. We were well equipped, however,
and with a convoy of two cars declared ourselves ready to set out.
The desert we went through at the start was completely arid, and
although the rainy season had started farther south, we had no
evidence of it. The roads, those that existed, were pretty bad. We
followed the railroad tracks, but still got lost a few times and only
managed to cover 110 kilometers that day. Next day we got into
the real desert, which was sometimes as flat as a floor; we made
good time until evening, when we had to laboriously dig ourselves out of muddy riverbeds and then drive the cars for several
miles along a railroad bank, without managing to find the road
again. We continued the trip to San Luis Potosi in this interesting
and exhausting fashion. All told, it took us five days to get there.
The last stretch was wet, and we were surprised by a couple of
downpours, the result of which was that we and our Jewish
friends got stuck a dozen times. But we always managed to dig
and pull each other out. There is actually nothing dangerous
about this trip, though delays and similar inconveniences are
legion. After ten days we finally arrived in Mexico City. Aunt Nita
had been worried about my absence. A letter that I'd written
never arrived. Having to stay in bed for a couple of days nursing
my stomach, I didn't have the chance to look around the city right
away, but was taken care of in a touching and most efficient way
by Nita and her husband. I admire Carl Axel very much. Nita has
inherited your eyes, and resembles Ebba Bonde and her sisters
more than ever. They have a beautiful home, although it's rather

large and hard to keep up. They are talking about getting a smaller one that's easier to manage, for the servant problem seems to be a nightmare. I'll be here for a while. Then we may go down to Oaxaca. Nothing has been said about the trip home yet.

Fondest greetings to you and Fina
Raoul

Nita and Carl Axel send their love. Mother is feeling very lonely, so it would be nice if you would send her this letter.

[Fina Johansson was GOW's housekeeper.]

ISTANBUL
AUGUST 25, 1934

My dear boy,

Thank you for your letter of the 5th from Mexico City. I have also received one from your mother and one from Nita, who writes of your visit with great enthusiasm. What she had to tell me made me very happy.

I will now broach the question of the immediate plans for your future. Two major alternatives present themselves.

One is that upon graduation you join the line of employment seekers and earn your own livelihood. This will mean the drawing table and the office chair, and you will enter a world of more or less industrious young people quietly intent on making it only at the expense of their friends. A bit of sports activity and an occasional visit to a café will lighten the existence, true, but the heavy clouds of the struggle for existence will mean that when they turn in at night, exhausted, their reflections on the day are likely to be dark. Competition today is not at all pleasant. The question of how to make it weighs constantly upon you. And in that struggle the qualifications of the competitors are all about the same. The skills required for translating or typing don't vary greatly. The supply of people with equal qualifications, nice clothes, solid schooling, and a university education far exceeds the demand. The growth of the intelligentsia proletariat is happening everywhere. With time, the feeling of camaraderie, respect for the rights of others, etc., become dampened. The net result is that problems preoccupy you more and more.

The alternative is to find something outside the usual order of things, to find a place among the leaders, not just among your peers. Like all other successful ventures, this demands an organization of its own. In the beginning it is less a question of realizing something that you yourself think you would like than it is of making others, the decision makers and those in positions of leadership, aware of your usefulness. During the Napoleonic wars corporals were said to have carried a marshal's baton in their knapsack. It symbolized their determination to achieve a position of leadership outside the usual bothersome order. You expose yourself to the envy of your peers, and you may even be accused of ruthlessness, but this is outweighed by your duty to put your gifts to good use. The well-being of the masses depends on capable leaders. It is to our country's advantage that the energy of her native sons be maximized. All potential should therefore be developed, no matter the field. Money is in no way the decisive factor in this, for history will never recognize a Rothschild as a Rembrandt or a Beethoven. *Sans comparaison*, of course, for you will not be the like of either. There must be leaders and models. It is the duty of those who have the talent to carry out the great tasks, to rise above their contemporaries.

It is not presumptuous of me to count on your talent. You have it, through your blood, your inheritance, and through the wonderful gift of a cool head. I have always spoken of the importance of self-control. The qualities I have enumerated, more than family connections, justify my conviction that you should be directed toward becoming a leader, not just another hard-working worker among many.

It is easy for a young man with talent to become *primus inter pares*. It is always to be desired. But it is one thing to be the equal of a bookkeeper and another to seek a position among the groups that are above the one you yourself belong to. To be a climber, to put it vulgarly. This you can often do through connections, though climbing that way benefits neither the individual nor those interests that would be served. Climbing by someone skilled and talented is fully justifiable, however. In fact, modern views on equality and equal opportunities, about which you have probably heard about in America, even demand it.

The idea behind your education has been to help you qualify. I have tried to equip you with something that we are not accustomed to here in Sweden, and that in fact we ignore — knowledge of the world and familiarity with other people, understanding their way of thinking, their customs, and their way of seeing. I thought that this would give you an advantage over your contemporaries. The conviction here at home that we are better than anyone else needs to be shaken. No country can do without contact with other peoples. This requires understanding their habits and customs. Anybody can see that life abroad is more difficult than here at home. A trailblazer discovers the good to be found out there among the foreigners. He studies them and broadens his horizons.

Your stay in Ann Arbor has been useful, but the theoretical part of your education will soon come to a close. We are now entering a new phase: the *practical* part. You yourself once said in a letter that you knew nothing about practical things. You are right, and the problem has long occupied my thoughts. I do not like the way young people live in Stockholm. There is too much frivolity and fun, and a young man from a good family is exposed to risks that may harm his future. We have several examples of that within our own family, and there are even some within the royal family. I have therefore decided that the practical part of your education had better take place abroad. During the seventies Knut worked briefly at the Crédit Lyonnais in Paris. Marcus's boys have been both there and in America. In both cases it has worked to their advantage. But I am not convinced that working for a *large* bank or business institute is very useful to a young man. You are placed in a department. As a rule your work is of a completely unskilled nature. You never come into contact with those who make the decisions. It will be of a nominal usefulness and not give you any real qualifications, as can easily be seen from the fact that employees of such institutions advance to positions of importance only rarely and even then very slowly. I therefore think that there is much more to be gained from being employed in a *small* company. It is easier to get an overall picture. Everybody comes into contact with everyone else. It is easier to understand how things work. The crucial point is to come into contact with those who make the decisions, and that will happen in a small company. Working there will be the springboard up into the circle of the leaders, into becoming "inter pares" with them. For some time, my research has been geared toward finding you a direction that might interest you and be of use to you.

I have already spoken of South America. The reason is that I think that I have found a leader there who would suit our purposes. Our best commercial attaché, A. C. W. Wingqvist, born in 1885, lives in Bogotá, Colombia, and has been stationed there since 1930. I don't know him personally but have made very thorough inquiries. He is not married, and his territory consists of Venezuela, Colombia, Central America, the West Indies, and Mexico. These countries are among the richest in the world. Like everywhere else, they have been hit by the depression. A German consul general I know, who recently spent six years there, has told me that much is to be learned by going there. From what I have learned about Wingqvist as a person, I believe he will be interested in you. He has an enterprising spirit. You will probably be able to find employment in an American office of suitable size through him. In addition to the contact with W., work in such a place would have beneficial results. You would get a practical complement to your education within six months or a year, and an overview of the operations of a commercial office, which undoubtedly will come in handy at a later point. I am not talking about sight-seeing. That is secondary. The point is to come into contact with the management of a company that has had to compete for its position.

Once you have agreed to this, I will begin writing W. I am already familiar with many of the details through Mr. Backlund, who works for the Swedish legation here as a copier. He spent four years in Bogotá. His father is an officer, and his grandfather, whom I met in Petersburg in 1916 at the Nobels', was a world-famous professor of astronomy at Pulkovo University. One day, after he had told me quite a bit about his experiences there, I asked B. why he hadn't stayed on. He answered simply: lack of talent.

If you approve of my plan to send you to Bogotá toward the end of March 1935, following a short stay in Stockholm, you should begin learning Spanish immediately. I am certain that there are ways of doing this in Ann Arbor. They tell me it is easy if you already know French. You will find books about these countries at the library.

I may also be able to arrange it through my good friend Kampmann, one of the directors of Kampmann, Kierulf, and Saxild, responsible for undertaking the large railroad projects here and starting even larger ones in Persia, that you be given the task of inquiring into — and reporting about, following precise questionnaires — the possibilities of contracting for a subsidiary company in those countries. This is not to open doors for possible employment with them (I would not dream of doing this since you do not as yet possess any skills), but only to give you the opportunity to show off. What I have discussed above constitutes only one phase of your practical education. You should be able to finish it sometime in 1936. I now come to a possible second stage.

For the past fourteen years I have been in close contact with one of the directors of the Dutch Bank, Ervin Freund. He is a Jew, Czech, 42 years old, and spent his entire career in banking. He is highly talented, and I consider him the best banker in C-ple. He has been appointed to head a new office opened by his bank in Haifa (the head office is in Amsterdam, with branch offices here, in Buenos Aires, Rio, and São Paulo, among other places). One of England's most famous men in the economic arena, Lord Metchell, said of that city, shortly before his death last year, that within twenty years it would be the equal of Alexandria and Genoa. It is the central point for the Palestinian railroad network and the English pipelines; and the English have just completed the only big port in Palestine there. That and Tel Aviv are the centers of the activity for Jewish immigrants, who have already amassed a large fortune and deposited as much as 12 million pounds sterling in the banks in the area. It is teeming with more activity than anywhere else on earth. Freund has a first-rate pioneering spirit. We have had innumerable discussions over the years, though oddly enough we have never once dined together. Our contact has always been talking about trade political questions. He considers me an expert in that area and for my part I have long expected him (and still do) to become foreign director in a future Swedish bank in the Orient. It is true we are not there yet, but we will get there eventually. We could not find anyone better suited to fill the current void in the area of foreign banking. A couple of months ago I spoke with him of my plans for you in

South America. He burst out, "Have him come see me in Haifa after that." I take this seriously. Having worked for a commercial firm in Bogotá, you would then have the best possible inside view of the activity inside a frontier bank. No one would be a better teacher than Freund. No one would interest him more than my grandson. He has no children of his own. In the course of your employment you would have the opportunity to observe many areas, such as the projects undertaken by the Jewish immigrants, whose talents and experience are considerable. Haifa is very much a community in expansion.

What makes such an opportunity especially valuable is that you would come under the tutelage of my highly valued friend. The idea would be for you to arrive in Haifa in the middle of 1936. I am counting on your practical education being finished by then. How long you would remain with Freund is your decision; but both he and I would dislike any limits to be established before you begin your employment. It would not look good. It goes without saying, however, that you should not feel forced to commit yourself for life.

Well, there you have some food for thought. Let me know what you think, but tell only your parents about this. It is no one else's business. Do not discuss it with any of your friends in Ann Arbor.

Reading all this will lead you to conclude I am illogical. I start by belittling bookkeeping and end by offering you exactly that. But the prospects accompanying it are exceptionally favorable.

[GOW]

ANN ARBOR
SEPTEMBER 23, 1934

Dear Grandfather,

Many thanks for your long letter, which Mother forwarded to me, and which contained plans for my education following the end of my studies in America.

In principle I am in complete agreement with the program. I

think Mexico would be a better field of operation than Colombia, but they're probably about the same.

As to the timing of the Colombia trip, I suggest early summer 1935, rather than March, 1935.

The trip home went smoothly except that on one occasion a truck had to tow our car by its axles for a mile and a half. The wheels barely touched the bottom of the tracks.

We brought back lots of Mexican things and we're trying to sell them, and this seems to be going quite well. We're not selling what we have but ordering them from the manufacturers we got to know last summer. Mostly what we offer are table cloths, napkins, mats, china (rather poor quality), and straw items. Our business is fairly small-scale of course, but that doesn't matter. My friend Dick Shields quit school to do this full-time. I don't think it worth it. The items we're selling are no more attractive than those produced in Europe or elsewhere. The price is good, but not as cheap as Japanese items. Their attraction is a certain originality and primitiveness. You could build up a good business doing this if you took the time. It depends on what happens with customs and currency. So I think I'll go to Colombia.

My final architectural courses are keeping me busy, as is a course in "decorative design," a course in Spanish, two courses in concrete, and a thesis on Swedish architecture (that I've been postponing and now have to do).

I'm so happy I had the chance to go to Mexico. Carl Axel is a wonderful man, and I found the entire Swedish colony pleasant. I met a lot of people of whom I am now very fond. The country is beautiful, even though the climate is a bit cold for my taste. The Mexicans, and especially the Indians, are childishly happy and kind and harmless. I am sure it's a land of the future, given its enormous natural resources, which will increasingly be exploited as communications improve. The Great Pan-American Highway to Mexico City should be finished in a little over a year and a half. It runs through very inaccessible areas of enormous natural beauty. Tourist traffic alone should bring in large amounts, for the simple reason that certain beautiful parts of Mexico are closer to the east than to the west. The temperature stays cool when the worst heatwaves hit the States. Furthermore, there are plenty of picturesque monuments in Mexico and it's very romantic. There's no reason why the same class of Americans that go to Europe shouldn't go to Mexico as well. The country is less expensive and getting there takes less time. Once the country acquires a reputation for safety and progress, American capital will find its way there, more than is the case now, and a real golden age will begin.

But I don't think it will ever be a U.S.A. in miniature. It's too mountainous and inaccessible for that. Geologically speaking, the country is young; the mountain slopes are steep and there are few wide valleys. The population is not highly cultured, but they don't appear the least bit lazy. It's amusing to see the peons *run* along the roads from their distant villages to the central marketplace in one of the cities, loaded down with enormous cargos of vessels or brooms or mats or whatever their native region produces. This habit of running stems from the days when they didn't have any beasts of burden. When the Spaniards arrived, there were neither horses nor donkeys. They say a message from Mexico City could be sent just as quickly as one from Rome.

I'll write again when school is in full swing.

A thousand kisses to Grandmother and greetings,
Raoul

ISTANBUL
OCTOBER 30, 1934

My dear boy,

I have received your letter of September 23, and I am pleased that you approve of the plan I proposed in my letter of August 25.

As you are aware, I have — at least up to now — had some qualms about your mother's eagerly insisting that you become a banker. I'll tell you the reason for my qualms, and start by quoting some lines from a letter I wrote her that accompanied a copy of my letter to you. That she might better understand why I think it useful for you to work for some time at my friend Freund's bank in Haifa, I pointed out that what a frontier bank does reflects all aspects of commerce, and that some knowledge of it would be extremely helpful. It is a kind of nerve center, and the surest way of acquiring information. No other channels provide so accurate an insight into the economic situation as banking. By being given an opportunity to study the scrupulous methods by which a bank tests the credit of various companies, you would receive training assessing the prospects for financial gain, a training applicable to a number of professions. I am certain it will always be useful to see for yourself how these things get done, and to know when not to engage in some business undertakings. But the greatest benefit lies on the purely personal level. Freund is unusually alert, skillful, and experienced.

You will see that I am of the opinion employment should be *of maximum general educational use to all sorts of activities*. My belief that you would find employment in a *small frontier commercial office* more useful lies behind my choosing this comparatively *small bank* in Haifa. You would be closer to the action. Most of the employees will be new to their surroundings, and you won't encounter the sort of reserve that always characterizes certain circles of older civil servants, so full of imagined wisdom but also quite often ill-concealed disappointment about not having advanced beyond the edge of the counter. There will be more of a *fraternité*. Your talent and experience will make it easier to find a good position within the inner circle. Enough about this.

As for your wish to spend several months in Sweden after completing your studies in Ann Arbor, that is for you to decide. I will give you my opinion, however.

For you it will be a pleasure to come home, and even more so for your mother, and I am therefore in full agreement even though I see some negative aspects. I have already pointed out that life in Stockholm is dangerous for a young man. The restraint that you find in other countries, not least in Paris, London, and Nice, as a result of the depression, is not to be found in Stockholm. They are still living the good life, dancing, speculating, ignoring the fact that an enormous revolution is taking place all over the world, both in society as a whole and in business. Look at Italy. Mussolini's strong spirit has found favor even among the fiercest cynics. This frivolous and carefree culture has taken heed of his warnings and come to find a single focus of strength. This is self-control at its highest. It can also be found in Germany, but of a completely different sort — the bitter feeling of *having* to undertake the greatest national rallying of resources that the world has ever seen. They do so to salvage their existence. That movement may fall apart any day, however. In Italy, it will survive because it is founded upon a conviction of its usefulness; the one in Germany on fear and inevitable necessity. In Stockholm you will find no signs of this frame of mind. The prevailing system of *laissez-aller* has weakened individual resistance among the men, especially the young ones, and exposed them to temptations that, with mathematical certainty, will lead to dire consequences. Those involving passion I will not enter into here. You know my thoughts on them. I will, however, touch upon an aspect that you may not have considered, one in which what I say is governed by memories of my own experiences as a young man.

You will certainly be very warmly received by our families. Maybe too warmly, since your qualities may have been generously exaggerated during your long absence. You are surrounded by a nimbus, and this means very high expectations have been placed on you. This is a dangerous situation that unless handled correctly may easily lead to dire consequences. I realize full well that my pointing this out may to some extent destroy your pleasure, but my age and my love for you leave me no choice except to mention the matter. I want to steel you. Among the older generation of men you will meet are some who have accomplished a great deal in life. They will be pleased by your talents, and look for all the good things they can find in your character. But they are also experienced men not fooled by nicely combed hair or an unabashed torrent of words. Do not ever forget when dealing with them that you know nothing, and that your experience of people and the world is slight. They have much to say. Listen attentively to everything they utter. If they hint that they would like to help you, accept their offers most graciously, always by pointing out that your practical education is not yet complete and that you will probably not be ready for any tasks at home for several years. You must not fail under any circumstances to do this, for should it be arranged that you find work at home you would become part of a collection of clever and select young men all competing for the fleshpots. Your future would be uncertain, because you know nothing yet about practical life. You would be in a completely different position should you wait until 1938. By then you will have insight into commerce and banking *abroad,* about which very few know anything here at home. You would have a complete understanding of business, acquired under the best tutelage, which absolutely no one in Sweden will have. I stressed the value and importance of this in my letter. You will be able to carry on a completely different kind of conversation with the older generation than the one you can today. Now, clearly, they have the upper hand. Afterward, the upper hand will be yours, because no one in Sweden will have seen or experienced anything like what I have discussed. You will be worth something, not just in our own circle but also among those who eventually will realize, in coming years, that Swedish industry lags behind, and whose thoughts increasingly will revolve around how to remedy its backwardness. They will need what they currently lack — a strong presence, a person acquainted with business abroad on a large scale. You will be unique, provided you manage — during your short visit — to establish a solid impression of attractive personal qualities that may lead to a desire to use your services. The bread that has been given you will become a gift of grace.

You will find it easy to take care of these things during a brief stay in Stockholm. You may say *once* that you know nothing, but to repeat it might give rise to ridicule. It might cause one to ask why you are having a good time instead of acquiring what you need. There is a much greater risk that they will find weaknesses during a long visit. And once found, those weaknesses will become the topic of discussion, having first been magnified. My advice is to stay home for as short a time as possible. It is human nature for people to seek to bring everybody else down to their own level. Your current popularity will give rise to an urge to destroy any halo, even if it contains no element of arrogance.

I have written a letter to legation counsel Wingqvist and enclose a copy. I am also in touch with Consul General Kastengren in Calcutta, whom I saw in Nice last year, in case Wingqvist's reply should be negative. K. is a solid man, but without the wide range of experience that W. has. As a training ground the two places may be equal, but it would be more unusual for a Swede to be familiar with the South American markets and possessing a command of Spanish. It is not part of my plans that you should train for a career in either place. It is more a matter of acquiring some insight into business abroad. The most valuable part of the program will be the time in Haifa, but it requires previous business experience of a general nature. You need not know anything to volunteer your services in Bogotá, but to work under Freund it would not do to be unfamiliar with normal office routines, correspondence, etc.

[GOW]

ANN ARBOR
NOVEMBER 13, 1934

Dearest Grandfather,

I haven't written for a long time, and I'm all the sorrier because I haven't yet expressed the full extent of my gratitude and happiness as regards your offer to send me to Colombia and later to Palestine.

I had already finished a letter when your letter of October 30 arrived. In it, I had proposed further reasons why I should stay longer than a month in Sweden. Now I will rewrite it, because your arguments for a brief stay in Sweden were so persuasive that I don't wish to make a fool of myself by continuing on with my line of reasoning.

I have already completed a term of Spanish and am now into my second. My trip to Mexico was of considerable help. I liked Mexico very much and would prefer to go there rather than to Colombia. But I understand that your choice has been dictated by personal considerations, and I won't ask you to change your decision.

I have expressed my interest in Swedish export and everything touching on international trade in general so many times that you know I'm in complete agreement about your plans for me, and will do my best to live up to your expectations.

I've enjoyed being here so much that I'm sad at the prospect of leaving in February, even though I'm obviously happy about going home. I'm now finishing my final course in architecture. This past month we've been working with so-called "cheap housing." The problem calls for constructing sixteen city blocks, with space for 4,500 people. The entire area — at least in my project — is designed as a park in which there are four-story lamellated buildings. We are also to include two churches, a school, a childcare center, a "community center," stores, a fire station, etc.

The whole project is very interesting, but very difficult, because every good solution calls for a compromise among several different viewpoints. The need for parks and the one for low buildings, for example, are contradictory. The one for narrow houses with lots of sun contrasts the need for inexpensive, wider houses with good insulation. My teacher is a Frenchman named Jean Hebrard, a longtime American resident who previously worked on projects in Siam. In 1913, he finished an enormous project for an international city, which was to have been constructed near Brussels on ground donated by the Belgian state. It was supposed to house functions such as those the League of Nations now performs, in addition to all kinds of scientific institutions whose mission required international cooperation, such as radium research, power transmission, etc. The city's design was extremely grandiose, and everything was grouped around a 300-meter-high skyscraper (it wasn't until five or six years later that the first skyscraper to exceed 300 meters was constructed). It took him and his coworkers seven years to finish the hundreds of plans for this project, which cost 100,000 dollars. Working under him has been wonderful, although he's very European. That is to say, he maintains a certain aloofness, and it would never occur to anyone to address him with anything but the greatest of reverence and respect. American professors, on the other hand, without in any way sacrificing their authority, feel embarrassed if you scrape and bow. In American slang this is known as "polishing the apple." How the expression originated I don't know.

I'm happy the Democrats won the election. Not that it is a foregone conclusion that they will do a better job of governing than the Republicans, but because I've always argued in my letters home that Roosevelt is still the nation's strong man, and that it would take more than a couple of bad winters for the nation to lose confidence in him. And there is absolutely no doubt that times are much better now than when I arrived, certainly better than in 1932, which was a terrible year. It wouldn't surprise me if this country underwent fundamental governmental reform before long, particularly in the area of "states' rights." It is more and more apparent that the political organizations of the individual

states are corrupt and incompetent. One thing that has high-
lighted this is the action of the federal police against "kidnappers"
and others. They've had great success and this has aroused general admiration, while giving rise to invidious comments about
the ability of the individual states to tackle crime on their own.

The politicians are opposed to any change toward a more
centralized government and quote Jefferson, who wanted the
sovereignty of the states to remain inviolable. But had he been
alive today and seen how high the levels of communications,
mass production etc. have become, he would probably have
laughed at those who invoke his name for the dubious purpose of
keeping an outmoded and inefficient organization going. It will
be fun to see what the future brings.

> With fondest regards to Grandmother,
> Raoul

HOTEL D'ANGLETERRE, NICE
DECEMBER 20, 1934

My dear boy,

Thank you for your letter of November 13. I am glad you approve
of my plan for your immediate future. The centerpiece, of course,
is Haifa. What comes before is merely preparation, so that, as I
have already said, you do not have to be ashamed before Mr.
Freund with your total ignorance of office work. I had put off
writing you until hearing from Wingqvist or Kastengren. I have
now had a late reply from W. through the Swedish embassy in
Paris. It is not definitive, but he will write again. I am sending you
a copy of both my letter to him and his response, which proves
that he is more out of touch with the commercial world than I am
here in the East. The two missives provide plenty of food for
thought. It appears not at all easy to volunteer one's services.
They are afraid you would gain insight into their methods, and
that is precisely what we are out to gain. I am rather proud I was
already able to see the significance of that as far back as twenty-
four years ago. Now I'm wondering what would be best — to

wait for another letter from Wingqvist or to write the minister in
Peru, Einar Modig (Lima), Avenida 28 de Julio, Miraflores (I still
prefer Bogotá to Lima on account of the climate, which is better),
or to have you yourself write to Carl Axel Söderlund. Since it
would probably be wise to have several arrows in your quiver,
and since you seem inclined to go to Mexico, you might write Carl
Axel and ask him to look into the possibilities for volunteering
your services, without remuneration, at some import/export office in Mexico. It makes no difference whether it is Mexican or
American, but it mustn't be too large. Make certain that all correspondence is *par avion* because I am anxious not to lose any
time. In your letter to C.A. you may want to employ some of the
arguments I used in my letter to Wingqvist, unless you think it
better just to refer to them. Don't be discouraged by the fact that
finding a job seems to be difficult; this should only act as a spur to
renewed efforts to reach our goal. I remain convinced that the
main thrust of the program is right. We must not lose sight of it. I
noted with satisfaction that paragraph of your letter in which you
tell me how often you have written of your enthusiasm for Swedish export and everything involving international trade, which
proves that in that respect we are of one mind. As soon as I hear
anything I'll let you know.

I have had bad news from home. In a fit of nervous reckless-
ness, Nita has signed a petition for divorce. It is in Carl Axel's
possession. Then she left. As soon as she got home she became
inconsolable, regretting her stupidity, and offering to do anything
for a reconciliation. I have wired C.A. and asked him to hold off
submitting the document. I do not know what he will do. We have
kept the whole thing a secret, the Falkmans and I, primarily for
Grandmother's sake, and therefore you must not breathe a word
about what I've told you; I think it might help resolve the matter,
though, if you resumed your correspondence with C.A. as if
nothing had happened.

I was very interested by your account of your work in the final
architecture course and the so-called "cheap housing" project. I
did a similar one when Saltsjöbaden was being founded. If we
have a chance to meet I would like to know more about it, and if
you can lay your hands on a copy of the plan, it would be fun to
see how far they have come in America. When you get to Stockholm, you should make sure to visit Alsten and other private

housing communities. It is true they haven't skimped on the size of the lots, primarily because the lots are only leased for a specific amount of time, so that their value keeps climbing in anticipation of more "compact" utilization in the future.

Keep me up-to-date on your trip home. I would prefer not to go to Stockholm but am naturally most anxious to see you. We will have to see how it might be arranged. The reason is that Marcus and I are rather at odds on the subject of our trade policy. It is regrettable, but he is somewhat of a despot — as all great financiers were wont to be — and has a hard time realizing that the world has undergone considerable change. I'm quite unhappy about this but find myself unable to play the penitent. We are living in a crucial period. The new generation will view things differently. The older generation *does not want* to accept any modification of the old views, and it is futile to try to teach old dogs new tricks. I'm better off sticking with the younger generation, which is beginning to wake up to what's going on.

Wishing you all the best for the New Year.

Your devoted,
[GOW]

[The Falkmans are Karin and Oscar Falkman, GOW's daughter and her husband].

ANN ARBOR
JANUARY 1, 1935

[Written in English]

Dear Grandfather,

I hope you will pardon my writing in English: this typewriter has no Swedish keys. I have spent this entire Christmas in Ann Arbor, as I had quite a lot to do, writing my thesis in architecture and also completing a rather elaborate notebook in a course on decorative design that I am taking. Everybody leaves town within a few hours of the last classes before Christmas, and from then to the seventh of January the place is like a tomb. However, I have been busying myself rather constantly with my work and I haven't bored myself at all. None of my friends stayed here over vacation, so I certainly didn't have any temptations to keep me from it.

We have been having a fine weather, snow most of the time and a few days of quite severe cold. One morning something peculiar happened. Due to changes of temperature, I presume, the street pavements, lawns, and even tree trunks were coated with a layer of perfectly clear ice almost an inch thick. It looked very strange and very beautiful.

Christmas Eve I felt rather lonely and gloomy, but I went to the show ("cinema" in British English) as I often do, and it was so funny that when I returned at midnight I laughed out loud. I go to the show usually a couple of times a week; maybe I've inherited that taste from you, for if I remember correctly, you and Grandmother and I went there almost constantly that summer that I was in Istanbul.

I don't yet know exactly when I'll arrive in Stockholm. School is over in the first week of February, but I'll take my time leaving here. I also intend to go to Boston before I leave. So the beginning of March is a probable date, nicely coordinated with the disappearance of the worst cold spell.

Did I tell you that my grade on the Housing Problem, which we have been having, was "excellent"? I'm very happy, for it was quite an important problem, the solution of which required over ten weeks of study and draughting. However, there is not much to show for all that, because it all goes on one single sheet of paper.

I had a letter from Grandmother, who was so contented at being out in Saltsjöbaden, where she amused herself hugely digging and planting in the garden.

Tried to get ahold of Gustaf Sundberg's book on the Swedish National Character, but could not find it in the large library here. I thought I had seen it somewhere in the United States but I must have been mistaken. It would have come in handy at the writing of my thesis on Swedish Architecture. Instead I found an old Statistical Yearbook from 1904, written by him, and there I found a summary of his views on the subject.

The prospect of leaving the United States does not please me at all. From the way you talk and write about it I feel that you became just as infatuated in it as I have. It is a wonderful place and I am sure I will long to go back to it. If I ever do get a chance to get back I hope I will not find it too different from what it is, but I imagine that as soon as prosperity is back again things will start happening with a vengeance.

Colvins have gone down to Panama where I think he is Commander of Fort Sherman. Fitz is still at Harvard, however, where he is studying at law. That is why I want to go to Boston on my way home. I think Lucette, his sister, is also up for a visit, but I don't know whether she will be there by the time I am through school.

I long so much to see you and I hope you will be in Sweden sometime during the early spring or else if I could meet you on the continent somewhere.

One thing I would like to clear up now is the military service problem. I hope they give me a chance to complete it sometime because I long to go back to the army. It is a vigorous and healthy life. They don't seem to have a habit of ever answering letters at the "rullforingsexpedition" or at least they don't answer me, and I have written a couple of times. If I could complete it by a special arrangement during the spring I would not mind.

To tide me over the dreariness of the vacation I have borrowed a radio, which affords me a great deal of pleasure. American radio performances are quite wonderful, going constantly from early morning until late at night. The quality is also very high and one can at any time hear good classical music if one does not like the jazz music which of course accounts for most of the programs. Yesterday afternoon, that is during the last day of 1934, I heard the midnight New Year's celebrations from Manila in the Philippine islands. It came through absolutely clear, due to the use of short-wave transmission. Another musical pleasure which Ann Arbor offers is Handel's "Messiah," which is sung every year at a free concert for five thousand people at the University Auditorium. I have heard that now every year since I came here, usually with my friend Miss Bernice Ringman, who is of Swedish ancestry and who has been in Sweden. It is a wonderful piece of music. I don't think there is anything I would rather hear.

As to my year of study in Colombia, I would like to say that I think I would prefer to have a job there connected with a salary, be it ever so small. I have a feeling that if I were merely to act as student not much would be accomplished. If I were to have a little job connected with an income I would still have the benefit of Mr.

Wingqvist's expert guidance. On the other hand if I were to work in some office without salary my chances of getting in touch with Mr. Wingqvist or my superior at the office would not be increased. Naturally I know that there are practically no jobs available anywhere but if I could have a choice I would choose the small job with a salary to the position as student. I have been going to school now for such a long time I begin to feel rather useless. I understand that all this is preparation for a definite type of activity later on, but I do think that if I am to learn office manners, and that is one of the purposes for working in Colombia before going to Haifa, then I would learn that better if I were in the ordinary position of the office worker rather than in a sort of privileged one.

I shall be very glad to meet my parents and you again, and will again take the opportunity of thanking you for all your generosity and love in making possible for me the wonderful experience of spending these years in America.

> With warmest regards and Happy New Year,
> Raoul

> HOTEL D'ANGLETERRE, NICE
> JANUARY 12, 1935

My dear boy,

The last letter I had from you was dated December 20. I'm quite anxious to have some news of your graduation, of how you did in your final projects, and of your trip home. Crossing the Atlantic in February can be a bit rough. I once had a very bad crossing with a White Star ship by the name of the *Teutonic.* But it should be all right, and the voyage only takes a few days. Let me know the date of your arrival and send your letter by air.

Lilly Crafoord, who arrived here a few days ago, tells me that your mother told her that you would be arriving in Sweden around February 20, but I have not heard from Maj —

I repeat what I already told you, to pay close attention to the older generation, always keeping in mind that they are not the ones making the decisions nowadays and, even less, have the future in their hands. In my opinion, Jacob and Dodde are the most important members of our family. Both are capable men and have managed to acquire a very good reputation. Their methods are much more up-to-date than those of the older generation. They are valued. The older generation was feared. That, I think, is the general opinion, roughly speaking. The adulation of financiers that has disappeared in America is still alive to some extent in Sweden, though it is fading. Naturally we all admire the older generation, first and foremost Father, who gave the family its leading position.

You should visit Fredrik Wallenberg at Drottningholm. He has spent most of his life abroad, mostly as a journalist. He worked for many years for the *Daily Mail*, whose director was Mr. Harmsworth, later a most dangerous and clever minister of propaganda during the world war who died as Lord Northcliffe — Fredrik has much to tell about international journalism. His specialty was political caricature, which has always been one of the most potent English weapons against their opponents. Along with Trafalgar, it sealed Napoleon's fate. He once told me that he'd done more than 15,000 drawings during his time in London and Paris. He is talented, very knowledgeable, and likes to talk, which is why it should be particularly tempting for you to meet him. He is blind but manages to correspond admirably on the typewriter. You'd better go to see him by yourself, after calling him first at Drottningholm 40. You will get more out of your visit that way —

Don't forget to let me know, by airmail, whether you've written to Carl Axel and what he has replied.

Your devoted
(GOW)

[Lilly Crafoord was GOW's sister. Fredrik Wallenberg, the journalist, who was married to GOW's sister Ingeborg, was his prime source of information for family news.]

[Written in English]

Dear Grandfather,

I have received your interesting letters and the book, which lately I have not had time to read due to a lot of work which has accumulated.

I have not yet had an answer from Carl Axel whom I wrote a short time ago. The letter from Bogotá of which you sent me a copy interested me much. I liked the character of the writing, and I think I would also like the man.

Lilly Crafoord was misinformed. I will not arrive home by the twentieth of February but will probably leave here (Ann Arbor) by that time depending on how fast I can wind up my work here.

From your letter I can see that you are leaving the arrangements for my trip home to me. In order that our plans should tie up with each other I would like to consult with you. Since you do not cherish the idea of visiting Sweden, particularly not during the cold season, would it meet with your approval if I went home over France? I have been looking forward to seeing you and in that manner that could be arranged. Later I could return to Sweden over Berlin, where I would like to see my favorite cousin Maj Nisser, who has recently married Count Heinrich von Plauen, and whose home is in Wisenburg close to Berlin.

My last problem after the Housing Problem, on which I received the grade "Excellent," was a Natural History Museum. This problem was quite unlike the previous one. It was almost entirely an aesthetic rather than an economic problem. The whole thing was a sort of memorial affair with an imposing approach in the grand manner. The building was supposed to be designed to balance an existing very large museum group situated on the other side of an intervening boulevard. It also had to dominate a park which constituted its immediate surroundings. The required cubage was probably not more than 200,000 cubic feet but I succeeded in finally designing a building containing not less than 1,500,000 cubic feet. I am quite proud of having suceeded in wasting that much space for it is almost as difficult as saving it. The front of the building consisted of a semicircular concave colonnade of impressive dimensions (it was about as high as the colonnade of the Concert Hall in Stockholm but wider) which overlooked a large plaza and a formal garden 450 feet by 450 feet. A building like that, where no practical considerations are taken, would of course never be built, but it was a lot of fun designing it after the slightly arid housing problem. It is being judged right now as I write this, and I don't know the result yet.

I had my last day of school yesterday. It felt very peculiar to end these pleasant and interesting years of study in America. I have had a wonderful time and the parting was very sad. The next weeks are taken up with examinations. I am quite fearful for the outcome of one subject, concrete, where, by the force of circumstances I had to take a harder course than my program required. Everything hinges on the final examination next Thursday.

As I write, Carl Axel has not written but I do know that the Mexican laws with respect to the employment of foreign non-specialized labor are quite stringent. An employer is required to keep ten Mexicans for every foreigner employed. Whether these regulations hold true for unpaid office workers I do not know.

Times still seem to be getting better and better at least in the Detroit area where automobile production is leading all industries in a small boom.

I will write you again after examinations or when Carl Axel answers me.

My warm regards,
Raoul

ANN ARBOR
FEBRUARY 11, 1935

Dear Grandfather,

Today I got a letter from Carl Axel, from which the following: "Spoke the other day with an engineer by the name of Ramirez, who owns a construction company and who at the same time is the representative for Mo-Domsjö here in Mexico. He will be delighted to have you on his office staff. His father-in-law runs the agency for Otis elevators in this country, and if you would prefer to work for him that could be arranged. What remains to be dealt with is the immigration problem, but from what I hear it will not present an obstacle if it is handled in a sensible manner. You would probably first have to ask for permission to enter the country for six months and apply for an extension later on. Moreover, I believe all this would be best handled here in Mexico City, so let me know when and if you decide to come and I will take care of everything for you. Your grandfather sent me a wire a few months ago informing me that he had sent me a letter. However, that letter has never arrived. Please give me his address so I can write him." In case there's been some mistake this is Carl Axel's present address: Compania Mexicana "Aga," S.A., Apartado 1474, Mexico, S.F. He is a very fine man and I like him very much. Either one of the two positions mentioned seems attractive, although Carl Axel does not say very much about the characters or accomplishments of the two Mexicans. But I would think he is a very good judge. I submit these two for your opinion and judgment.

I'm now entirely done with school and busy working on my thesis, which seems to be taking longer than I'd expected. I find it somewhat difficult and futile to write about a subject like Sweden, when there is nobody to talk to and match wits with. As a result I am proceeding slowly and without much enthusiasm. My grades have come in and they are a bit lower than usual. One of them seems to be a mistake, but I'm not going to bother about it. However I'm all finished with school and that continues to amaze me.

My thoughts of Sweden had been lying dormant for three years and now suddenly they are breaking out in full bloom, and I'm actually dreaming about home every night. I long to get back soon to see my parents and everybody else.

Will write or wire as soon as I know my date of departure.

Warmest regards,
Raoul

[Telegram]
WALLENBERG
1021 HILL STREET
ANN ARBOR MICHIGAN

It is preferable your going direct Stockholm stop Will join you
there later stop Wire date arrival in Gothenburg

Wallenberg
Nice le 12 fevrier 1935

STOCKHOLM
JUNE 9, 1935

Dearest Grandfather,

It was so wonderful seeing you and spending time with you. I want
to thank you again for all you're doing for me and assure you that I
will always try to do all I can to be worthy of it. We had such a good
time together, and I'm glad that you enjoyed my company.

I've had word from Oslo that the boat will be leaving on the
15th and so arriving in the morning of that day should give me
enough time. I will therefore be able to leave here on the 14th, as
you wished.

There has been nothing about the Riddarholm swimming pool
in the newspaper as yet, but when there is I will send the article
to you.

I'm told some young people whom Mother knows will be on
the boat, so that I may not be as bored as I feared. In addition, I'll
take along some work, which will be more than enough to keep
me busy for three weeks.

You were interested in reading the letter I got from the school in
America, informing me of my medal. I'd thrown it away since in
and of itself it wasn't very important. I have now retrieved it, however.

Dear Mr. Wallenberg:
It was a great pleasure to receive your letter of April 24th.
[*RW's note:* Newspaper clipping of the Riddarholm pool] We

posted the paper on the Bulletin Board so that your friends would see your lively and interesting reaction to the problem in Stockholm. I wish it were possible for you to continue your contact with the project.

Perhaps you know that each year we award a medal on behalf of the American Institute of Architecture to the student who has in our judgment distinguished himself in the work of the school. I am happy to write you that the faculty has selected you as the recipient this year, and accordingly you will, in the course of time, receive the student medal from the national body. I congratulate you on behalf of the faculty.

South Africa sounds far away from the world and from architecture, but I am sure that wherever you go your friends will enjoy your fine spirit and cooperation.

Mrs. Lorch and Betty were pleased to hear from you. I remain, with cordial greetings,

Sincerely yours,
E. Lorch

Nina went down to Germany two days ago to stay with Maj von Plauen for a month. Mother is beginning to feel a bit lonely, but she still has her Kevinge.

Mother and Father both ask to be remembered to you.

We had Nita here for dinner the other day, and that might have done some good.

Fond regards from your
Raoul

The name of the South African firm is:
Arderne, Scott, Thesen Ltd
Lower Church Street
Woodstock
Cape Town

The address of the Consulate General:
Boston House
Strand St.
Cape Town

*[The Riddarholm Pool. Riddarholm was a somewhat seedy and
abandoned wharf close to the Royal Palace in Stockholm. A
decision had been made to build a swimming facility there. The
project was canceled, however, and construction of a harbor in
Riddarholm had been proposed as an alternative. E. Lorch was
dean of the school of architecture at the University of Michigan.
During RW's return to Sweden, South Africa replaced South
America as the place to continue the "second phase" of his education, and it was arranged that he work at a company called
Arderne, Scott, Thesen.]*

CAPE TOWN
JULY 8, 1935

Dearest Grandfather,

Today at two o'clock the *Hammaren* cast anchor outside Cape
Town. It was Sunday, and since no ships are allowed into harbor
unless absolutely necessary, we had to sit there until six o'clock
this morning. Cape Town is unexpectedly beautiful. I had imagined something flat and cold and forbidding. Nordic and English
and boring. Instead, it seems extremely southern and picturesque. The city is partly situated on the steep foot of Table
Mountain, which rises up right behind it. You often read in books
about various cities that are said to lie in the shadow of such and
such famous mountain. Then it turns out when you actually get
there that you can't make out the mountain at all except on really
clear days in September. It's not like that here. Table Mountain is
incredibly majestic, very nearby, and in some kinds of weather,
probably a little threatening. The city faces north, oddly enough,
even though it is situated on the southern coast of Africa, in a
deep bay surrounded by hills like the ones that surround Constantinople, and also by jagged mountains. I have now settled
into a hotel, a type of boardinghouse right outside the city. It is
located on the Atlantic shore, only a hundred meters from the
water, and faces the sunset.

The trip was excellent. I had the company of two Swedish

fellows, one named Björn Burchardt, 24 years old, the son of an ironworks owner in Norrland and who visited South Africa during a seven-month stint on a whaler. He's come to stand on his own two feet. He intends to work in the paper business, and will probably succeed since he's very energetic and intelligent. He's traveling with Göte Spets, also from Norrland but less intelligent and self-assured than Burchardt. He seems to be along for the ride. He's one of Sweden's leading motorcycle racers, the son of wealthy parents in Hudiksvall, and wants to become more independent. Both have come with little money, although they appear to have decent prospects. We had lots of fun together on the trip, although I became more and more absorbed in my Umeå firehouse, an architectural competition that I've entered. Doing the detail work on it was hard when the ship pitched violently, as happened toward the end of the trip when we faced a strong southeaster with high breakers. My proposal is now practically finished. The only thing missing is a perspective drawing. Not bad for three weeks' work. I'm not entirely satisfied with the result and intend to work out another proposal, which has to be sent off in exactly one week on the last mail plane to Sweden to get there before the application deadline. I think it will be a week well spent, for if the last three weeks' work has brought me only up to the level of the last of the participants (the contest had been going on for a long time before I entered it), another week might bring me closer to a possible prize. I don't think that I have the remotest chance of winning, but I really enjoy participating. I will start at Arderne, Scott, Thesen in a week. Parenthetically, they are commonly known as Thesen Ltd. or Thesen & Co.

We saw sharks twice during the voyage, and I was amused to note that they actually do have a triangular dorsal fin, and that it actually does stick up above the water when they swim. What they need it for I do not know. We were followed by an albatross for a couple of days. It was very graceful, gliding along the surface of the water and dodging the waves with lightning speed.

I was surprised that we saw land only three times during the whole trip, namely in the Channel, the Canary Islands, and the small West African port city of Dakar, whose existence we could divine by the reflection of the lighthouse just beyond the horizon as we passed by at night. Dakar is the starting point for German and French airplanes crossing the Atlantic to South America, from what I am told.

For the time being, Burchardt, Spets, and I are living together at this hotel, which seems to be an excellent place for getting to know the surroundings. I've met Consul Hegardt, who appears to be very nice and well liked. I've also heard nothing but good things about Fevrell.

Hegardt is evidently very efficient. A message was waiting for Burchardt when he arrived, telling him that an agent was ready to avail himself of his services as an expert and salesman. Hegardt was the one who recommended that we put up here. It's usually not my habit to live with Swedes, and there are other Swedes besides us, but as I am here precisely to study what the Swedes are doing or not doing in trade I think it just as well I get to know them.

The day has been very hectic, as arrival days tend to be, what with getting used to new circumstances, customs officials, and other nuisances. For me it may have been especially so because for the last part of the voyage I was working very hard and sleeping very little while giving birth to my fire station. It's a shame that in all likelihood nothing will come of it.

We are having the strangest summer weather even though it's the middle of winter. Apparently this has never happened before; at least not since the days of Vasco da Gama. It's as hot as a midsummer's day, even right now, at night. Once more, as always, my deep thanks for all the love and kindness you have heaped on me, of which my presence here is yet even further proof.

> Many regards to you and also
> to Fina from
> Raoul

Dearest Grandfather,

I am still not completely settled in and still living very primitively (there are three of us in the room) in the same hotel as when I first arrived. I got so completely absorbed in my drawings of the Umeå fire station during my first week that I didn't have time to go out hunting for a better place to live. When in ceremonial fashion my proposal had been handed over to the post office I caught a bad cold. That was about a week ago, and I haven't been doing much of anything except sitting here pining, feeling too low to do anything useful. I did start at Arderne, Scott, Thesen Ltd. a few days ago, however. Their office, an ugly and old-fashioned three-story building, is situated on the other side of the "Downtown district" and because of this it takes me half an hour to get there. Everyone has counseled me to stay out here, for better people supposedly live here and nowhere else, but I think I'll move into the center anyway. It's too early to say much about my job. So far all I've done is sit around, checking bills and receipts. The office appears to be big, maybe even too big, and the work can't be all that illuminating. I will ask them to move me around from one department to another. So far, my strongest impression has been the horrible cold and draftiness of the place. Everyone has a cold, and some are sick at home with bronchitis or worse. Consul Hegardt, who is a very kind and thoughtful man, brought me over to the company and introduced me to the directors, who I have to say didn't seem particularly interested. I will be able to judge the work better in my next letter, however. Admiral Evans has been in Durban, so I haven't been able to visit him (his wife is Norwegian and a friend of Aunt Alice's, as you may remember). I am not overly happy with my architectural proposals. Furthermore, the post office told me that they will probably arrive in Umeå in complete ruins and tatters, which is too bad, given the amount of effort I've put into them.

Cape Town has turned out to be a disappointment. My last letter was written when I was still under the influence of the favorable impression I got when the *Hammaren* came into port and the city seemed to have an almost Italian air about it. It was warm and beautiful then. But I had barely sealed the envelope when the temperature sank to almost nothing. And when it is cold here it is *really* cold. I have never been so cold in my life as during this past week. There are drafts from every corner, and the only source of heat in the hotel, an open fire in the parlor, gives off so much smoke you can barely see your hand. Just like the Swede you met in Peking who arrived wearing eight jackets and over-coats, I have now begun to assume fairly rotund proportions. It is actually probably a good thing that there are three of us in the same room. We can generate some heat for each other.

The city is more old-fashioned than I'd thought. There are hardly any buildings in the center, and from what I hear the boom is limited to Johannesburg, where there is lots of building activity. Wages are higher there. If Thesen turns out to be unsatisfactory I may eventually go there. It is also a nicer city.

The military service authorities proved less generous than they have up to this point and did *not* allow me to defer my military service. However, I have again applied for deferment for valid reasons and hope that they will give in. I told them that 1936 would be a good year, since I would be much closer to my native country then. If they refuse my request there is nothing for me to do but wait until I get home. Any penalty should be minimal, I think.

The food is good but monotonous. Like everything else here it is also expensive. Clothes etc. are extremely expensive. Going to the movies, one of my favorite pastimes, is very difficult. There's only one evening performance, tickets are usually two kronor, and you have to travel long distances by streetcar to get there. The programs are excellent, at least, with lots of short features before-hand.

Went up to the American consulate the other day to inquire about traveling to the United States, and they told me I could even get an entry visa from another country. I am homesick for it from time to time, and if I ever did decide to go back I wouldn't want to find that there was some formality I had failed to observe. He was generally very nice, the consul.

One of the attractive features of life down here is the drinking of tea. The tea is really excellent and we even get it at the office twice a day. The rest of the food is very rich and English.

I'm sorry I don't have anything special to relate, but as I said

I've spent most of my time recuperating. Mr. Dahl, the gentleman Hegardt originally talked to at Arderne, Scott, Thesen, is in Norway at the moment. His return will probably mean that I'll be better taken care of than at present. The company has close ties to Transatlantic, since they fill three Transatlantic ships a year. Twice a year the directors are invited aboard a Swedish boat that docks here and buttered up with a superb Swedish dinner. Thesen Ltd. deals in lumber and construction equipment, including iron-building products. As an architect I probably have quite a lot to learn. When they heard I was an architect they offered to put me in an architecture office, but I declined. That was not why I came here. The office is about as big as a closet, and their layout is, at least at a cursory glance, miserable. But then they are only interested in selling wood and not in building houses.

A thousand regards from
Raoul

ISTANBUL
JULY 21, 1935

My dear boy,

I have just received your airmail letter of July 8th in which you describe your trip and your first impressions of Cape Town. It amused me, and I am happy that everything went well and that you sent the letter by air. I have never been in Cape Town myself, but have heard quite a bit about the place, partly from consuls and partly from naval officers. When Marcus and I were taking the entrance examination to the Naval Academy in September, 1870, we had an officer who was quite well known at the time, Captain Georg Trolle, as our teacher to help improve our rather poor English. Trolle was a friend of our parents. Later, in 1881, he was in Cape Town on board the corvette *Gefle* and brought us back a couple of assegais (spears) as a present. He insisted they had been the very ones used by the natives during the hidden attack and assassination of Napoleon, son of the emperor, number III, that is. . . .

I have been thinking about writing a résumé of my impressions of you after your return from America. You might find it useful to have a recapitulation from time to time now that you are beginning to find your direction in life. One never has time for things like that in Stockholm, as there is too much going on.

As you probably noticed, I was a little bit worried about your visit to Stockholm, which explains a certain resistance on my part to the idea of your staying at home too long. I was afraid of Stockholm and all its idle amusements. Fortunately, I was mistaken, which is why you never heard anything from me about cutting short your stay. It was a high point for me when one of my friends told me that after a week at home you were running around town looking for a "job." Job meant a variety of things, and was indicative of energy and the desire to be active. I finally urged you to leave because I didn't want you to get too stuck in some artistic architectural activity. I want you to be better trained in the art of business techniques (a good word), so that you would have an opportunity to learn how to earn money — crass, I know — but you will never achieve a satisfactory kind of self-sufficiency unless you become financially independent. The program in Cape Town, as well as in Haifa, is designed to teach you that art, which dominates developing countries. I don't mean that you now should start amassing money, only that your attention be directed toward availing yourself of all opportunities. It is consistent with what I often urged you to do during your travels, namely get to know people's frame of mind and way of thinking. When I was young, the military was regarded as the best career, but I understand now that regimentation is no substitute for individual thinking. In developing societies alertness and observation are sharpened to the maximum.

It was a joy for all of us to have you in Stockholm. You handled yourself well and it was useful to you. You became known, which is invaluable to a young person, and this was not only because you had been in America, California, Canada, or Mexico, but because of your own innate qualities. I do presume to believe, however, that your being accustomed to dealing with people of varying caliber contributed to the ease with which you were able to enter into discussions, even with men of importance. You must not draw the conclusion that the important men of Riddarholmen would be easy prey. You were at a slight advantage in a field in which they were a little out of their depth, except for Professor Östberg and Carl Laurin — architecture, and they happily yielded to your lively conversation. If you think about it you will realize that this advantage was due largely to your having learned to deal with people. I tell you this not to flatter you, but to spur you on to even greater efforts at cultivating your natural talents.

To sum up: I was very satisfied with your stay in Stockholm. You have given your parents and me great pleasure.

I have no recommendations to make about your work at Thesen's. You will do that better yourself. But I want you to start *a course in bookkeeping* immediately. While it's true you won't need to rely on this skill if you want to be a boss rather than a bookkeeper, you should know it to keep a check on the work of your subordinates. It would be better to find local friends instead of Swedes. Swedes often fail to do this.

My next task is to make arrangements for Haifa and to make absolutely sure Freund won't fail us. There's no hurry, but I'd like you to inform me soon of what routes there are — straight through or with stops — along the east coast of Africa from Cape Town up to Suez. This is not to say that I'm eager for you to leave the Cape, only that I'm so anxious to see you under Freund's tutelage that my thoughts often revolve around the moment when that may be realized.

I was pleased with my ten days in Nice after the witches' sabbath in Stockholm. . . .

Stay well and accept my fondest regards,
[GOW]

ISTANBUL
AUGUST 2, 1935

My dear boy,

In my letter to you of July 21 regarding the Cape-Suez trip, I wrote that you should advise me in good time of what shipping lines exist. I have found out from a travel bureau here that there is a German boat leaving once a month. . . .

I will enjoy hearing your impressions of your co-workers at the office and the other people with whom you come into contact. Let me know how many there are, how long the company has existed, and if they're planning to expand their market. I would imagine that in an area like the Cape there is constant talk of new directions. Talk from the mouths of adventurers has no value, but the comments of experienced men are worth taking seriously. I would also imagine that the ways of the native element and those of the British diverge, as has happened in India. Forty years ago, when the British were implementing a far more demonstratively imperialist policy than today, 25,000 young men from the leading English families were employed in India. This was regarded as quite natural, and I used to say that the British could handle India so long as they maintained such a large contingent of their nation's finest there. But if the time comes when for whatever reason this will no longer be possible, things will change. Just like in Rome, the leaders will prefer to stay at home. And then you will see the final act of the great drama of world imperialism.

I'm having a pleasant time with the new Swedish minister Winther and his wife; much better than under his predecessor. This gives me much pleasure and satisfaction.

I have asked Miss Wernberger to send you another letter of credit in the amount of £200. Eventually you will have to tell me if you need more.

Your devoted
[GOW]

[Wilhelm Winther *became the Swedish minister to Turkey after GOW's retirement.*]

CAPE TOWN
AUGUST 8, 1935

Dear Grandfather,

Received your letter of July 21 and thank you very much. I'm glad you're having a pleasant time and that you've had time to recover from the unpleasantness in Stockholm.

I myself am thriving, maybe even too well. I haven't been going to Thesen's as regularly as before these past few days, since from the point of view of acquiring useful skills the company is only of limited use to me. The office is rather large, and all I am given are routine tasks from which I'm not able to draw any specific conclusions. In the architecture office I feel overqualified and at the same time not of any use, since the task of the office is to do pedestrian and standard drawings that require no thought and are designed to promote the sale of wood products. It has been worthwhile from a technical point of view to be in the office and to learn how simple it can be to build a house. I have also learned something about building material, construction plans, etc.

What has been the most fun recently has been accompanying the salesmen on their rounds of the city and the surroundings. It's interesting to see how they treat their customers. All in all, however, I have to say that I haven't learned very much at Arderne, Scott, Thesen.

You will therefore be pleased to learn that I've found a new position, and I guarantee it will be more instructive. It's with a Swedish company, the Swedish African Co., Dir. Carl Frykberg. He sells paper, wood products, imitation leather, and lots of other things. Björn Burchardt, my traveling companion from the *Hammaren*, works there. He sells paper, keeping one-third of the commission and giving Frykberg two-thirds. After he'd spoken to Frykberg and I'd spoken to both Fevrell and Hegardt, I decided to join Frykberg. This is exactly the kind of office you wished for me. In addition to Frykberg, Burchardt, and myself, the staff consists of a secretary, and that's it. He's very friendly and eager to help. I have much closer contact with Frykberg than I did with the gentlemen at Thesen's. Even though I hadn't been to see him and he only knew of my existence through Burchardt, he was kind enough to inquire a couple of days ago through Burchardt whether I'd like to go up to Table Mountain on Sunday, yesterday. Table Mountain is fairly high, about 3,500 feet, and steep. The trip took seven hours, and today I'm stiff all over and my feet hurt terribly.

My first task at Frykberg's will be rather interesting. It involves an invention that makes movie film last longer, so that you don't have to make so many copies. It is Swedish, and the idea is either to sell it to a large movie company here, or else to establish our own laboratory, probably the latter. It should be a fun job, but I have no idea how things work. What's most fun is being allowed to do things more or less on my own. In addition, I also get to handle lumber sales (i.e., if I manage to find a buyer). The whole setup really is much better than at Arderne, Scott, Thesen.

I was out at Arderne, Scott, Thesen all morning designing the interior of a café in Worcester, which is about 85 miles from here. Tomorrow I'll go there again, and that will probably be my last day there. I'm sure that there are many fine men among the salesmen (my superiors I have only met to bow to every morning). One of the salesmen, Mr. Evans, who sells waterproofing material, is Australian and has spent two years in America, three and a half in the war, partly at Gallipoli and partly on the western front and in the air force. He was wounded, gassed, and spent most of the time in the hospital. I am told he is a clever salesman, completely dominating his special market here in Cape Town, and makes more money than three of the eight directors of AST. But like all salesmen he talks a great deal about himself and uses a specialized "supersalesman" jargon.

I can't stay at the hotel I told you I was moving to. Hopemilt is its name. It is crawling with cockroaches (which are not too bad once you get used to them, and which devour each other when you kill them). In addition, the food is bad and the water supply sporadic. I've been pestering them for two weeks about putting a lamp in my bedroom, with no result as yet. Burchardt and I now intend to join forces and get a little apartment and find a maid to order about who will do things the way they should be done and not the way the traditions passed down from Vasco da Gama prescribe. You cannot accuse this country of being comfortable and pleasant. Possibly it is for those with money, but not otherwise. It is beautiful and the climate is fine now, but as I said, conveniences are conspicuously lacking.

We have been out hunting for an apartment every Saturday afternoon of late, and we've started to think we can find one as cheap as a boardinghouse.

I spent lots of time with the Fevrells during their last few days here. Aunt Ebba is really very funny and rather like mother in the way she talks. I think she's taken the family's treatment of Madeleine very hard, and he has too. Otherwise he speaks of you with greatest admiration and seems very optimistic that your ideas will eventually prevail at home. I'm beginning to realize firsthand the usefulness of a bank such as the one you recommended.

The other day, Aunt Ebba and I went to see Mrs. Evans, the admiral's wife, whom Aunt Alice had asked me to look up. She was Norwegian and fat and seemingly rather boring, although in her official capacity friendly enough. I didn't know it at the time, but her husband the admiral is the much admired and, a few years ago, quite famous leader of a punitive expedition dispatched against one of the Negro tribes here. A white man living in the wilderness had raped a Negro girl and been sentenced to be whipped by the chief of the tribe. This constituted a threat to the authority of the white man here, but since the chief was morally in the right the situation was extremely delicate. Evans handled his expedition so well that all the parties were happy and satisfied. He's supposed to be only 49 years old and "self-made."

The social life here is hardly what you would call booming and for my part has been limited to movies and drinking beer or whisky in one of the innumerable old-fashioned bars around the city.

I hope you're happy in Constantinople and that Fina's food is as delicious as always.

A thousand greetings from your
Raoul

[Aunt Ebba *was married to Thomas Fevrell, one of Gustaf Wallenberg's colleagues from his days in Japan who had become the Swedish consul in Pretoria.* Madeleine *was the Fevrells' daughter.*]

Dearest Grandfather,

I'm having an excellent time at Carl Frykberg's "Swedish African Company." Arderne, Scott, Thesen really wasn't the best place. I was lower than a supernumerary stamp-licker there. At Frykberg's, however, I work independently and yet am still in direct contact with him. I find this ideal. He mainly sells lumber, but almost every week he gets offers to represent new companies. He declines them, for he doesn't find it worth wasting his time on them. Instead he gives them to me. I'm currently in the process of trying to introduce a Swedish method for improving film, but it probably won't work. I'm also selling sports equipment, luggage, tents, etc., from the Claeson Brothers Company of Gothenburg, and chemicals for Elof Hansson in Gothenburg. In two weeks I'll start with wood products for an American firm. This way I learn both office work and how to do business, because I have to take care of the correspondence. I'm learning how to buy and how to sell merchandise. The entire office consists only of Carl Frykberg and young Björn Burchardt, of whom I am really quite fond, and who represents Forsså Bruk, AB Kraftbox, and Strömsnäs Bruk. He's now expanding his contacts and is very enterprising. Then there is only the secretary and me and a black "boy." Burchardt and I are thus sort of second-in-command.

We intend to move into an apartment that we've rented. We even have a Swedish maid. In the long run it will be only insignificantly more expensive than the boardinghouse, and we won't have to fight the cockroaches and the filth. The place where I'm currently living is horrible, even though I selected it carefully.

Burchardt and I are co-workers, and he has a quite a lot to teach me. He's very much at home with everything involving wood and paper. His father owns Forsså Bruk and Kraftbox. He's very modest, natural, intelligent, and "forward-looking." The boy, that is, not the father. He worked for Strömsnäs for three years before coming here. I'm very happy to have made his acquaintance; he is actually the first young Swedish businessman I've gotten to know. And I think it's good to know someone your own age, someone you really believe in and who is your friend.

I know that you object to my hanging around with Swedes, and I will remedy this bit by bit.

Our apartment has two rooms and a beautiful location, and since we no longer have that many extra expenses we're able to save money. We found it by luck. A family wanted to go away for six months and was renting the apartment cheap and fully furnished.

After a lot of persistent badgering, I have managed to get keys to the office (in this country, it's often hard to get anything, including duplicate keys). I don't have time for all my work during the day. There are so many things to be done: running around seeing customers, writing suppliers in Sweden, writing the consulate, writing potential clients in the countryside, visiting the library to learn about some new merchandise, etc.

In spite of my two — as I myself think — eloquent letters to the military authorities, there doesn't seem to be anything to be done about their original refusal of my request for deferral. There appears to be some sort of legal obstacle to granting a postponement for longer than three years. I have therefore appealed, whatever good it may do.

My social life has been entirely limited to the movies, but on the other hand I've gone quite often. I seem to have inherited Grandmother's phenomenal ability to laugh long and heartily at the silliest things.

I have had a letter from Woodard, the young man in America whom I've told you about in my letters. He may be coming here this winter, and it would be good to see him. I went to the American consulate to inquire about a job for him.

We have had a lot of rain recently: sometimes it begins to feel like a real Swedish fall, but as soon as the sun comes out again it turns incredibly hot.

Your last letter made me so happy. It was so kind and I wish you were here.

I've been rather upset the last few months, including when I was in Stockholm. A girl whom I used to spend all my time with in the United States and whom I liked very much unfortunately fell in love with me, and I've had a very difficult time of it, when everything I wrote or did only hurt her. I have found it depressing to be the cause of so much pain. About two weeks ago, I decided to tell her that we should stop writing, but it was difficult. I think it was for the best.

I attend night school two to three evenings a week for about two hours at a time, and in six months or so I will have mastered bookkeeping, typing, and business terminology.

I have not hurled myself into society life, and in fact it is so tiresome that I may skip it, even though it was supposed to have been part of my program. The city is so long and narrow that it's hard to get to people's homes without the most strenuous of efforts.

I'm hoping to sell 200 pounds of chemicals in a couple of weeks. Then I'm hoping for more.

A thousand greetings and once again thank you for the lovely letter you wrote for my birthday.

Raoul

ISTANBUL
SEPTEMBER 23, 1935

My dear boy,

What you told me in your letter of August 26 about a love affair in the States has caused me great anxiety. You must let me have the full details of how this has developed or I will not be able to advise you. It is imperative in a matter in which you yourself have no experience. It would be fortunate were this simply a question of an honorable relationship. Then, as you yourself say in your letter, you could write her after you had had time to think the matter over and tell her that everything was finished between the two of you. If, on the other hand, you have seduced the girl, then things are very serious. I am very worried about this, and you must hasten to enlighten me. If you seduce an American girl you are trapped. Then all the castles in the air I have constructed on your behalf will tumble. If this is indeed the case, your future is very bleak, for it will necessarily call for a complete change of plans. You will be forced to make a career in America. That, too, may work out, of course. But what a tremendous difference to what your prospects might have been at home in Sweden, where they might have flourished in a climate in which you belong, as you do, to a respected family with a name that predisposes people to receive you well, since those who carry it have universally been recognized as a benefit to society. Sweden is too small for you to live with a wife who has been tarnished by an illegitimate liaison. I fully realize how easily the sexual urges of a young man can lead to a liaison with a young girl, but he must not let them put his future at risk. I therefore do not blame you for being led to this, but I am terrified — should it turn out that you have seduced the girl and that she is pregnant — of the possible consequences for you.

Circumstances like these are in no way uncommon, however I cannot help but view your case very pessimistically. You must therefore enlighten me right away so that we might find a way out. If it should turn out that my fears are unfounded, you must break off all correspondence forthwith. If she writes, leave her letters unanswered. It may seem cruel and heartless, but believe me it is an absolute necessity.

At the age of 72, I have been able to gain some insight into the way people think. Today, Great Love belongs in the realm of fiction. It too has been mass-produced. Young women use any and all means at their disposal to get their claws into whatever young man suits their designs. They want to be taken care of. They want to have an opportunity to dress, dazzle with their looks, and acquire social standing. The male is always driven by sexual urges, girls much less so. All her energy, obviously with many exceptions, is directed toward tempting and attracting him once she has realized the advantages to her, and he will give in to temptation if he does not watch out. The danger is greatest from that class of girls who come from humble circumstances. It is far smaller with girls from our own class. Nonetheless, they all use the same weapons — the attractiveness that is part of youth, beautiful curves revealed more and more for the purpose of enticing, and where nature is lacking, cosmetics, which have developed into a colossal industry.

All this is nothing but a beautiful surface. But what of the substance, the race and genes that determine the offspring, the character and quality of mind that a good life together requires? The latter you will discover soon enough; the consequences of the deficiencies in the former when the children start to grow. Human beings pay great attention to the pedigree of their chickens and pigs, but they unthinkingly accept almost any risk to their own. Many turn out to be a credit to themselves — good mothers, full of character and self-sacrificing. They bring happiness and satisfaction. But just study all those poisonous old ladies once their youthful charm has fled and their horribly misshapen figures no longer can be covered by artificial means, who, dissatisfied with themselves and everything else, no longer make an attempt to hide the hyena within. They become the tormentors of those closest to them. Strange how much hyena there is in women.

A young man with your prospects does not have time to tie himself down until he has had time to organize his life and his work. A young wife wants everything to revolve around her. She wants to be entertained and amused. She wants to travel. If she has any spirit, she wants to stand out among her women friends. She always wants to run before she can walk. He usually makes the mistake of telling her that he is more important than he really is. She magnifies his status to boost her reputation in the eyes of her friends. The tendency toward competition inherent in our time (mostly at the expense of others) means that the peace necessary to life together will be lacking. A young man absorbed by his sexual urges pays no attention to any such considerations. He wants her body. He wants the pleasure of the moment, and she does nothing but offer it. Those who are not from his own class are the most skillful and therefore the most dangerous. They have nothing to lose. I am generalizing. In your case, I assume that the fault is yours. You have not been careful and prudent enough, and that is what makes the matter so tragic. But you must not give up your life. You must not deprive your mother and me of our expectations of you. You must not pay attention to this foolish love. Romantic love is part of the decadent nature of our culture. The orientals view it completely differently. Their ideas are geared to maintaining the lineage. By creating fashion plates with power, Westerners have hastened their own decline.

I am touching on things that you do not share, but I cannot help myself, for I am so upset and sad at having perhaps lost that which I had made the object of my dreams. Nothing can make me happy except the news that you have managed to extricate yourself completely from this unpleasant affair.

Your devoted
[GOW]

Tesiz telgrafname:
Wallenberg Swedish Legation
Istanbul

168 Cape Town 16 11/10

Please dont worry/no complications/affection her part only/
correspondence finished = Raoul +

Cape Town
October 14, 1935

[Written in English]

Dearest Grandfather,

I have received your letter of September 23 and avail myself of
today's airmail to answer it. As it appeared from it that you were
very worried, I permitted myself to wire you an immediate answer to allay your fears. I do not quite understand what in my
letter of the 26th August could have given rise to your anxiety in
regard to the American girl. However, I do not at the moment
have a copy of it before me.

I never was in love with the girl and have told her so often. On the
other hand I liked her very much and we were together, too much
perhaps, during the greatest part of my stay in Ann Arbor. I did
not know that she was in love with me and it did not become apparent until she had been writing me for some time while I was in
Sweden. I answered in a manner calculated to tell her in a friendly
and mild manner that although I respected and admired her, I did
not love her. She evidently did not or did not want to understand
the nature of my feelings for her and her letters became more and
more expressive of her love for me. I suspect, though, that the fact
that I was absent and she alone accounted for the greater part of
her fervent pleas. On my birthday I received a cable asking me if I
loved her. I immediately wired back a negative answer, and the
day after I wrote a friendly letter telling her goodbye and wishing
her the best of luck. I should have received an answer to that letter
three weeks ago, but as I have heard nothing from her I presume
that she has preferred to break off the correspondence.

As you can readily understand, the matter has been rather harassing for me because I liked her so much and hated to know that I was the cause of her unhappiness. Unfortunately, too, she was older than I and therefore it will be rather more difficult for her to recuperate. It also upset me to know that there was nothing that I could do.

Although I have caused you worry by not expressing myself clearly in regard to this matter, I am glad that I did so, because the resulting letter which you have written serves as a new proof of your love and care for me. I am so glad that you spoke so clearly and that you immediately offered your help and your advice even in the case of the girl being pregnant. I suppose you had drawn such a conclusion from the worried styling of my first letter. However, that is not at all the case. My worry was entirely due to anxiety in regard to the girl and her unhappiness. I only hope that time will cure her wounds.

In the "Byggmästaren" for the 21st August there appeared the following article headed "Riddarholmsbadet" [The Riddarholm pool].

[Continued in Swedish]

Of the approximately eleven different proposals for a swimming pool centrally located in Stockholm, a topic officially debated since 1922, not a single one involved the Riddarholm Island. [. . .] We are, therefore, all the more pleased to note that the initiative of a proposal to locate Stockholm's main swimming pool on the Riddarholm Island has originated with the head of the Djurgård Commission.

[. . .] In a little brochure containing a preface by Lieutenant Colonel Petterson, architect Raoul Wallenberg has now proposed seven preliminary alternatives to constructing the pool on Riddarholm Island. The idea of locating the pool on this site is worthy of careful consideration. The island possesses all the requisite qualifications for offering a happy solution. It is completely centrally located and without traffic routes that would in any way interfere with construction. The location is airy, with water on three sides and one of the most beautiful views of Stockholm.

[. . .]

If the pool is constructed on land, that is, which is the intent of all seven alternatives. But this is absolutely not the best location.

Whether or not the water of the Mälaren will one day be cleaned up and suitable for swimming, an open-air pool on Riddarholm Island would never have to be provisional. The site is too valuable for that. This is therefore no reason to propose a floating pool. But there are other reasons that make us wish for an investigation of the possibilities for completely separating the pool from the shore.

[. . .]

Whether the pool is located on land or in the water, the investigation now completed has demonstrated the great potential of this site and its superiority to functions debated earlier. Rescinding the City Council's decision in favor of the Ström pool and negotiating with the crown about the Riddarholm Island Pool — without tying it into other underlying objectives — are to be wished devoutly.

I'm very happy with the journal's position. The fact that they are critical of the details doesn't mean that their support on the Riddarholm front isn't welcome. As far as their purely architectural view that the pool shouldn't be located on land, I don't agree at all, but think it vandalizing, impractical, and ugly. However, I intend to write them a letter thanking them for their opinion and asking their advice, which I hope will flatter them. The "Byggmästaren" is a Bauhaus-oriented journal and rather extreme in its views.

The Swedish trade delegation has been here and I've met with all the members twice. They will only be staying for two days and are out eating most of the time. Since they're paying their own expenses you can't expect them to stay very long. Dr. Dalén will be staying here at the Cape for as long as seven weeks, while the others are going on to Johannesburg and then to Australia. He has promised to come and see us and eat clabber [cottage cheese], which he likes a lot.

A thousand heartfelt regards from your devoted and grateful

Raoul

[Dr. Dalén refers to the inventor and Nobel laureate Nils Gustaf Dalén, who was then director of AGA.]

ISTANBUL
OCTOBER 20, 1935

My dear boy,

I was so pleased to receive your telegram reading "Dont worry — no complications — affection her part only — correspondence finished." I have considered the message from every conceivable angle to see if there was anything hidden or omitted, but I have come up with nothing. I found it clear and straightforward and was reassured. Thank you for sending the wire! A letter with further information is probably on its way — if such is necessary. The post office here is no longer accepting airmail for the Cape. It is after October 1, so correspondence will be slower.

Your descriptions of your life and your work interested me. Acting as an agent is a good idea, because it will give you insight into how customers should be treated. I also enjoyed your description of Frykberg and Burchardt. They seem solid. But if either of them suggests that you make some financial commitment, you must decline. We must hold fast to our program, which is that your stay in Cape Town is for training purposes only. If you commit any money you will get sidetracked. It would lead to your being obligated to recoup what you have invested. To offer you a chance to earn something on an occasional item is all right. But you must not under any conditions listen to proposals to make a considerable sum of money. It is too early. You don't yet have enough judgment and experience, and it would also interfere with our plan.

My greatest wish now is that you should be installed in Haifa. There I see possibilities for you — under Freund's guidance and after a little time has passed — to profit from your architectural skills by assisting an occasional bank customer. It will help the bank and will bring you income. And there is a kind of security in only associating with that sort of people (the bank's clients) whose reliability may be vouched for by a man as experienced as Freund. . . .

I have also had a letter from Freund, in which he says explicitly that you are welcome as a volunteer. I have been the one using the term "volunteer" in my correspondence with him, partly because it wouldn't be reasonable for me to ask for paid employment without giving him the opportunity to form an opinion of you, and partly because I want to make absolutely certain that I don't run the risk of being turned down. . . . It is therefore absolutely decided that you will be received by Freund in his bank, Hollantsche Bank Uni, as a volunteer. Nothing has been said about when your employment would start. Tell me when you think it would be good.

I suggested in an earlier letter that the best thing would probably be to take a ship along the east coast of Africa, from the Cape to Port Said. If I were in your shoes I would do just that, as you would then be able to see all the places on the east African coast. But when I suggested this war had not yet broken out. Perhaps that should give one pause. It has not in my case, and I will present my reasons. Because of the zealousness of the journalists and the newspapers' greed for sensation, people here at home think that we are facing a new world war. My opinion is there is no danger of that happening, at least not for several years yet. The disturbances in question, the Abyssinian conflict and French nervousness, cannot lead to an international conflagration. The former is so far removed from the center of the political treadmill that it hardly affects the general situation. The newspapers have given the general public a skewed picture of the situation: nobody wants war, of which everybody has already had more than their share. Everybody is afraid of it. The result will probably be the same as it was in China in the nineties: England and Italy will divide the spoils while solemnly maintaining that they will respect the sovereignty of Negus [Haile Selassie] and his country's [Ethiopia's] integrity. . . .

I am well and leading the kind of empty life that is always the fate of old people. Write me soon and tell me whether you've been successful in your agenting. Also, tell me about the visit to the Cape by Fevrell and the delegation. I am quite interested and curious to know what they are up to.

Your devoted
[GOW]

[Ethiopia was attacked by Italy in October of 1935. Haile Selassie *(1892–1975) was emperor of the country between 1930 and 1936, and between 1941 and 1974.]*

CAPE TOWN
NOVEMBER 15, 1935

[Written in English]

Dear Grandfather,

I'm writing to tell you that this afternoon Mr. Frykberg, Björn Burchardt, and I will be leaving for Johannesburg and other parts of the Union.

We'll be away on this business trip for five weeks or longer. I will look Fevrells up in Pretoria, though I fear there will not be much time for me to meet them, as we will be very busy.

They called us up from Doctor Dalén today and invited us for dinner next week, but unfortunately we couldn't accept as we will not be here.

The heat is arriving and normally the temperature ranges between 25 and 32 degrees [77° and 90° F]. The weather is always beautiful and it's hard to imagine that Christmas is just around the corner. We swim daily in the pool outside our window.

Business is all right, that is, I'm not selling a great deal, but at least I'm learning how. It will be interesting to see how things go in Johannesburg from that point of view. I'm told there is a considerable boom going on up there. On the other hand life is even more expensive there than here. My friend Göte Spets, who at the moment is down in the Antarctic catching whales, worked up there for some time and he tells me that people are fairly rolling in gold in Jo'burg. That, of course, will drive prices up.

I look very comic at the moment because I've had my hair cut. The hair was falling out, not visibly, but getting thinner every day, and my doctor told me cutting it off entirely would be a good remedy. I hope it works and think it already has done some good.

Merry Christmas and a Happy New Year,
Raoul

[P.S.] Your last letter — which gave the reasons why one should not expect a general war — was most interesting and very welcome too, as I saw that my cable with respect to the American girl put your mind at rest.

JOHANNESBURG
NOVEMBER 29, 1935

[Written in English]

Dear Grandfather,

I've been in Johannesburg for about two weeks with Frykberg and Burchardt. We have been given an awful lot to do and been working from about seven o'clock in the morning till late at night almost every night. I especially have been busy because I have so many different things to take care of. Lately I've been concentrating on sanitary goods and sports goods, including suitcases.

We've been pretty successful here, as Johannesburg is the world's boomtown of the moment. Everywhere houses are going up or being torn down. It looks more like America than any place I've seen.

Lately I've been thinking seriously about what to do with the months between the beginning of next year and September, when I have to show up for my military service. There is of course always the possibility of making that nice trip you suggested along the east coast of Africa, going to Palestine, staying there a few months, and then heading home to Sweden. However, I've been wondering whether it wouldn't be a great deal more useful for me to stay under the excellent instruction I am now getting until such time as I'm needed for my military service. That way I would not go to Palestine until October, but I wouldn't miss much, as the three months or so available before leaving could not be of great use. On the other hand, if I stay here I can get six solid months of valuable experience, and that ought to put me in a position to learn and understand better than before what goes on in that bank.

This argument sounds right but I wanted to find a better authority than myself. I went to Fevrell, and he strongly recommended I stay here in Johannesburg until the military training begins and then go to Palestine.

Frykberg has asked me to sell boxes and greaseproof paper for him if I stay here, so I will learn yet another branch of our exports. For Florén I am doing a great deal of preparatory work involving water closets, wash basins, etc.

Tomorrow we are continuing down to Durban and then on to Cape Town. Around New Year I will be coming back up here, when the buying season for some of my articles starts.

Should you definitely wish it, though I strongly recommend against it, I shall of course leave for Palestine right away, that is in March, when my lease is up.

Merry Christmas, dear Grandfather, and my best regards,
Raoul Wallenberg

ISTANBUL
DECEMBER 22, 1935

My dear boy,

I have received your letters of November 15 and 29 and thank you for them. I am glad that you are active and interested in your work. . . .

I want to discuss the issue you touched on concerning the timing of your departure from the Cape. As you have noticed, I have hinted at my wish that you come under Freund's guidance as soon as possible. The reason is that I consider that part of your training of primary importance. The work in Cape Town is secondary. Another reason is that I want to accelerate your education, for I am getting old and I would so very much like you to come to the end of your education.

I do not in any way mean to criticize the usefulness of your work at the Cape. I also understand Fevrell's good intentions when he eagerly supports your staying on. But whether you devote nine or fifteen months to your present occupation makes no difference. I do not know how long your military service will last, but I assume from the wording of your letter that it is more than just a refresher course of a month or so. If you arrive in Haifa in March, there will be enough time for you to get settled before you would have to go to Sweden. That you are somewhat hesitant is only natural, I think. You are unwilling to interrupt your work in the Cape so soon, having just got into it. I see that as nothing more than proof of your energy and sense of duty. I found the same thing in Stockholm when, after having started to work on the Ström pool, you clearly had a difficult time tearing yourself away. You found it hard, as you do now, to abandon a job that interests you. I see both cases only as providing training in details, though I appreciate your sense of duty. That was my motivation in Stockholm and it is my motivation now. The stay in Stockholm was good in that it established you. Now you have had an opportunity to work in the field and it is time to change to staff work. Its purpose is to give you an idea of the philosophy at work in a number of areas of intelligent business management.

There is a German boat leaving for Port Said around March 20, one on April 23, and one on May 26. If you take the first, you will be in Haifa in April and have time to get sufficiently settled, so that it will not matter if you are gone for a month and a half. I am absolutely certain that you will be at least as interested in your work there as you are in your work at the Cape. The work will be of a different nature, and intelligence and alertness will be decisive. It will give you insight that your contemporaries in Sweden will never master. I also hold forth the prospect of my coming to Sweden in September — if I am still alive — while you are doing your military service, to avail myself of the opportunity to do some planning for your future by having you meet, in my company, people in leading positions who might be able to use you. I will look for them primarily outside the Wallenberg group, which is not to say that I am averse to your being employed by them, but the point is to widen whatever possibilities there might be. I want to eliminate any thought of acceptance based on your "being part of the family," and I know that young men with your qualifications are not very easy to find there. My articles have earned me considerable notoriety, and I have had occasion to talk to several persons about issues I have raised. It will involve top people within banking and industry: and should I be so fortunate that a committee on trade and shipping gets formed, I will once again take my place among the ranks of the famous at home, for I will be the guiding spirit in a plan of action that becomes more and more necessary with every passing day.

I am sure you understand that I would not want to miss such an opportunity of being useful to you. Of course we are not there yet, but prospects look good. It would be most desirable to reveal the entire idea behind your education. In no way is it my intention to wangle a position for you, only to plant the thought, among those we meet, that it might be advantageous to snare a young man with such considerable experience. For all these reasons it would be best to get you started in Haifa. It would therefore be desirable if you came home for a while in September.

Give some thought to this and decide for yourself what you think best. I am sending a copy of this letter to your mother so that she may have an opportunity to think it over and then tell you what she thinks.

I am going to Nice on December 26 and will be staying at the Hotel d'Angleterre as usual.

Your devoted
[GOW]

CAPE TOWN
JANUARY 9, 1936

Dearest Grandfather,

I've just received your letter of December 22 and hasten to answer.

As things stand now, given your urging I go to Palestine as soon as possible, I will probably be leaving on March 20. I don't have to make up my mind right away, but, I repeat, that is when I will probably leave.

I had intended to go to Johannesburg in the New Year, but it turned out that one of the items I was supposed to sell there, and which probably would have been the most lucrative, financially speaking, i.e., Olofström's stainless steel implements, will be sold by another agent, rather than through my boss, Mr. Florén. This made going there less appealing, and when it also turned out to be difficult to find someone suitable to take my place in our little apartment on short notice I decided to postpone my trip.

Since I'm not going to Johannesburg in the New Year, one of the main reasons for my going there at all disappears, namely that if I went there right away I would have a couple of uninterrupted months to develop some business that later might pay off. If I went on March 1, for example, I would hardly have enough time to do anything before it was time to leave. Björn Burchardt did promise me that if I went in March he would let me handle cardboard sales there, and that would be highly advantageous. Not that I could make any money whatsoever from it, but it would have been very good for me to get acquainted with such an important basic as cardboard. This is why I'm still tempted to go to Johannesburg.

This brings me to another matter and that is my stay in Sweden during my month of military service. I have already discussed the matter with Björn Burchardt and he has promised to help. I would like to get to know something about our leading export industries while I'm in Sweden, preferably not just in a theoretical way but also from seeing them from the inside, so to speak. Through Burchardt, I would be able to see two of Sweden's most modern factories, i.e., Strömsnäs and Forsså. I'm probably going to take advantage of this opportunity, partly because my general understanding of Sweden is somewhat incomplete, since I only know Swedish school life and not Swedish working life, and partly because I believe I would be able to profit from what I learn out here if I knew more about production at home. Fortunately, this will not delay me for long. A month should be about right to visit each factory for a few days, and to follow an order from the moment the airmail letter from overseas comes in to when the roll of paper or piece of machinery is loaded onto the railroad car to be carted off.

I have a bit of a cold right now and don't feel very well, so I leave further writing until the next mail.

A thousand regards,
Raoul

CAPE TOWN
JANUARY 13, 1936

Dear Grandfather,

I am only writing to tell you that barring any unforeseen events, I have decided to leave for Port Said or Suez by the German ship *Tanganyika,* which leaves from here on February 14. I'll be taking this boat because it puts in at more ports than the English ship leaving a week later.

I may leave here even earlier to go up the coast on the Swedish boat *Kaaparen.* If I did, I would join the German ship in Durban or in Lourenço Marques in Portuguese East Africa.

I don't know what I'll do along the way. I would prefer to have maximum possible freedom so that, for example, I might stop in Egypt for a few days. Therefore I don't want you to expect me in Haifa on a certain date. When I arrive I will immediately go to the Swedish consul. It would be best if you sent my latest instructions there. I don't know the precise name of Freund's bank. The German boat should arrive in Egypt around March 21.

A thousand regards,
Raoul Wallenberg

[P.S.] The ship puts in at Port Elizabeth, East London, Durban, Lourenço Marques, Mozambique, Port Amelia, Dar-es-Salaam, Zanzibar, Tanga, Mombasa, Djibouti, Aden, Port Said, Suez. This in case you should want to reach me on the way.

CAPE TOWN
JANUARY 20, 1936

Dear Grandfather,

My plans have changed somewhat since I wrote you last. It turns out that the travel agent, in spite of his assurances to the contrary, wasn't able to get me a ticket on the German east coast boat *Tanganyika*. The next boat, which was British, was to my way of thinking fairly slow in arriving in Egypt and didn't put in at as many ports as the German. There were no other ships in the inexpensive category.

I might have taken one or gone first-class on the German boat, which naturally wasn't full, had I not realized that now that I'm all set to go and have wrapped up my work here it isn't worth continuing with the kind of small business transactions I could have engaged in during a trip up the coast.

I have therefore decided to take advantage of an excellent opportunity. The Italian ship *Duilio,* the largest boat on the South Africa route — 24,000 tons — is leaving from here for Genoa on February 7, where it connects with the *Esperia,* also Italian and equally up-to-date, arriving in Haifa on February 27. The voyage goes via Dakar, Gibraltar, Marseilles, Genoa, and Alexandria. It therefore offers quite a few things of interest, and the price is really remarkable: 32 pounds. This is considerably less than tourist class would be on the east coast, even though you waste a lot of time on the trip and the standard of comfort is low. On the Italian ship, I would have a first-class cabin all to myself, with bath, window, a sofa, and two beds. You have to eat in the tourist-class dining room, however. There is only second class after Genoa, I am told. The ship would have been quite empty because of the boycott against Italy if two hundred Jews on their way to a Zionist conference in Palestine hadn't booked passage. Knowing the average South African Jew, I'm a bit pessimistic, but the trip may turn out to be pleasant nonetheless.

My arrival date will be February 27, as far as I can determine, but I may break up the trip by staying in Genoa for a day or so. I've now been informed by the consulate here that there is no vice consulate in Haifa as yet. You had better address your letters to Poste Restante in Haifa.

I'm pleased that things have turned out this way; it puts me in Haifa almost a month earlier than my last plan. I'm sorry to miss the pleasures of the East African coast, but to my way of thinking the savings in money and time make up for it.

I feel sad leaving South Africa and take with me the very best memories. I have also gotten to know some people of whom I am very fond.

A thousand regards,
Raoul

NICE
FEBRUARY 4, 1936

My dear boy,

I must thank you for your letters of January 9 and 13 and have not answered because I did not think that a letter would reach you before your departure. Now I have had the idea of sending a copy to all the consulates, wherever we have them on the East African coast. I do not know whether it will work. I see that you have decided to take the German boat *Tanganyika* on February 14. I am sending these letters by airmail, but without much hope that one of them will reach you, since I do not expect that they have modern things like that on the East African coast.

You don't mention anything about money, so I assume you have been able to arrange everything.

If you get to Cairo you must naturally go and see the Swedish minister, Harald Bildt, who is an old friend of mine. He was my secretary in Tokyo in 1907. His father's second wife was a sister of Beatrice's, my brother Oscar's wife, née Keiller. They lived in Rome for many years, and his widow still does. Harald's mother was an American by the name of Moore. Harald will be happy to see you. He is very interested in our family.

The vice consul in Cairo is called Ekberg, a representative of SKF [Swenska Kullager Fabriken] and one of my friends. Very capable. You must absolutely look him up since he is very experienced in Oriental trade matters. And very nice besides.

The consul in Alexandria is named von Gerber, an older man, a lumber dealer who has lived there for a long time. I don't know him personally.

I wrote Freund to find out what was needed to get a permit for an extended stay in Haifa but have not yet had an answer. His bank is called *Hollantsche Bank Uni.*

Maj writes in her last letter that she has spoken to a Major Thott, who told her that the service in question is only a refresher course. It starts in early September and ends twenty-five days later in October. There is absolutely no reason why you could not get a deferment for another year. So in that respect you are completely free. It is much better because this way you can be flexible about a possible trip home and have complete freedom of action depending on how things work out in Palestine. Haifa is, to my mind, the main thing. I continue to worry that you're considering going home before your commercial training has been concluded. Our plans constitute an entity and should not be fragmented.

Ah, I forgot to tell you that Dodde is in Egypt, convalescing after a serious illness. Nunne is with him. His illness, a clot in his lungs, was very dangerous. He was within an inch of losing his life. They say it will be a year before he can go back to work. I would like you to establish a good relationship with him because he is more in tune with the times than his brother.

Both are quite well liked by the customers of the bank. But Dodde more so, I think. Jacob is more like his father Marcus, somewhat in the style of a Rothschild of the first part of the nineteenth century. Democracy has broken the power of finance in most countries, and I think you are wise to realize this. Politics looks rather messy right now. Everybody is arming themselves, and you can't tell where it might lead. Try to stay completely neutral. The prevalent attitude in Sweden is, to my way of thinking, not wise. People are angry with the Italians, but that is unimportant. If the Italians have a bone to pick with the black-amoors in Africa, that is their own business. By taking sides we have lost the Italian market completely. In countries that are far removed from ordinary world events it is much better to refrain from taking sides. The Italians were badly treated at Versailles and want to acquire more territory. I find it rather natural from their point of view, but they have proceeded unwisely and collided

with the British. That is their business, not ours. The stay in
Palestine will also be good for you from that standpoint. When
you have occasion to spend a lot of time among minorities you
arrive at the conclusion that their rights are not always well served
by the great powers. A great part of politics has always been
egoism. The best thing is, as I said, to refrain from taking sides. It
has served me well. I am sure you have had occasion to realize
this during your stay on the Cape. You have to keep eyes and ears
open to make observations, but should refrain from passing judg-
ments.

Siri and Lilly are on the Côte d'Azur, Siri at Cap-d'Ail and Lilly in
Condamine, which is close to Monte Carlo. I see them often and
this gives me pleasure. Grandmother has told me that she is
coming here. I am very happy about that, but I don't think she
wants to leave until after February 16, which is Great-
Grandmother's 93rd birthday. Annie likes her mother very much
and always tries to please her.

The king arrives here Friday, February 7, accompanied by an
old friend of mine, Admiral Ehrensvärd, Count Bonde, Lord-in-
Waiting Klercker, and Dr. Casserman. I don't know Klercker, but I
have been told that he is married to one of Boheman's sisters. I
have greatly enjoyed the company of my old friend Colonel
Schenfeldt, whom you know, and Captain Frösén, who is of my
age. We play vira twice a week, which is nice.

In the beginning of my letter I said that I would send a copy of
this letter to the consulates, but as I have learned that there are
very few of them on the African east coast and as I have found out
that your ship belongs to the German East African line, I have
decided to address it to the agencies of the company, in the hope
that at least one of them will reach you. Be careful about eating
fruit and other things in the various places. You must not take
unnecessary risks. Do write me a line from time to time.

Your devoted
[GOW]

*[Siri is Gustaf Wallenberg's sister. Her married name was Ox-
enstierna. Vira is a Swedish card game similar to bridge.]*

GENOA
FEBRUARY 24, 1936

Dear Grandfather,

I am in Genoa at the moment and it may turn out that I will have to stay here for some time. I was misinformed and therefore failed to get an evidently crucial visa for Palestine while I was in Cape Town.

I tried to get one through the British consulate general but had no success. When it comes to visitors in Palestine the restrictions are apparently much stricter than you would think, and the moment that the consulate found out that I intended to stay there for six months they pricked up their ears and refused to issue a visa. They wanted a letter and a paper from Freund's bank, and these, if I understood it correctly, must also be approved by the Palestinian government before a visa can be issued.

There is a boat leaving for Palestine this Friday, and if everything can be settled by then I will take it; otherwise I will stay on here for another week. Meanwhile it would be nice to see you. It would be easy for me to get over to Nice from here.

You can reach me here at the hotel Helvetia, Piazza Annunziata, even if I move elsewhere.

Fondest regards,
Raoul

P.S. Am I right that the name of Freund's bank is *Hollantsche Bank Uni?*

GENOA
FEBRUARY 28, 1936

Dear Grandfather,

I was lucky with my passport, and after arguing with the British consul for an hour managed to get a tourist visa without a deposition. There is no regular boat until March 7, but I'm planning to take a smaller boat belonging to the same line, and it leaves tomorrow night (Saturday) and puts in at plenty of interesting ports, among them Piraeus, so I may be able to see Athens. I'm glad that the problem has been resolved and that I will be able to leave.

It was good to see you and Grandmother. I was especially pleased to see how well you looked.

As to our latest conversation about whether to interrupt my stay in Haifa, I want to apologize again for losing my temper. I'm far too aware of my debt to you not always to yield to your decisions. But I was sorry that you sought to find ulterior motives in my objections. All I wanted to do was contribute to the planning of my program, to make it broader and more effective. That was why I proposed studying conditions at home before concluding my stay in Haifa. I have no particular objection to living abroad and no particular urge to go home at this point when I have not earned any money.

Thank you very much for your kindness toward me in Nice.

Affectionately,
Raoul

Haifa
March 12, 1936

Dear Grandfather,

I'm now settled here in Haifa and started working. The morning after my arrival I went to see Freund, who was sitting in an inner room of an office brimming over with people, mostly young people. He received me graciously but was surprised; he had not thought I would be coming for another year or so. He hadn't gotten the letter you sent him some months ago. He asked me to come back the next morning at the beginning of the workday and he would find something for me to do. After leaving him I went to see his secretary, a Dutch Jew by the name of Gerson. I had heard about him in Cape Town from our neighbors and closest friends, a newly married young Dutch woman named Fieta Pretorius, who went to school with him in Holland. She told me that she thought he was working in some bank in Palestine. It is a fairly amazing coincidence that I should land in his bank, of all places. I'm now living in his boardinghouse, Jewish of course, and rather good. He is only 21 and has an uncle in Holland to thank for his excellent position. Now he intends to start a riding school here instead, which I think a fairly peculiar career.

I haven't done anything particularly bank-related as yet, but have copied some letters, gone through documents to learn what they look like, compiled some statistics on the fluctuations of the New York stock market, etc. Freund is sort of a nervous type but evidently has me in mind, for I have something different to do all the time.

We work from 8:30 A.M. until 1 and then from 3 P.M. until 6:30. Fridays, Saturdays, and Sundays we stop working at 3 P.M. and have no lunch break. In other words, we're open seven days a week and you can choose whether you want Saturday or Sunday off. I have decided to work Sundays and take Saturdays off, since most of the others seem to do so. Everybody in the office is very friendly and pleasant to work with. They are phenomenally good at languages and I'm almost ashamed, but my German is rapidly returning, as is my French. The bank will be moving into a beautiful new Bauhaus building across the street in a few months. We are some thirty employees at this point, and a year ago there were fewer than ten. We are also supposedly in a crisis situation here because of the Abyssinian question. The largest industry in Palestine appears to be fictitious at a cursory glance, that is to say, immigration, which is resulting in an enormous construction boom actually larger — at least relatively speaking — than the one in Johannesburg. Haifa is brand new, except that there are still some Arab huts. There are three times as many Arabs as Jews in Palestine.

The region is beautiful, reminiscent of Cape Town, the same bay, same mountains — although Table Mountain is missing — and the same orientation. From where I live, the port and the center of the city look exactly the same. The harbor is filled with English cruisers defending the oil pipeline from Iraq. There are also a couple of large factories, and now an oil refinery is scheduled to be built.

The trip here was interminably delayed by a slow-loading

process and took three or four days longer than estimated. The food was horrible, and I got seasick toward the end. One thing was excellent, however, and that was the fact that we put in at Piraeus and I therefore got to see Athens. I was not disappointed in the slightest. On the contrary, it was much more beautiful than I'd expected. We also were in Alexandria for almost a whole day, but I didn't go up to Cairo. There were close to a hundred English warships, among them three battleships and one aircraft carrier. It took us more than ten minutes to pass through their ranks, and when we left again at night they were all lit up like a great Tivoli. It was a wonderful sight. In Port Said, a picturesque and quiet town except in the bad quarters, which really were bad, was yet another British battleship. As we were leaving, an Italian troop transport filled to overflowing with soldiers and workers came steaming into the mouth of the canal. Our crew and I and the 2,000 men on the troop carrier waved frenetically at each other, yelling wildly and screaming "Duce, Duce, Duce." Then we sang the nice new Italian song, "Facetta nera, bella Abessinia" ["Black jewel, fair Abyssinia"]. After that the other boat disappeared in the dark. We were followed for a while by a motorboat filled with Italian girls and rented by the Italian consul in Port Said to meet each new troop carrier as it enters the harbor. One of the girls got on a bicycle and followed the boat through the canal along the bank, still singing "Facetta nera."

The trip was also very interesting because the passengers were a mixed bunch and this gave rise to a multitude of discussions. The atmosphere was especially jolly the evening a rumor went around that the Germans had occupied the Rhineland, that the French had mobilized, and that the British navy had left Alexandria to anchor outside Kiel in protest. The news service was poor, as you can see, but that rumor really lit a fire under the Germans on board. I was sorry to find such universal gloominess as to the prospects for the future of Europe. It was mainly concentrated among the Jews, though they had their reasons, I think.

I'm here on a tourist visa, yet don't work any the less for that. I think it's a bit silly and undiplomatic, but Freund told me to do this. He said that I should not apply for an extension until some time had passed, because my application would probably be rejected if it followed too closely on my arrival.

The Jews here are afraid of the Arabs, who are beginning to

wake up and dream of an empire. Poor people, they evidently have to adjust to being in a minority wherever they go. They have boundless enthusiasm and idealism and these immediately strike you as the most common characteristics of Zionism. It is truly a gamble on their part to try to settle hundreds of thousands of Jews in this dry, stony little place surrounded by and already teeming with Arabs. They are nevertheless optimistic to a man, and were energy a guarantee for success the results would be excellent, for they seem to work practically around the clock.

My fondest regards to my dear grandparents. How is your foot?

Raoul

HAIFA
APRIL 3, 1936

Dear Grandfather,

Very slowly, I am learning about banking technique. I find it complicated and difficult to understand. For the first few days I was put in the correspondence section, but for the last week or so I have been in current accounts, and I still don't understand much of what is going on. Everybody is very nice but also very busy, and they don't have much time for explanations. I see Freund only when he comes out of his office to take care of some paper or to introduce a customer to the department manager. He apologized for taking so little care of me, but I asked him not to trouble himself in the least until I felt better able to assimilate his superior knowledge. He is very well liked by his employees even though he's somewhat nervous and throws tantrums every now and then whenever anything goes awry.

One thing that I like about my Jewish friends is that they don't criticize their bosses at all, nor usually each other. Many are from Constantinople, among them a Mr. Carasso, who knew you and evidently used to see you often. He functions as a sort of liaison with the customers here. There's also a young Dutchman by the name of Euyen, one of only two non-Jews, who lived in Constantinople for nine years and worked in the office there. Apart from them, there are people here of every possible nationality, from Russia, Romania, Germany, and Holland. They speak all kinds of languages, but now I'm beginning to feel relatively comfortable in the three main languages. I'm thinking about learning Arabic instead of Hebrew, which is what everybody recommends even though Hebrew is the most important language here, rising like a phoenix from the ashes; there are large quantities of books and newspapers being printed in Hebrew and only Hebrew is spoken in the theater.

I usually go to bed right after supper, or else go to the movies. I'm feeling incredibly tired for some reason; they say the climate affects all newcomers that way, but I find that strange, as it has been excellent so far. We have had real Swedish summer heat, maybe even too much heat. I had forgotten to get my typhus shots before coming, so I'm in the process of having that done now and it has been an unpleasant experience. Sundays, I usually take a walk up on Mount Carmel (where the Carmelite fathers originated) and admire the view. During Easter, my friend Gerson and possibly one other and I are planning a trip to Tiberias, or some place like it, to go swimming and horseback riding.

I haven't made any acquaintances outside the office worth mentioning, and I still haven't been invited to Mr. Freund's. Oh yes, I met a Swedish-speaking German gardener who has been at Svalöv (agricultural institute) and who insisted that I come for dinner tomorrow. Someone also told me that a Swedish Jewish family by the name of Melamede lived here, so I was evidently mistaken in assuming that there wouldn't be any Swedes here.

The people at my boardinghouse are mainly German Jews and very nice and funny. One day, one of them told me in passing that her brother had been murdered by the Nazis. Otherwise, people here don't talk much about the past, but almost exclusively about the future of Palestine, in which everyone believes wholeheartedly — it would be a pity if they didn't, since Palestine is their home and the realization of a longtime dream. There is a kind of self-generating boom caused by the steady stream of new immigrants bringing ever growing needs that can only be met by a continuous process of starting up and expanding enterprises. As long as people remain optimistic and believe in the future of the country, the construction will continue and there will be a lot of money floating around. But should that faith ever fail, I believe there will be a terrible crisis. Palestine's hope is to become the industrial center of the Near East, and they already have lots of industries, though they are designed primarily to satisfy the domestic market and export hasn't yet started. Because of this, their economy is rather fragile, but the Jews are firmly convinced that all will work out. They are used to suffering worse things than a financial crisis, so they don't care about the risks and, besides, they have no choice except to settle here. I never knew that so many Jews were as deeply and fanatically religious as many here are. To them, Palestine is much more than a mere refuge; it is the promised land, the land designated for them by God. It will take an enormous effort to make the country suitable for farming, for there is very little water and much too much stone. Before they arrived there were only about 800,000 Arabs, if that many, and they would like to reach a Jewish population of 4,000,000. When a foreigner asks how the country will feed that many, they reply with a beautiful fable. Palestine, they say, is like the skin of a deer. When the skin is removed from the animal, it shrinks, and you wonder how it could ever have covered the animal. It is the same with Palestine: so long as Palestine contains a Jewish population, it drips with milk and honey and can support a large population; when there are no longer any Jews, it shrinks in value, unable to support even a small Arab population and its minuscule demands.

I have no news about myself. Give Grandmother my fond regards.

Raoul

NICE
APRIL 4, 1936

My dear boy,

Thank you very much for your letter of March 12. Unfortunately, it had to remain unanswered for a week and a half. I have been bedridden since you left. I had to take to my bed as soon as I had taken care of your little banking business in the Provincial Bank. It cost me £1.5 and I have a receipt.

What a nuisance that I should have trouble with my leg. I felt something for several days, but since there was no fever I assumed that it was not phlebitis, the symptoms of which I know very well. When it did not get better I thought it best to call in a specialist on phlebitis. I found one right away who explained that the lymphatic vessels in one leg were inflamed and that I had to lie still with my leg in the air. It is terribly awkward. I also had to have a nurse come in every morning and every evening to change the compresses. It turned into phlebitis of the lower leg. Now everything is almost healed. I have to be very careful but went to the taverna once, which I enjoyed very much, and yesterday we went for a ride. Everybody has been terribly kind and inquires about my health, from the king to all our acquaintances. I find it hard to write. It is impossible in bed when you have your leg raised. I am now able to sit with my leg propped up on a chair, and therefore seize the opportunity of writing my dear boy. I wrote a letter to Freund a couple of days ago but did not send it, because I wanted to wait until I was able to write you first, so that you would have a letter when you heard that Freund had one.

I enjoyed your letter very much. It gave me a good idea of your life in Haifa, and I look forward to accounts of the contacts you will be making there. Being with talented people is always interesting. You are cut down to the right size and subconsciously try to avail yourself of their experience and views. The latter pertains to young people starting out under conditions new to them. Hearing these views stimulates discussion and the desire to formulate one's own. It is also useful for linguistic ability. Orientals are wonderfully gifted in languages. Benghiat knows nine languages. Turkish, Greek, Hebrew, Persian (he worked there for several years in his youth), Italian, Spanish, German, French, and English.

It seems about right that Freund's bank should now have thirty employees. When the Dutch bank opened in C-ple it had only around ten. Eight years later there were 120. Freund started there. . . .

I have not decided yet how long to stay here. It depends primarily on when I feel well again. However, I am tentatively considering taking a boat leaving Marseilles for Istanbul on April 27.

I will write Miss Wernberger and ask her to send you a letter of credit for £200.

Grandmother is well and sends her regards. Write soon and tell me in detail about your acquaintances. Both older and younger.

Your devoted
[GOW]

[Benghiat was an employee at the Swedish legation in Istanbul.]

HAIFA
APRIL 20, 1936

Dear Grandfather,

Thank you very much for your letter of April 4, which I have not answered because — like you — I have been in bed. I went to Tiberias and another town called Safed with some friends during the Easter holiday. That is probably where I caught a touch of a fever called Papadatschi, which is very common here. You run a very high temperature and stay in bed for a few days, then it is over. It's not dangerous.

Unfortunately, the Papadatschi was joined by something that, judging from the symptoms, I took to be my old Mexican dysentery cropping up. Instead it turned out to be an inflammation of the large intestine, although the doctor thought it might have been associated with my old Mexican malady. I was in bed for about ten days. I still haven't gone back to the office, though I feel well now. I must stick to a diet for some time and hope that it won't recur or become chronic.

I am very happy to learn that the phlebitis is better. I was a little worried when I left Nice, as I remember you said that it was nothing to trifle with.

I have nothing new to relate; I've almost forgotten the office, even though I did read a book on "Banking" and took some contract forms home to see what they looked like. Otherwise I have amused myself with a few novels from a lending library and by drawing additions to the house that my parents are building and to which they sent me the drawings made by an architect named Ahlberg. I enjoyed going through them and revising them. Unfortunately, my little changes will probably arrive too late, as the foundation has already been poured. I would really like to do those plans for Mother.

I had a good time on my trip to Tiberias. I went with a couple of friends from the bank, both from Constantinople. The first day we went by Volvo-bus from Haifa through Nazareth to Tiberias. The bus driver was an Arab who sang loudly the whole time, and most of the passengers were wild Arab types. The next morning we went swimming in the lake, which is situated a couple of hundred feet below sea level and is the one on which Jesus walked. Then we visited the Tiberias Hot Springs, famous old springs packed with old Arabs with ghastly sores. We didn't go in the water. Then we went to one of the new socialist Jewish colonies, located where the Jordan flows out of the lake. It was truly admirable. The Arabs don't like selling their unused and neglected land to the Jews, and when they do they jack the prices up as high as possible. The Jews therefore try as hard as they can to farm efficiently, to get maximum yield. The organizational form is that of a socialist collective and made up mostly of young people who work terribly hard in the worst possible climate. Hundreds of lives have been lost to malaria. They are doing well with all kinds of fruits and vegetables, but grain apparently doesn't work too well.

That same evening, we left the hot cauldron formed by the lake for the heights in the north, Osh Mina and Safad. These are old and beautiful towns with a larger proportion of Arabs and an excellent climate. We took a long walk at night between the two towns, and this was wonderful. On one occasion, thinking we were lost, we met two Arab women and asked for directions. They lashed out at us with the most horrible insults and continued to curse and yell at us until they were out of sight. We ran as fast as our legs would carry us, for we suddenly realized we had committed a grave sin by addressing veiled women, and Arabs quickly draw their knives. We had proof of this a few days later, when riots broke out in Tel Aviv and some twenty people were killed. The disturbances have now spread to exactly the same towns we went to during Easter, namely Tiberias, Nazareth, Safad, and Acre. The latter is an entirely Arab town on the bay of Haifa, which we are able to discern as a distant white spot in the sunny haze. It is one of the most picturesque places I have ever seen, with extremely narrow, mysterious streets and surrounded by huge walls. It used to be an important port city. Napoleon once laid siege to it unsuccessfully.

Now it is full summer and we have had several days of intense heat, the so-called Hamsin that blows in off the desert. Earlier, the heat had been primarily political, and trucks loaded with soldiers and machine guns still patrol the streets. No disturbance is expected here; Haifa lies outside the traditional trouble area, for one thing, and the British have an especially good opportunity to monitor the situation, since part of their fleet is in the harbor.

Freund still has not taken me in hand; he is very busy.

Thank you for the new letter of credit, which arrived a few days ago. Miss Wernberger enclosed a very funny and interesting letter. She really is a kind person.

I very much hope that the phlebitis is all gone and that you are completely recovered. If you're still in Nice, say hello to the colonel for me; he's a very nice person. I was very surprised that he recognized me, since he only saw me once five years ago.

Thank you very much for your trouble and the outlay at the Provincial Bank.

> Greetings to Grandmother and thank you for the card.
> Raoul

[The disturbances RW refers to occurred between native Palestinians and Jewish settlers. Palestine was still under British rule in 1936.]

HOTEL D'ANGLETERRE, NICE
MAY 21, 1936

My dear boy,

Thank you for such a long and interesting letter. My health is much better now and I can move about freely, but I am still being quite careful.

The newspapers are full of the trouble in Palestine. I have not paid attention to it, as I am quite familiar with the foreign correspondents' love of sensation, and it might just be that the Italian correspondents have an interest in embarrassing the English. *But do not take any unnecessary risks.* Even if I have not paid too much attention to sensationalistic news bulletins, the purpose of which sometimes is to hide the real truth — I came across many similar instances in eastern Asia and the Near East, when firebrands in those regions were giving off quite a few sparks — I nevertheless have reason to discuss the matter because of a message from Oscar Falkman that reached me today. A relative of his, Willy Falkman, a correspondent for *Dagens Nyheter,* has just returned from Palestine, and he thinks that *the situation is more dangerous* than the papers say and that they fear an explosion. Given this, I cannot help but wonder whether you should leave Palestine. First of all, we have to gauge the risk. Your boss ought to know, for banks are naturally very well informed, and a neutral bank has less reason to gloss over circumstances than those of a more political nature. If you feel there is a risk, I advise you to leave. But you have to decide for yourself and also consider to what extent staying would be useful to you.

Should you decide to leave, I think it unwise that you go home and do nothing this summer. I want to propose that you go to Istanbul, where I would greatly enjoy your company for a few months until this fall, when the plan we have discussed previously goes into action. I am sure that I could find a position for you as a volunteer at the Dutch bank here, the head of which, M. Gassner, I know well. You may even profit from being with M. Benghiat, an unusually talented and experienced man who has taken a great interest in you. Your time would not be wasted. You would have the opportunity to make a few new contacts. Think about this and let me know what you decide.

As for me, I had intended to leave for C-ple a few weeks ago, but I have postponed my departure, partly to wait until my leg is completely healed, though primarily to await some news from Mr. Wener Gren, with whom I have begun a correspondence the purpose of which is to interest him in my plan for increasing our foreign trade. I won't stay here much longer, however. In any case, Fina will be happy to receive you should you decide in favor of the C-ple plan.

Has your hair grown out again, and how is your health?

Your devoted
[GOW]

Nice
May 28, 1936

My dear boy,

Today I will write you in greater detail to discuss what you relate in your letter of April 30 about the confrontations between Arabs and Jews, and about the fact that "Freund has not yet taken you in hand," — as well as what you tell me about your touch of Papa-dataschi and its possible connection with your Mexican dysentery.

I will begin with the latter. You may recall that I gave you careful instructions on what to do while traveling in hot climates when you undertook your trip to Mexico two years ago. Malaria is a nasty illness, and very hard to cure, but you don't have to get it if you use a mosquito net. One is sometimes tempted not to, but you may be unlucky and therefore *you must never neglect this kind of protection.* In Tokyo there was not a single Japanese dwelling in which the entire family did not use a mosquito net. It was like a tent under which the whole family slept. You could see it at night when you went out and all the sliding paper windows had been left open for ventilation. It is the same thing with dysentery, which you get by not being cautious about food. There is no protection against it other than avoiding those restaurants where you have reason to suspect that the owner, for the sake of economizing, has bought unsuitable *matières premières*. You always have to be very careful about water. It must always be boiled. In a place like Palestine you must be extra cautious, because Jewish immigrants, who have lived under quite different

hygienic circumstances and don't have too much inclination toward cleanliness, by both habit and choice, are easily remiss.

I am glad to be able to tell you that you are mistaken when you
write "that Freund pays no attention to you." The day before
yesterday I received a letter from him, sent on from Istanbul,
which made me very happy. I hesitated about sending you a
copy, but I will anyway, while also warning you not to breathe a
word to anyone out there that he has said such nice things about
you. It is nothing but an acknowledged and successful banker's
statement outlining your work, your direction, which he obviously understands quite well, and your preeminent qualities as far
as practical work is concerned. You could not ask for a better and
more persuasive testimonial. It will be of the greatest value once
you are home and looking for a position. He shows his concern
about you by making plans for you to go to Beirut, to work for a
banker there. It will be extremely useful, and you must accept the
suggestion at once. I hope it is his intention that your stay in
Beirut only be temporary, and that you will then return to Haifa. I
immediately wrote a letter back, of course, thanking him for his
interest and concern. I wrote that I liked the Beirut plan very
much, but thought it best to mention that I hoped that you would
be allowed to go to Sweden this fall to complete the required
military service, adding that I would like it very much were you
allowed to resume your work with him after that. Guard well that
copy of Freund's letter (perhaps you had better make a new copy
on better paper), for I am sure that those at home seldom see such
a glowing testimonial. You should value it highly and appreciate
its future usefulness to you.

Finally, the disturbances in Palestine. I myself am not afraid,
but you must always be cautious. I have experienced many
similar occurrences in China, Japan, Siberia, and in the Balkans,
so I know that newspaper journalists' accounts are always sensa-
tionalized. That is their job; the readers want it so. One exposes
oneself to equally great dangers when one visits Paris or London,
where it is difficult to maintain order. The thing is, you must not
and should not visit places where local authority is ineffective.
Those in banks have learned that. In Haifa, which is England's
most important port on the coast, you can be sure they will
always deploy sufficient forces to cover any eventuality. It is also
obvious from Freund's letter that he is of the same opinion, as he

says that the disturbances that had been dormant for many years and recently erupted will soon be taken care of. That the Arabs are annoyed at old man Balfour's promising their country to others is hardly surprising. But I don't think that there are any religious considerations behind these disturbances.

Freund's suggestion that you go to Beirut comes at a very good time. You must immediately accept and thank him. This is the best way to avoid looking to those at home as if you are afraid and want to flee. I am also certain that instinctively you rebel against this. I do, although I do not want you to take any unnecessary risks. That must not happen. To my mind there are none, however, only if you make sure to avoid foolishness. The best solution is accepting Freund's offer of a temporary stay in Beirut. That takes care of any further discussion of "whether it is dangerous to stay in Haifa." To phrase the question thus offends me. It also appears from both English and French newspapers that the British have sent troops and that they have the situation under control. The unrest appears greatest in Jaffa and Tel Aviv, and less in Haifa.

From the length of my letter you can see that I am in good spirits again. I am catching the *Théophile Gautier* in Marseilles on June 8 and will be in Istanbul on the 15th. I will be lunching in Naples at that nice restaurant inside the Forte del Ove and will remember our pleasant time together there five years ago.

Your devoted
[GOW]

[Old man Balfour *refers to Arthur James Balfour (1848–1930), who as British foreign secretary announced to Parliament on November 2, 1917, his endorsement of the establishment of a homeland for the Jewish people in Palestine. This became known as the "Balfour Declaration."*]

HAIFA
JUNE 19, 1936

Dear Grandfather,

I am writing this in a café where I've been sitting for several hours having tea. Haifa is still fairly peaceful, and going out is not dangerous so long as you avoid the Arab quarters. There has been some bomb throwing, with meager results. They usually explode prematurely and kill the would-be assassin.

Thank you for your two letters, the ones you sent before your departure for Istanbul. I am glad to hear that you're better, and I very much hope that it will stay that way.

Reading between the lines, I see that you worry about my safety here, since you keep dwelling on the situation here in Palestine. I have made up my mind right away to leave immediately should the situation so warrant, i.e., without first asking permission. If I did, I would probably go to Beirut. Aside from that, I have no special urge to go there just to work for Zilkha Bros. because I wouldn't learn much in one month's time and I've hardly had enough time to get into my work and the situation here.

I'm sorry that you were so impressed by Freund's letter, as I myself find it a rather devious piece of writing. The fact is, he hardly knows me, has met with me for a total of 4 hours or so, and has not inquired about me or my busywork from my colleagues at the office. I'm generally not too pleased with what I have learned in Haifa. No doubt I will have become sufficiently acquainted with things by the time I leave for home to tell whether it's worth returning or not.

I went to Tel Aviv to have a look at the exhibition. Not much to it, but the city is pleasant, the architecture better than in Haifa, and some of the streets are tree lined. The effects of the disturbances have been disastrous, but I still don't think there is much physical danger. The total number of Jews and Europeans killed is 33. I have a vague feeling that this week and the next will be decisive; we'll be able to form an opinion on whether this will continue or not. I think most of it will be over in three weeks, but others are more pessimistic.

My stomach illness is long gone and my hair has almost completely grown out. While in bed I devoted myself to my parents' house, and I was happy to hear that two of my suggestions were carried out. I've had a lot of fun doing the drawings.

I regret not having a regular, long-term, paying job, for it's not easy to work with any kind of energy when the goal is so distant and hard to discern as in this case. I'm not working for anything as immediate as advancement, only to acquire knowledge.

One nice thing here is the climate, day after day of sun and warmth, sometimes almost too much of a good thing, but in any case better than snow and slush. There's a seaside resort just outside the city where I go with friends or young ladies almost every Saturday afternoon. I am now working on Saturdays, along with a handful of Christians who work on the Jewish sabbath and thus are off when my Jewish friends are working. I don't particularly like this arrangement, but luckily working hours are very short on Saturday and therefore I'll be able to continue going to the seaside place (Bat Galim).

The nature of banking, such as I see it manifested in the Holland bank, has surprised me in one respect, i.e., in its civil service capacity. I had always thought banks were the apotheosis of "rugged individualism," a concrete example of the superiority of private enterprise to state ownership.

Now I see that though it is privately owned rather than state owned, it is so mechanically managed that it might as well be run by the state. The salaries of the bank employees are based on merit, but other than that they have no interest in the bank. From their point of view, it makes no difference whether the bank is state owned or not; they would work as intensely and efficiently under one system as under the other. What I have seen of banking so far makes it seem like a kind of glorified pawnshop; I have not seen any "financial transactions." All the work not done by the management, i.e., everything not associated with estimating financial conditions and political development, new industry, or other forms of company activity, seems like routine work to me. I would guess that once you've mastered this routine, there are few areas in which you have a chance of finding yourself faced with a new situation calling for an extra measure of intelligence or imagination. All the rules have been written, everything has been foreseen. If you compare the amount of intelligence needed or the degree of independent thinking called for in a bank (except among the management) with what is needed in an architecture office or even a commercial agency, you immediately see that these latter are on a completely different level. One thing that I do find interesting is the organization of the work itself, the structure of the office, etc.

Today we learned that my best friend, the Dutchman who left for Tel Aviv a few weeks ago to study riding schools, has come down with typhus and we are quite worried. There are always plenty of minor fevers around and you don't seem to be able to do anything about them, but typhus is relatively rare.

A thousand regards to both of you,
Raoul

ISTANBUL
JUNE 26, 1936

Dear Maj,

I am sending you a copy of today's letter to Raoul, in which I discuss a trip home and what the possible benefit of it might be. I wish you would tell me what you think about it so that, as always, we may cooperate fully in the best interest of our dear boy. Obviously, the main thing for you is to see him. I can understand that. But I want to consider what might be useful. I would appreciate your understanding the importance of not talking too much about his staying home. I am not seeking a "place" for him so much as looking for the best prospects, to prepare the way for a good position.

Freund tells me in a recent letter that foreigners are not in any danger in Palestine. You can trust his judgment. Newspaper correspondents always exaggerate. Writing about the sensational is their profession. The general public likes that. So I do not think you have to worry about anything happening to the boy. Nevertheless, I would like for you to admonish him to be very careful about going to places where there is trouble.

Let me know what you think about my letter and whether you have any comments.

Fondest regards to Fred and the children
Your devoted
[GOW]

[The letter referred to by GOW, dated June 26, is not included in the correspondence.]

HAIFA
JULY 6, 1936

Dear Grandfather,

I've received both your letters, and I thank you very much. In a way, these letters have made me happier than any others you've written to me. You cannot have helped but notice that my letters this last year have betrayed a certain anxiousness, stemming from the fact that while I thought my present course of study — which is entirely your doing — clever and logically directed toward *the goal you set,* namely a foreign bank, it didn't serve the purpose of preparing me to earn an income in the near future. It's true that a couple of years of working in an agency and in bank branches as an unpaid volunteer does provide a suitable direction for your purposes, but it doesn't help when it comes to getting a well-paid position *right away.* I had a feeling, and I still have it, that being a volunteer is dangerous. A recommendation is only worth something if whoever has written it has had to pay your wages. I was also afraid that your plan was too inflexible. I had a feeling that you had made up your mind that I was to stay in Palestine for a couple of years, no matter what I felt about the place. I have already seen once how different a company can be from the inside, namely in the case of Arderne, Scott, Thesen in Cape Town, which was a complete waste of time. All this is why I'm so happy about your last letter, because I detect a willingness to adjust the plan to the circumstances. On those terms, I'm willing to be cooperative and accommodate myself to your wishes more than I had thought lately, as I don't want to hide from you my thought that during the last few months, I had begun to think that I would have to cry "wolf" in order to make myself heard.

The question is this: does the Holland Bank offer me my best opportunity to learn what I am supposed to learn? Up to now, I was certain that it did not and have already told you so, but I think I detect an improvement. I have been promised a move to another section — and high time, for I have been in "Foreign Exchange" for almost three months, doing routine work. There are too few employees and the bank put me there simply because there was nobody else. I have spoken to Freund about returning, and he told me I would be welcome, and I said that I probably would be back. So the formalities are taken care of. The only thing remaining now is the immigration authority. Actually, one bad thing about Haifa is that I will probably never be paid here, since it is impossible to get that kind of visa even if I were to be entitled to a salary from the point of view of the bank. We also spoke about Zilkha and agreed that I would go there this fall. If I return, that is. The reason I don't want to go there now is that so long as I am only staying here a total of five months, I think it silly to split up that short a time; it would only make sense to go to Zilkha if I were coming back, not just for a month, but with the idea of being flexible, so that if it turns out to be a good place I might stay longer. We also talked about the bank in general. He promised that later on, when I was more experienced, he would write to the main office and ask if I could go to Buenos Aires, should I so desire. It is a larger branch and more of the kind of frontier bank you were thinking of. No one is propagandizing Dutch products here, for example, and the bank doesn't represent Holland in the least. Thus — and this is what seems bizarre — Dutch companies with accounts in Dutch banks other than the Holland Bank are sending their export documents to their own banks, which, in their turn, send them to one of our competitors here for cashing. I don't know how to avoid this, but I think it unreasonable, *a priori*, that as long as there is a Dutch bank right there documents from Dutch companies not be sent to it; a great deal of Dutch money is lost.

You mustn't lose sight of one thing, and that is that I may not be particularly suited for banking at all. Do you think, for example, that you would have thought me capable of assuming your mantle in this area if I were not your grandson? Architecture is an entirely different matter. I have an aptitude for that profession; I have been interested in it my whole life, and ever since my elementary school days, I've been running around all the building sites in Stockholm, looking around and making friends with the engineers. To tell you the truth, I don't find myself very bankerish: the director of a bank should be judgelike and calm and cold and cynical besides. Freund and Jacob W. are probably typical, and I feel as different from them as I could be. My temperament is better suited to some positive line of work than to sitting around saying no. The South African venture was a success, and I enclose copies of letters about me written by Florén and Frykberg. I apologize for not sending them before; I thought you already had them, but your last letter from Istanbul shows that I was mistaken.

My request for three weeks' extra service was turned down for the second time, and consequently, I don't report until the beginning of September. I haven't started planning for my return yet, but I would like to visit my cousin Maj Nisser, now married to a von Plauen, whom I haven't seen for several years and who was my favorite cousin. She lives at Wiesenburg castle, Mark, outside Berlin. Another thing that Freund and I talked about was my going via Amsterdam to talk with the gentlemen there about a job in South America. The idea would be to become permanently employed in order to determine whether I was at all suited for this.

Mother has repeatedly written that she is looking forward to having me home, and I have therefore taken the attitude that I will stay abroad so long as it is *definitely* better and so long as it really does provide me with skills I cannot get at home and benefits the development of our plans. I still maintain, however, that I need more insight into how things are done at home. On the one hand, I admit that being abroad is a good way to hide flaws and deficiencies. On the other you also hide your potential talent and may be met by skepticism when you finally do go home.

As far as the Falkmans' Johan is concerned, I would suggest that if his parents neglected to tell you that he did not advance, it might be because they wanted to wait for results of the special tests he takes this fall before giving up hope. It was possible, at least when I was in school, to make up failing grades by studying over the summer, then taking tests in the fall. If you passed you were not held back. If he spent the summer in England, this would be an indication that he had failed English, and he will undoubtedly pass the tests after a whole summer in England.

It will be interesting to have you introduce me personally to the great men at home this fall. The love and care that you devote to me (not to mention the money) are always in my thoughts, and I take your coming trip home as further proof of them. Were I a worthy grandson I would thank you by following your directives without questions or objections. I am therefore ashamed of the comments and suggestions I occasionally offer, but I don't regret them, since I don't think it would do me any good to hide my apprehensiveness. That, as I said before, is precisely why I appreciate your last letter so much, for it demonstrates a more flexible position vis-à-vis the question of what I should do, whether I should stay here, etc.

How are you planning to go home; when, etc.? My military service will be finished sometime during the first week in October.

The disturbances here are tapering off, but I will postpone my trip to Jerusalem as long as possible because the interesting parts of the city are off limits. Besides, there is still a curfew, and nobody is allowed in the street after seven o'clock, which should make life rather boring for those people, especially the young ones, who work until seven and then have to go home to their rooms without the chance to go to the movies or out for a walk. A sort of three months' prison sentence for the poor Jews.

Say hello to Fina and many regards from
Raoul

[HAIFA]
[AUGUST ? 1936]

Dear Grandfather,

I will be leaving here on the 18th aboard the Polish ship *Polonia*, passing through Istanbul on the 23rd. The boat will be there all

day, and then I continue on to Constanza, Kattwitz, Warsaw, and
Berlin. It is the least expensive route and should also be very
interesting, as I have not been to Poland before. I have only
bought a ticket to Istanbul, as I wanted to wait to hear your plans
for your trip home before I bought the final one. I presume,
however, that you are not planning to go home until later, since
you said in your letters that you wanted to introduce me to some
of the important men at home *after* my military service. My
military service begins on September 10. I will be staying in Berlin
for three or four days and should therefore arrive home about
September 3. My service ends on October 6th. If for some reason
you would like for me to go home some other way, or if it could
be arranged for us to travel together, which I would really enjoy,
send me a cable, because I don't want to put off making my
reservations too long, as boats are full.

Thank you very much for your letter of the 13th. When I read
the first sentence I suddenly had an urge to ask you to tell me
something about my father. Preferably in a letter, so that I could
always carry it with me. I have always half subconsciously felt
very much his inferior. In the pictures I have he looks so good and
honest and self-sacrificing, and I feel like a bad substitute.

Last night I came back from a few hours' visit to Jerusalem —
my first visit. It was wonderful, but because of the bad conditions you aren't allowed to see anything. The Old City, with all
its monuments, is entirely closed off, and in the new city, too, no
one is allowed out after seven o'clock. This has now been going
on for more than three months. The trip went well and no one
shot at us. You see soldiers everywhere on the road from Tel
Aviv, and the taxi drove like a fury, evidently to reduce the risk
of being shot at.

I happened by chance to pass by the Swedish school, and went
in and met the headmistress, Miss Ekland or Eklund. She's been to
Constantinople, staying with the Kolmodins, and evidently knew
you and especially Grandmother. She has single-handedly built
the school up during a fifteen-year stay, and now has two hundred Arab pupils and eight or nine Arab women teaching under
her direction.

It was vacation time and we had coffee together, just the two of
us. The day before, she'd written to Willy Falkman, whose articles

she had read, asking him to come and see her next time. She also knew the Fevrells.

I haven't heard from home for a long time and am a bit worried. Have you had some news?

You must not worry that my reason for wanting a paying job is so that I can go and get married right away. I do have a strong desire to earn money, preferably lots of money. I want a wife as well, but for the time being I think money comes first.

Regards,
Raoul

Raoul Wallenberg
c/o von Dardel
Kevinge Strand
Stocksund
Sweden

[GOW's letter of July 13, in which he apparently mentions Raoul Oscar Wallenberg, his son and RW's father, is missing from the correspondence.]

STOCKHOLM
OCTOBER 12, 1936

Dearest Grandfather,

We have all been expecting you for some days and wonder when you're coming. My military service ended on the 6th, and since then I've been hanging around doing nothing in particular. I have not wanted to inquire about a job so as not to anticipate you. As far as Sweden is concerned, that is. I have, however, had some talks with Frykberg, who would like me to go back to Africa.

My parents' house is now almost finished. It's very nice and gorgeously situated. Mother drives her new car with great assurance for a beginner. Nina, and especially Guy, have grown and are now "adults." Guy is first in his class.

My military service wasn't too bad, except for the occasional disagreement with my company head, Captain Kallner, who bawled me out on several occasions and called me just about every name he could think of. The maneuvers were fine. We did only get a couple of hours sleep at night, but the whole thing was very exciting, and the weather was better than it has been during a maneuver for a long time. It took place in Gästrikland, with airplanes and tanks and 20,000 men, so this was major warfare.

I've seen everyone in the family and was happy to find them in good health. I am sorry to say that I found our Aunt Amalia feeling very poorly during my visit to Malmvik, however. She'd been that way for several months. Little Marcus has also been ill and doesn't give the appearance of having fully recovered. His features are drawn and hollowed, and he doesn't at all look as healthy as during my last visit. I very much hope that both will improve.

We're anxiously awaiting a line or two telling us when to expect you back in your native country.

Your
Raoul

c/o von Dardel
Kevinge Strand
Stocksund

OCT. 22, 1936

Dear Grandfather,

The other day I heard through Karin that ill health is preventing you from returning to Sweden and that you've had to go to Nice to recuperate. I was quite worried, and hope to have a line or two from you before long telling me that you're well again.

Since I do not wish to be a burden to my stepfather nor live off my assets and, as you told me in Istanbul, will receive support from you only when abroad, I find it necessary to find some work. I would prefer to wait until you got home, so that I not contract any obligations before we undertake the famous tour of introduction.

When I went to see Uncle Marcus he mentioned that he'd spoken with the head of Atlas Diesel about a job. I went out to Atlas Diesel, and Mr. Jacobsson, the director, told me that I could go through their training program, which prepares you for sales jobs abroad. It takes eight to ten months, however, and in the meantime you only earn 175 kronor a month. There's no guarantee when it's over that you'll be picked for the foreign sales staff and reach a higher salary level, other than luck and skill. I went to see Johansson in Kooperativa, but he only had time to tell me that there was nothing. The same with Graffman of AB Transfer. I also went to see Axel Andersson Johnsson, who put me in touch with the head of Avesta, with whom I had a talk today. He will let me know in two weeks. Here too, it is a matter of foreign sales, and they also have a long training period, although not as long — about six months. Both these offers involve the risk, however, that if accepted I may get stuck abroad somewhere with no way of being heard or promoted. Andersson of the Persian Company has no use for me at this point but asked me to send in an application and said he would keep me in mind, etc. Norlander of Sveaexport didn't think me technically qualified. Wenner-Gren of Electrolux was out of the country when I was there. I wrote to and visited a few minor companies, but they were not interested. I now await your instructions with great impatience, and I sincerely hope that soon you will be in robust health.

Your
Raoul

STOCKHOLM
[UNDATED 1936]

Dear Grandfather,

I heard through Grandmother yesterday that you had arrived in Nice and that you were well. I don't deny I have been a little anxious and worried, but I knew that it couldn't be too serious or I would have heard something. Nevertheless, I was very happy to get the word from Grandmother, and I hope that you will soon be as well as you were during my last visit to Constantinople; I really enjoyed our time together there, even though it was only for a few hours.

The delay in your arrival here has obviously altered my plans to some extent, since I'm anxious to find something to do as soon as possible. I have ceased my attempts to find a good position for the time being, so as not to anticipate things by flooding the market with news of my availability before you get here.

If you let me know when you think you might be allowed to come home I'll find out what I can do in the meantime. I will not take the position at Atlas Diesel, since I don't find their offer too tempting at this point.

Jorden Runt [Around the Globe] will be out next week, and in it will be my article about South Africa; I will send it to you as soon as I get it.

I trust that you will not, out of goodness, leave Nice before you are truly recovered; I will be all right until then. I'm sure I'll find something to do.

Our house is now finished; I'm looking forward to showing it to you.

All the best from me and from my parents.

Your
Raoul

STOCKHOLM
NOVEMBER 4, 1936

Dear Grandfather,

I'm writing to keep you up-to-date on developments on the job market here.

Sometime after my visit to Mr. Andersson, the director of the Persian Company, I received a letter from him telling me that he didn't think he had anything, but asking me to go see Harald Malmström, the future head of their office in Teheran. I had a long conversation with him and liked him very much, and he told me that they would eventually be reorganizing their Persian operation and that they would be needing another person in Teheran. Without committing himself in any way, he gave me to understand that I might be considered, but not for the next few months; furthermore it is up to the board to decide whom to employ. He thought my education quite well suited for their purposes. The salary would be good, but I got no details. It appears to be a rather long-term position if I get it, although the prospects are probably shaky, as it is a new business. Bofors, Nydqvist & Holm, and Kooperativa are behind it. My task would appear to have something to do with purchasing.

I will let you know as soon as there is something new.

Your
Raoul

[Letter to Karin Falkman]

NICE
NOVEMBER 23, 1936

Dear Karin,

All is well with Grandfather as far as I can tell, and I don't think there is any cause for concern.

He met us at the station when we arrived. Of course he looked thinner than usual, but you would never guess that he'd lost 13 kilos. He is no longer losing weight. Aunt Lilly and he spent their days playing solitaire, all meals have been taken outdoors, we have been to see Uncle Knut and even gone to the movies a couple of times. He slept during the first one for about fifteen minutes, but the second time he was very interested and amused.

As for the rest, he is being sensible and does not appear depressed; he does not stay up until four in the morning and is livelier than one might think after so much dieting. He is allowed to eat meat and have a beer, etc., again.

Aunt Lilly has not yet talked to the doctor, so I can only report my own observations. His prostate is not causing him pain, he says; no drainage or other operation is necessary. He is able to take care of himself in every respect. There is no kidney pain, and he sleeps well at night.

This is very good news both for me and for you, and I just hope that Aunt Lilly's talk with the doctor will confirm what our eyes tell us.

I am leaving for home on the 26th or thereabouts but will probably make a few stops along the way.

Raoul

FÄHRSCHIFF, GERMANY
DECEMBER 12, 1936

Dear Grandfather,

I am now on my way to Neustadt (not far from Freiburg, Breisgau) to look at a factory that makes zippers. I'm going on behalf of Uncle Marcus and the Investment Institute, who want to buy a patent for this zipper as the basis for a manufacturing plant for the Scandinavian market, and which I, somehow, would be part of. Whether this company is founded or not partly depends on what I find out. The whole thing sounds very tempting. I should be able to give you definite information before New Year's about what my job for the near future will be.

Grandmother will be coming down around the 15th or a little later.

Everybody sends their regards, hoping for a speedy return of your very best health.

Say hello to Aunt Lilly.

Raoul

STOCKHOLM
DECEMBER 20, 1936

Dear Grandfather,

My best wishes for a merry Christmas and a speedy recovery. I
heard that you were beginning to gain weight and am happy to
hear it. I'm convinced that before long you won't even know that
you had jaundice and prostate trouble.

As I am terribly busy looking into the Swedish possibilities for
the new zipper that the Emission Institute has acquired, I don't
have time to write as much as I should. It looks fairly promising,
but they won't make up their minds until my report is finished,
i.e., in some weeks' time, and then only if I advise my client to
pursue it further — something that I am as yet unable to say.

I have talked to Karin Falkman about your black vase and will
give you a report on it later.

Grandmother and Miss Wernberger told me about your generous Christmas gift; thank you very much, it was most welcome.
I am going to buy something for Guy and Nina with it.

Again, Merry Christmas to my dear Grandparents.

Raoul

STOCKHOLM
JANUARY 5, 1937

Dearest Grandfather,

Thank you very much for the generous and very useful Christmas
gift you gave me and my brother and sister.

Since getting back from Germany I've been busy calculating
operating costs and such for the projected zipper factory, doing
the best I can. I have also asked various buyers how they would
react to this kind of product. I was supposed to report my findings
to Uncle Marcus and August Nachmansson on December 28, so
that they could make a decision. Since I wasn't able to come to a
definitive conclusion in so short a time, we asked the Swiss man
who holds the license to extend the option period, so that we

could have more time to consider. I am therefore still busy calculating and making inquiries, and I really cannot tell yet what the outcome will be. If we were to start manufacture I would be given a well-paid position, but on the other hand it might be a disadvantage to be tied to a venture that might fail. I am therefore weighing the pros and cons with utmost care before making a decision.

The weather here has been very warm and beautiful, and we haven't had any snow, for which I am quite thankful. Our house is completely finished, and Mother can finally catch her breath. The interior, especially, came out very well, and it has a beautiful view of Ulriksdal Palace across the bay, about 400 meters away.

I attended the early New Year's service in Katarina Church; the entire family was there, including Uncle Marcus, Oscar, Victor, and Fredrik. Of my aunts, only Siri and Ruth were there. Loads of young people: Jacob, Little Marcus, Knut Bergenstråhle, Haakon Mörner, Ernst Killander, all with wives and some children. Several others too. Uncle Knut, Aunt Alice, and Aunt Amalia stayed home, but I saw the latter at breakfast afterward and she really looked much better than I had dared hope after last fall. She's almost back to normal, although she complained of headaches when there are a lot of people around.

Aunt Lilly has been very kind to me and sends me a card from time to time.

I'm glad to learn that you are improving from day to day; I am eagerly looking forward to the day when you will pay us a visit as we planned before you fell ill.

Greetings from my family and me to you, Grandmother and Grandfather,

Raoul

STOCKHOLM
JANUARY 19, 1937

Dearest Grandfather,

A few weeks ago Mother put the letter you had enclosed for me on my desk, among the papers that are piled almost up to eye level, whereupon it disappeared, only to emerge today. She forgot to tell me it was there.

I'm still just as busy as ever with my zipper, but the data I'm looking for is taking a long time to find, so that the last few days I haven't had much to do. I have not seen Uncle Marcus at all since the New Year's service and the breakfast afterward on Strandvägen 27. I do go up to see Director August Nachmansson of the Emission Institute from time to time, however. He is my immediate employer and also a very pleasant person, very businesslike and enterprising.

A few days ago I had lunch with Uncle Knut and Aunt Alice, but it wasn't as convivial as last time in Nice, for Aunt Alice got the time wrong and naturally thought that it was my fault. Uncle Knut was criticized for drinking strong tea and kept muttering angrily, "Don't make such a fuss." Olga was there. I like her very much, and it's always fun to see her. The first time was in Paris when you and I paid a visit to the Ritz.

My parents and I are invited to dinner at Little Marcus's in a few days. His new wife is generally well liked and is probably very good for him. She accompanies him everywhere on his trips, to sporting events and entertainments, and I think he appreciates it quite a lot, for as far as I can see she's a nice and tactful person.

Winter arrived today with severe cold but no snow. Nina and Guy, who are quite grown up now, went skating and skiing around the house. Guy will finish school this spring and then enroll at the Royal Institute of Technology. Then he might go abroad. He doesn't quite know what he wants to do yet, however.

As far as trade policy is concerned, the talk of the day — i.e., in the newspapers — is the lowering of tariffs among the Nordic countries. Everyone is dazzled by our domestic prosperity, to the point that no one sees the shadows on the trade front.

All best wishes from your devoted
Raoul

[This is the final letter in the correspondence between RW and GOW, who died in March 1937, during a visit to Sweden.]

[Letter to Nita and Carl Axel Söderlund.]

STOCKHOLM
AUGUST 13, 1938

After October 1, 1938
Östermalmsgatan 7, c/o Dardel

Dearest Nita and Carl Axel,

Many thanks for the nice telegram on my birthday. The day itself was spent in the simplest possible way: sitting in my cousin Lennart Hagströmer's 9-meter boat, which was being towed from Stockholm to a wharf in Norrtälje to have its broken mast repaired.

Last Sunday we were, as usual, out sailing in the archipelago and first lost a spar — which gave rise to some adventurous forays up the mast — and then the mast itself. We often go sailing with our friends and have a wonderful time — it is actually the empty bottles that keep the boat afloat these days.

I owe you yet another thank-you for the beautiful little Mexican silver hat, which adds noticeably to my room. I'm really sorry for my rudeness in not thanking you before.

Mother and Nina are, as you know, at the Colvins in Belle Haven, Greenwich, Conn., and are tremendously impressed by the many bathrooms.

Father has been in France and Germany, and Guy has ambulated between Kristianstad and Boden. I have therefore been alone in Stockholm, at Gösta Nisser's apartment, Styrmansgatan 57, where I will remain until October 1. It has been wonderful, as this is actually the very first time that I've spent a summer alone in Stockholm. A wonderful city.

In between, I have been up to see my friend from South Africa, Björn Burchardt, who has a hunting and fishing lodge at Lake Ross in Hälsingland. Once, we had two young ladies there over the weekend — we were all headed for a strange dance at a mountain pasture, referred to as a *bogäspe* — and we stayed on for the rest of the week. We consumed so much food in that short amount of time that we had to transport it in using a horse and a fully laden cart. It was a very remote area, and it was possible to fish, swim, and run around as undisturbed as anywhere in America.

I've been to see Grandmother a few times, and it has been a
delight to learn more about just how intelligent and interesting
she is. This last time she told me some hilarious stories of having
seven rooms full of furniture towed out to Saltsjöbaden on an
enormous coal barge as a newlywed. The monster tore loose
twice: once in Stockholm and once out at Baggen.

Speaking of funny experiences, I have to tell you something
that happened to me a couple of years ago, but which still makes
me wake up terrified at night: Professor Gerhard de Geer, whose
business is clay strata, the ice age, boulder-ridges, etc., is now
well advanced in years but has an ambitious wife, who wants him
to keep working and even expand his institute at Sveavägen,
even though he is getting old. She therefore decided to arrange a
nice dinner party for various leading lights among the moneyed
and aristocratic circles whom she wanted to work on. She evidently received many regrets, so I was invited the day of the
party, as she did not know very many whom she could ask at the
last moment. We were about twenty in all. The hostess sat next to
Prince Eugen, and I was placed next to an old wrinkled lady on
whose place card I could vaguely make out ". . . Pauli." "Pauli?
Pauli?" I thought. "Now that sounds vaguely familiar." It occurred
to me that she might be some kind of important cultural person,
someone like Anna Lindhagen, so I started a polite conversation
along those lines.

It turned out that I'd been right, she was indeed culturally
inclined; I even guessed that she might be artistically inclined. So
I asked her — oh, clever me! — whether she painted. When she
answered in the affirmative I asked politely whether she ever
exhibited her works.

At this question the charming old lady drew herself up and
said: "I do indeed exhibit, CONSTANTLY, in the National Museum."

After having my hand figuratively slapped, I drew a deep
breath and recovered by turning to the person on my left. I heard
the Pauli woman — not until then did I realize that it was HANNA
PAULI — talking to the person on her right. The first thing she
said was: "That one, the young man on my left? He's illiterate!"

At the end of the dinner there was one of those frightful silences
that always seems to occur when someone has said something
unsuitable. You could hear pins drop all around the room. The

charming old lady broke this silence by pointing a bony finger at Prince Eugen and saying in a voice that would wake the dead: "The Prince over there, *he is also a painter!*"

Have you seen Carmen? What is her name now and where does she live?

The weather has been unusually hot and in my opinion generally beautiful the whole year. Stockholm is always wonderful, and it is growing as rapidly as when you were here, except possibly for Lidingö. On the other hand, the plans for a navy base seem to be further along than before, and your house may turn out to be quite a good investment. They seem to have discovered that placing it farther out than Lidingö would mean so many extra costs that they would have to scrap the project.

Thank you once again, my dear Nita and Carl Axel, for remembering me. It reminded me of your last visit to Sweden and of Mexico before that, when I had the pleasure of seeing you often and under the most pleasant of circumstances.

Raoul

[Hanna Pauli (1864–1940) was a prominent member of the turn-of-the-century Swedish art establishment. Like Prince Eugen, also a respected painter, she was influenced by the French Barbizon School.]

[Letter to Nina von Dardel.]

STOCKHOLM
NOVEMBER 7, 1938

Dear Nina,

Thank you for your postcard and your long letter about slum clearances, etc. Today I've mailed you a booklet in English about Stockholm's social programs. I myself know nothing about the matter.

Comparing England and Sweden in this respect, you must bear in mind that Sweden has never had to confront many problems, and that achievements have therefore come more easily to the Swedes than to the British. For example, the population of

Stockholm has doubled in a little more than twenty years (I think). Those who have moved here needed to build new housing, and it is therefore necessarily newer and less run-down. If the population of Stockholm had remained static, we would have had proportionately more substandard housing.

Furthermore, Sweden has been able to live quite comfortably off its timber industry, since the whole world has suddenly developed a need for wood products, from timber and pit props to pulp and rayon. The income generated by this huge industry has obviously benefited the working class, i.e., the housing consumers. Had times been good for English coal and cotton, a large portion of their slums would probably have taken care of itself without any interference from the state or the municipality, since the workers themselves would have demanded — and could have afforded — better housing.

Finally, as far as the much-vaunted standard of living goes, this is naturally not the result of an especially highly developed social conscience among the wealthy of this country, but rather the result of increased demand for labor within the export industries. The farmers are not particularly well off. And lastly, I don't think that the wealth of the English millionaires ought to be compared with that of the Swedish against the background of the affluence of the working class in each country. English millionaires have earned their money largely off the British Empire, not England, and the English working class does not therefore have the right to begrudge them their income in the same way as ours may the income of our millionaires.

You are becoming terribly educated; I hope you survive. Your letters are read aloud with great admiration by the family. I'm doing marketing research for a coffee company for Jacob Wallenberg. Mother has the new apartment all set up in record time and is now mad about not having anything to do and nothing to turn to, while also turning down invitations, claiming that social life is the bane of contemporary society. I have given in and am due to begin bridge lessons with Mrs. Fagerberg next Friday. This way I hope to get an extra two hours' sleep a day, which I could use. Father is busy at the office every day with blueprints for our new house at Kevinge. Under Mother's influence, it has not shrunk to contain a spade, a bit of grass seed, and three long potatoes. The drawings are proceeding according to plan, so there is no longer any toilet paper left in the house.

Old Uncle Nils has turned 85, and it has given Mother much pleasure to offer him her congratulations. The old man is said to be in good form, recognizing those present surprisingly well. I myself was there the day before yesterday and was amazed at his control of the situation, and his never-failing good humor.

The other day I went to Cecil's with William Nisser and Ulla Dahllöf; they got engaged shortly afterward. She is very nice and witty. I also had lunch at Blue Heaven (pronounced *Blå Heeven* by the elevator operators) some time ago with your old classmate Viveka Lindfors, who is now a student at the Acting School of the Royal Dramatic Theater.

I have nothing more to tell you and therefore send my heartfelt sisters to my dearest greeting

from her devoted
Raoul

STOCKHOLM
DECEMBER 29, 1938

Dearest Nina,

Allow me to send you my best wishes for Christmas and also, under separate cover, a copy of the Christmas issue of *Veckojournalen* and a subscription for 1939.

Due to the extraordinary state of confusion that characterizes my notion of your current address as well as your future one, the magazine will in all likelihood never reach you so you won't have to go on reading this drivel.

All the store windows are filled with beautifully garlanded pigs' heads — I never could understand why they choose to display that end of the creature, as it is not the most delicious. Otherwise, the city has been in the throes of a paroxysm of Christmas spirit since the end of November. The merchants sell much more during Christmas and will consequently propose a law to extend Christmas to a year-round celebration.

Between Christmas and New Year I will either do nothing at all, or go up to see Björn Burchardt. Sometime after the New Year I hope to get a new job through Jacob Wallenberg, for whom I have been working on a project during the last few months.

I hope you have lots of fun during Christmas.

Your devoted
Raoul

[Veckojournalen (Weekly Journal) was a popular general-interest magazine. Today it is called Mänadsjournalen (Monthly Journal).]

STOCKHOLM
JANUARY 4, 1939

Dearest Grandmother,

I'm sorry that I will not be able to get out to see you myself, but I have two things to tell you:

1. I like you very much.
2. My best wishes on your seventieth birthday.

Your devoted
Raoul

STOCKHOLM
[UNDATED]

Mr. Jacob Wallenberg, Director
Enskilda Banken, AB
Stockholm

Dear Jacob,

I spoke with Mr. Ljungberg, the director of Swedish Match, on March 3 concerning a position in India, but have not heard anything as yet. I therefore later asked him whether there might be another opening within his company, to which he answered no, which is too bad, since naturally — no matter what the job, and all things being equal salarywise — I would prefer a job in Europe or America over one in the colonies.

Just hanging around waiting is rather depressing, and I would therefore be grateful for your opinion as to whether you still would advise me — as you did in early February — to keep waiting for the position you mentioned, or whether conditions are such that you would advise me to try and find something on my own instead. If the former, I wonder whether you have anything I could do while I wait.

Let me take this opportunity to thank you once again for your kind interest in me, and for your efforts on behalf of my continued employment.

Sincerely yours,
R. Wallenberg

FEBRUARY 28, 1944

Darling Nina,

It is frightfully boring here without you, and the dinner table at home is straight out of a play by Strindberg.

Mother is quite depressed, as you might imagine, since she may have to go back to the hospital for three months and undergo yet another operation, on top of everything else.

This letter will be rather choppy, since it has been written on different typewriters, for we have been terribly busy. The boxcars with oranges keep rolling in, one after the other, and so far without any hitches or problems. The market has been flooded with oranges this past week, because too much is being imported from different places all at the same time, making prices plummet. Thank God all of ours had already been sold. One customer took it into his head to go up to Bydalen on holiday, leaving no forwarding address and refusing to accept the goods.

The rest of the business is not doing too well; there are constant problems with the poultry men. We have some other major projects planned, but it's too soon to tell whether they are feasible or not.

The Falkmans had a magnificent dance with lots of pretty girls. There was, as you might expect, a touch of the mining district about the whole thing, with Johan Paues welcoming us in a speech teeming with expressions like "the folks down the road," and "yon neighbors," etc. The dinner, however, was very good. The following day, on the 19th, Gösta and Gittan gave a tremendously successful dinner party with Maj and Enzio, the Romanian minister, Lieutenant Colonel Drakenberg (my regimental commander — I obviously didn't tell him, or I wouldn't have been able to talk to him at ease), also a Mrs. de Vries, General Thörnell's daughter, married to the Dutch director of an insurance company. She told me some interesting things and is now intending to stay in Sweden. There was also a Mrs. Sten Anckarkrona, married to a lawyer. We had a spirited discussion about crime, with me claiming that everybody had a price, so to speak, and that it was just a matter of whether the temptation was great enough and balanced the right way and the risk of discovery minimal enough for anybody to turn into a criminal. I then brought up the usual question of what she would do if she could earn a million kronor by killing a Chinese with the touch of a button and with no fear of punishment. She haughtily denied that she would ever give in to such temptation, so I then listed a number of less dangerous things that she might accomplish by pushing the button while describing, in terms designed to be as tempting as possible, what she could do with a million. She would not be swayed, and Mother told me the next day that she was the world's stingiest mother. She and her husband, along with her mother-in-law, have ten million and own a newspaper.

Eva Odelberg was also there, and she told me that Hans Sjöqvist had fallen downstairs and cracked his skull so that he has lost the ability to speak and has become paralyzed. It is absolutely awful.

A week later, Göran and Märta Crafoord had a dinner party, this one also very nice. The kids acted as waiters and were given one kronor each if they didn't spill anything. We all signed solemn affidavits that the giant-sized spots and rivers of gravy on the tablecloth were already there when we arrived.

Last Saturday, finally, Byssan Wibom gave a very pleasant party with Prince Colonna and his very agreeable wife and Prince Carl Johan and all the usual crowd. Some seemed rather mean, like Maud Segerstråhle, for instance. A young man named Arbin went over to poor Gustaf d'Otrante and asked him pointedly, "Is it true that d'Otrante is the most important family in Sweden?" which made everybody laugh, since he reputedly maintains that this is the case. He recovered quite well, however, and said "No, but Schinkel is the least."

———

Yet another typewriter. Last Sunday I went to the office; afterward I met up with Knut von Horn and we went for a stroll in Djurgården. During our walk, we talked about the way the supply situation is developing. He works at the Ministry of Supply, as you know. We painted ourselves an alarming scenario, especially if there is peace in Finland. In that case, we guessed that we'd have a moral obligation to help them, out of our own rations. We thought it most unlikely that Finland would be permitted to import goods from South America. The painting was bleak even if there was no peace in Finland: in the event of a Russian attack we would have another half million refugees or more to feed. If Russia doesn't attack, the situation would improve, but even then could deteriorate should supplies from the outside be cut off — by an invasion, for example. Most people do not look at it this way, but I think that Central Europe is about to change political course again.

Guy is currently looking for a job, and Mother is after him not to sell himself too cheaply. He is leaning toward the aircraft factories in Linköping.

I have neither been out for a walk nor skiing in ages. There hasn't been a flake of snow in the city for as long as I can remember. This has really been a boring winter.

A week ago, I sent a letter to *Dagens Nyheter* [Daily News], suggesting that they do away with certain practices and change some of their permanent headings (type: "The Sports Section" and "Press Cuttings"). Three days later they took away a page heading, which had always looked awful, on their so-called Family Page, and yesterday I got a letter from Dahlgren, who thanked me for my kind interest and told me that the newspaper would "give my suggestions their consideration." Some of my suggestions were warranted. He thought that my suggestions might lead to changes in the present order of things in some instances, in others, not. I can't help but think that the latter may be at the heart of the matter.

Well, there is nothing more to report as far as I know, except to say that I hope that you'll be home for a visit, and the sooner the better. I send you my best wishes for a happy birthday, and it is my sincere hope that you will manage a whole year without any accidents. I'm enclosing a small gift.

Best wishes,
Raoul

[A note on RW's activities between 1936 and 1944:
Because RW had earned his advanced degree from an American university, he was unable to practice as an architect in Sweden. Unable as well to find a position in the Wallenberg bank, RW attempted unsuccessfully to start his own businesses. Eventually, through Jacob Wallenberg's connections, he was introduced to Kálmán Lauer, a Hungarian Jew who was director of a specialty export business called the Central European Trading Company, Inc. (Mellaneuropeiska Handelsaktiebolaget, or Meropa, for short). Because Lauer was no longer able to travel freely to Hungary, to which Meropa's products were primarily exported, RW went in Lauer's place, acting as his foreign trade representative and eventually becoming his junior partner. On June 9, 1944, Lauer introduced RW to Iver Olsen, the Stockholm representative of the U.S.-based War Refugee Board. They met at the Hotel

Salsjöbaden, the resort GOW had been so instrumental in constructing. Because RW was Swedish, fluent in German, and familiar with Budapest, Olsen wanted to recruit him to oversee a rescue operation of Hungarian Jews. RW immediately agreed, and his appointment was approved by Herschel V. Johnson, the American ambassador to Sweden, who informed Washington. RW left for Hungary on July 2.]

DISPATCHES FROM BUDAPEST

JULY 18–DECEMBER 12, 1944

INTRODUCTION

It was Sunday morning, the nineteenth of March, 1944, in Budapest. At six in the morning I was wakened by a telephone call from my chief, Minister Ivan Danielsson. "The Germans are taking over the city. Come to the legation at once!" What we had long expected now took place, and with lightning speed.

It was widely known that the Germans did not trust Hungary as an ally but feared that one sunny day the country would go looking for a way to "jump ship." The worse it went for Germany on the eastern front, the more the Hungarians wavered. The Germans had long mistrusted the Hungarian prime minister, Miklós Kállay. This was because he had declared publicly on several occasions that Hungary had been forced into the war against her will — needless to say, by the Germans.

Through his tightrope-walking policy, Kállay attempted, at one and the same time, to maintain correct relations with Germany, barring the way to further German demands and, behind the Germans' backs, to keep the door open for negotiations with the Allies, primarily the Americans and English.

The Hungarians anticipated the approach of Russian occupation with great anxiety and hoped to the very end that American and British troops would get there first. They even dreamed of being able to throw out the Germans, declare Hungary neutral, and thereby avoid occupation.

As a Hungarian patriot, Kállay had but one goal in mind: to keep the country intact as long as possible and to hold on to as much as possible of Hungary's resources, territorial gains, and social and political system.

The celebration of the national holiday on the fifteenth of March, 1944, was prepared for as usual. On the twentieth, there would be an even greater festivity because of the fiftieth anniversary of the death of Hungary's national hero, Lajos Kossuth. Parliament would meet on that day, and Kállay would make an important speech. The rumor was spread that he would then announce Hungary's surrender and the arrival of airborne British and American troops.

But fate ruled otherwise. Kállay would never again make a speech to the Hungarian nation.

The national holiday arrived, and the grand climax of the celebration was to be the premiere of a new patriotic opera.

Regent and "Administrator of the Realm" Miklós Horthy and his wife attended the event, along with a large flock of Hungarian celebrities. It was Mme Horthy's first public appearance since the tragic death of their eldest son Istvan, a fighter pilot on the eastern front whose plane crashed. I went with Danielsson to the opera. Between acts, one of the attachés from the German embassy confided to me that his chief, Minister von Jagow, had just given Horthy an important message from Hitler. Later we learned that the message was a summons to Hitler's headquarters, a prelude to the occupation.

Hungary was occupied, following the well-tested recipe, in a single morning. The border was overrun with swift motorized units, while parachute troops secured airports and other strategic points in the country.

In Budapest, all official buildings, radio and telegraph stations, were quickly invested by German forces. Kállay's regime was deposed and replaced by a government friendly to the Germans, with the Hungarian ambassador to Berlin, General Sztójay, as prime minister. His first act was to make sure that the Hungarian army, most of which happened to be at the Romanian border, offered no resistance. Named to head the most important ministry, that of the interior, were the former major of police Baky and the governor of Pest, Endre. Both were known for their fanatical anti-Semitism, and both belonged to the Hungarian Nazi Party, the so-called Arrow Cross Party.

Mass arrests of suspected persons were undertaken with the help of Germans who, in various guises, had resided in Budapest before the occupation, in collusion with the Arrow Cross.

The surprise was total, and Hungary capitulated without a struggle that Sunday. Everywhere there were traitors. Perhaps the most typical example was Horthy's own private detective, Peter Hain, who now revealed himself as the Germans' man and after a time was appointed head of the secret police. Through Hain, who had had Horthy's complete confidence, it had been possible for the Germans to follow the Hungarian leadership's moves day by day and thereby to decide the most auspicious moment for their own occupation.

The Germans did their work according to a carefully prepared plan. Their first act was to seize persons known as anti-Nazis: leading politicians, officials and scientists, industrialists and businessmen. The minister of the interior, Keresztes-Fischer, was arrested. Kállay escaped arrest by the skin of his teeth and succeeded in making his way to the Turkish legation. The Germans went from house to house, taking hostages, checking off a list. But this list was quite out-of-date. That is, it included the names of some persons who had already been dead several years, which shows that the German "master race" had long before thought about taking over Hungary.

Ullein-Reviczky, the chief of press relations in the foreign ministry whose dismissal Hitler had demanded, was no longer in Hungary. In the fall of 1943 he had been appointed minister to Sweden and was in Stockholm. There, at Kállay's bidding, he had followed up on the contacts initiated by the Hungarian journalist Andor Gellért and negotiated with the Allied missions on a separate peace for Hungary. However, these negotiations had not led anywhere, since those on the Allied side demanded unconditional surrender to all three allies. The Hungarians might consider capitulating to the British and American forces, but not to the Russian. Actually, all the Hungarian attempts to surrender unilaterally to the western Allies were doomed to fail from the start. It was not the Hungarians who got to choose their conquerors. What Kállay did not know, when he based his policy on Englishmen and Americans freeing his country, was that the three allies had decided in Tehran in November 1943 that eastern Europe would be the Red Army's territory of operations.

After the German occupation, Ullein-Reviczky resigned as official Hungarian representative in Sweden but was given the Swedish government's permission to remain as a private person with unimpaired diplomatic privileges. During the last years of the war, he worked vigorously for the creation of "Free Hungary" in other countries.

Hitler's hand-picked "Plenipotentiary of the Greater German Reich in Hungary," Dr. Veesenmayer, now moved into the German legation in Budapest. During months that would prove disastrous for Hungary, he would be the most powerful man in the country. The rumor of his cruel ravages in Yugoslavia, where he had earlier worked as Hitler's special emissary, had preceded his arrival.

A special unit headed by Adolf Eichmann was set up, its assignment the final solution of the Jewish problem in Hungary. Eichmann brought with him few but ruthless henchmen: Krumey, Hunsche, Dannecker, and Wisliceny. As additional help, Eichmann enlisted Otto Klages from the SS security service, who was assigned to conceal both the operation against the Jews and the goal of the deportations. The SS security service had long been in sharp opposition to the German armed forces' security organization under Admiral Canaris.

Thus the Hungarians, and especially Hungary's Jews, entertained no illusions about what was at hand.

We in Budapest became witnesses to something we had not thought possible in modern times: the beginning of a systematic extermination of an entire race. In various cases, desperate measures were taken to save Jews in our circle of acquaintances. One Swedish businessman, for example, declared himself ready to marry a Jewish woman who had been arrested. Someone tried to hide Jewish friends in his house or hire them pro forma as servants. But nothing helped. Those who were on the SS list when the Germans entered the city were hunted down and taken away, almost without exception.

The new Jewish ordinances, introduced in the spring of 1944, were a sinister omen of things to come. Step by step, the Jewish population of Hungary was robbed of all its civil rights. Jews were required to wear a yellow star on their breast, and failure to do this was punished with imprisonment or death.

I will never forget the day the ordinances went into effect. One could see Budapest's Jews, that is, every third and fourth person one met, marked with the yellow star as a sign that they belonged

to a despised pariah class that had been doomed to destruction.
Against the dark clothing most of them wore, the six-pointed stars
of a poisonous cadmium yellow seemed luminous. Some bore
them with the resignation of a thousand years of suffering, others
were too proud to show themselves outdoors with this mark on
their breasts. Some tried pathetically to hide their stars momen-
tarily with briefcase, package, or purse, the way one hides a
handicap. Of course this, too, was punishable. German soldiers
saw to it that the ordinances were obeyed, but the Hungarian
Arrow Crossmen, who willingly informed on those they knew,
were even more dangerous.

The property of the Jews was seized, and they were not allowed
to practice any profession. They were forbidden to visit restaurants or theaters. They could not sit on park benches or travel by
train or car. Later, they were concentrated in special camps or
buildings, marked with the yellow star, and were not allowed to
show themselves outdoors. Their suffering mounted in a daily
crescendo furioso. In the end, ghettos were set up, the last stage
before deportation to the gas chambers in Auschwitz or Birkenau.

During the spring and summer, practically all the Jews in the
countryside were gradually eliminated.[1] Eyewitnesses who visited the legation gave us terrifying descriptions of how various
parts of Hungary were "cleansed" of Jews. Then came the turn
of the Budapest suburbs. When I heard that a large number of
Jews from the suburbs — I was told around 15,000 — had been
taken to a brickyard outside the city, I went there to see it with
my own eyes.

Within the brickyard, thousands of Jews stood or lay tightly
packed together. They had been kept there for nearly a week
without food or drink and without shelter from weather or wind.
It was a terrible sight.

The area was fenced in and guarded by Hungarian gendarmes
equipped with submachine guns. The Hungarian gendarmes, as
distinguished from both the army (Honved) and the regular city
police, were known for their extreme anti-Semitism and their

---

[1]According to testimony revealed during the Eichmann trial in 1961, and confirmed in a conversation I had with the prosecutor of the trial during a visit to
Jerusalem some years ago, about 600,000 Jews were deported from Hungary
between May 15 and July 7. Most often, the frequency reached four trains a day
containing a total of 12,000 persons.

ruthlessness. They therefore became the Germans' willing tools
against the Jews.

Around this arena stood the inhabitants of the district, as silent,
frightened spectators. A German SS officer, a specialist in Jewish
matters and equipped with a long whip, served as "adviser."
While I stood there, a train with empty cattle cars was shifted onto
a spur that served the brickyard. The doors were opened and as
many Jews as possible — men, women, and children — were
forced into the cars with kicks and blows. Eighty or so persons
were stuffed into each car, which would normally accommodate
half as many. A mother tried to hide her child and prevent it being
taken along. A soldier saw this, grasped the child by the leg, and
flung it into the wagon.

As a kind of humanitarian gesture, a bucket of water was
placed in each wagon, then the doors were closed and nailed
shut with boards. The train is said to have steamed around Hungary for a week or so, during which time many died or went
insane. Those who survived continued their journey to the gas
chambers in Poland.

Because the deportations during May and June grew more and
more inclusive and proceeded in more and more inhuman forms,
on June 30, 1944, King Gustav V of Sweden sent the following
plea to Horthy:

Having received word of the extraordinarily harsh methods
your government has applied against the Jewish population of
Hungary, I permit myself to turn to Your Highness personally,
to beg in the name of humanity, that you take measures to save
those who still remain to be saved of the unfortunate people.
This plea has been evoked by my long-standing feelings of
friendship for your country and my sincere concern for Hungary's good name and reputation in the community of nations.

On July 12, the following reply came from Horthy to the Swedish king's plea:

I have received the telegraphic appeal sent me by your Majesty. With feelings of the deepest understanding, I ask Your
Majesty to be persuaded that I am doing everything that, in
the present situation, lies in my power to ensure that the

principles of humanity and justice are respected. I esteem to a high degree the feelings of friendship for my country that animate Your Majesty and I ask that Your Majesty preserve these feelings toward the Hungarian people in these times of severe trial.

It is said that after the Swedish king's intervention Horthy stepped in and succeeded, for the time being, in preventing further deportations from the capital. The Christian churches and the International Red Cross, too, protested, and the American secretary of state, Cordell Hull, sent through the Swiss legation a warning that, in the long run, Veesenmayer would go along with sparing the Jews of Budapest.

Now a difficult and trying time began for the legation and its members. We were besieged by Jews who suspected what was coming and pleaded for help. Supplicants jammed the reception room, and the line snaked all the way down to the street.

However, our ability to help all of them was limited. From a strict judicial standpoint, we could only intervene on behalf of Swedish citizens and citizens of those countries whose interests, because of the war, Sweden represented in Hungary. Yet something had to be done, and quickly. With every passing day the situation of the Jews worsened. In the beginning, we issued provisional Swedish passports — really a kind of travel document, which under certain circumstances could be given even to noncitizens of Sweden, that is, persons with especially close connections to Sweden through family relationships or business connections. The provisional passports at first gave no great protection, but the legation gradually succeeded through negotiations with the Hungarian authorities in winning the concession that the holders of such passes would be treated as Swedish citizens and be released from the requirement of wearing the yellow star. In this way, as a rule, they could avoid internment and deportation. To make sure that the value of these passports was not diminished by inflation, we were obliged to limit their number. This made it necessary to find other solutions, and our inventiveness was sorely tested. For a large number of the Jews, the application for Swedish citizenship had been made through Swedish relatives in Sweden, and for these Jews we issued certificates that read something like this:

It is hereby certified that the *Swedish* relatives, domiciled in Sweden, of John Doe, have on his behalf applied to the appropriate authorities for Swedish citizenship, upon which a decision may shortly be expected. For this reason, the Legation call upon all authorities, both civil and military, in any action concerning John Doe, to take due consideration of the matter cited above.

The certificate was decked out with the minister's signature, stamps, and seal, the whole panoply of authority.

However, a decree was soon issued to the effect that Hungary did not recognize any foreign citizenship that was conferred after the nineteenth day of March, 1944, that is to say, the day of the German invasion. We then began to fabricate similar certificates for those Jews who had been granted visas for travel to Sweden. The worth of these certificates, which became the forerunners of the so-called protective passports issued during Wallenberg's time, was perhaps at first sight debatable. Probably few who held these certificates allowed themselves any hope that these papers would help them escape from Hungary. However, the chief intention was simply to gain time. We were encouraged in our continued exertions by reports from those who got safely through raids and house searches by showing such documents to the usually uneducated and not overly intelligent Nazi functionaries.

In a rather short time, the legation issued no fewer than seven hundred provisional passports and certificates. The rumor of our work spread, and the host of supplicants swelled day by day.

The whole Swedish mission — the minister; the Swedish academic and Red Cross representative in Budapest, Waldemar Langlet; the consular officer, Dénes von Mezey; the typists, Birgit Brulin and Margareta Bauer; as well as I myself — worked day and night during these months. When it became clear that our strength would be insufficient for this new enterprise, the minister approached our Ministry of Foreign Affairs about reinforcing the legation staff.

Danielsson's request for more personnel happened to coincide with the negotiations that were going on in Stockholm between the foreign office and representatives of the American War Refugee Board, the World Jewish Congress, and the United

States' minister in Stockholm, Herschel Johnson, concerning the dispatch of a Swede to Hungary to head a rescue effort for the Jews.

The negotiations led to Raoul Wallenberg's receiving the assignment, and he was appointed secretary of legation in the Budapest mission.

Both my wife and I had known Raoul for a long time, and our friendship had been confirmed during the last few years when, as representative for a Swedish company — the Central European Trading Company — he had visited Hungary on various occasions.

I was convinced that no one was better qualified for the assignment than Wallenberg. He was a clever negotiator and organizer, unconventional, extraordinarily inventive, coolheaded, and something of a go-getter. Besides this, he was very good at languages and well grounded in Hungarian affairs. At heart, he was a great idealist and a warm human being.

Wallenberg arrived at the legation on the ninth of July, 1944, equipped rather oddly for a diplomat. He was carrying two knapsacks, a sleeping bag, a windbreaker, and a revolver. But this equipment would be put to good use in the months ahead. "The revolver is just to give me courage," he said to me in his typically joking way. "I hope I'll never have to use it. But now I'm in a hurry to get to work. I've read your reports, but could you bring me up-to-date?"

I related that the deportations from the countryside had been brought to an end and that most of Budapest's Jews had not yet been affected. The deportation of these Jews seemed to have been postponed, in accordance with the appeal by the Swedish king. "But everything depends on what the Germans have in mind," I added. "It's hardly believable that they will go along with sparing the Jews of the capital for good."

"What documents have you issued the Jews?" Wallenberg asked.

I showed him the provisional passports, the visa certificates, and the Red Cross protection letter. Wallenberg looked at the documents and said, after a pause: "I think I've got an idea for a new and maybe more effective document."

In this way, the idea of the so-called protective passports was born at our first meeting. These were the identification papers in

blue and yellow with the three-crowns emblem that would ultimately save tens of thousands of Jews.

As soon as he arrived, Wallenberg reorganized the rescue
operation, under the direction of the chief of the mission. This
operation came to be financed mainly by the War Refugee Board
in Washington, which, through the American legation in Stockholm, placed substantial sums at Wallenberg's disposal. But large
sums also flowed in from voluntary donations inside Hungary.

A special department was created, with Wallenberg as its head
and with mostly volunteer Jewish manpower as its personnel. By
this means, the other members of the mission could gain some
badly needed relief from such matters. For my own part, I could
now take up some long-neglected duties, such as preparing plans
for the possible evacuation of our mission from Budapest to the
countryside, putting the air-raid shelter in order, storing supplies,
and so on.

Wallenberg succeeded in gaining the agreement of the Hungarian authorities that the Jews on his staff should be freed from
wearing the yellow star, and this gave them greater protection
and freedom of movement. In his department, the protective
passports mentioned earlier were issued. They were furnished
with the minister's signature and explained straightforwardly that
the holder and his property were under the protection of the
Swedish legation until such time as his emigration to Sweden
could be arranged. That is, the Swedish government had declared
itself willing to accept all those Jews who were provided with
protective passports. But all attempts to transport these Jews to
Sweden ran aground, in the end, on the impossibility of obtaining
permission for passage through Germany.

The Hungarian government promised that holders of our protective passports would not be deported. They were allowed to
live in certain buildings on the Pest side of the Danube river
rented by the legation, the so-called "Swedish houses," while
awaiting their "emigration" to Sweden. The number of protective
passports approved by the Hungarian authorities rose to five
thousand. Later on, more and more Jews were spirited into these
buildings in secrecy, without the authorities' permission. Soon
the total number of Jews under Swedish protection rose to more
than twice the number authorized, or from 15,000 to 20,000.

In consultation with Wallenberg's department, the authorities arranged for a further number of dwellings to be placed at the disposal of Jews holding documents issued by the other foreign missions. Under Swedish leadership, the provision of the "foreign houses" with food was organized, and special hospitals were set up. After the war was over, it was shown that the total number of Jews who were thus rescued directly by the foreign legations and the International Red Cross amounted to nearly 50,000, of which almost half were saved by Swedish efforts, chiefly Wallenberg's.

During the summer, trying to get the deportations going again, the head of the Hungarian gendarmes, Lt. Col. Ferenczy, together with Baky and Endre, planned a coup to depose Horthy. The plans were supported by Eichmann, who had found the regent's presence altogether too much of hindrance.

On the pretext that they had to keep order in the capital, large forces of gendarmes concentrated in Budapest early in July, intending to overthrow Horthy. However, the regent had received word of this plan. He had time to call in several armored and infantry units, and with their help, he ordered the gendarmes to disperse.

Thereafter, the power wielded by Baky and Endre was considerably curtailed. Horthy's firmness was praised, and Budapest's Jews felt they might look forward to better days.

At the end of 1944, Romania surrendered, and it was only a question of time before the Russians would pour across Hungary's borders. Horthy, who had for some time contemplated deposing Sztójay, now seized the chance and replaced his government with a military government under General Lakatos. The Germans were presented with a fait accompli, and in this militarily critical situation they held back. Horthy apparently didn't intend to break with the Germans, anyway. Even if putting in a new government seemed to be part of his preparations for Hungarian capitulation, Horthy was still unwilling to open the borders to the Soviet armies. Evidently he still hoped to be able to stop the Russians till the western Allies could occupy Hungary.

After the Sztójay government was deposed, the situation of the Jews improved. The Germans agreed to let the Hungarians handle the Jewish question themselves. The bloodhounds Endre and Baky were fired, and Eichmann left Hungary.

The deportations stopped, and the Jews were gradually to be released from the internment camps. In Wallenberg's department, they could draw breath, and Wallenberg himself expected that the department could soon be shut down. He planned to return to Sweden, having completed his assignment.

But the Jews of Budapest had only gained a momentary reprieve, and instead of closing down, Wallenberg and his department would now face new and considerably more difficult problems.

On October 15, 1944, the Arrow Crossmen, with German help, staged a coup and deposed the Lakatos government. It was the same day the legation had arranged for the last of the Swedish women and children in Hungary to travel home to Sweden. Horthy gave in to superior force. He was forced to resign and to name Arrow Cross leader Ferenc Szálasi the new head of government, in return for the promise of asylum for himself and his family in Germany, as well as reunion there with his son, Miklós. The family was taken away and subsequently held prisoner in Hirschberg castle in Bayern, where they were freed by American troops at the war's end. Concerning young Miklós, however, the Germans did not keep their promise. When his wounds healed, he was put in concentration camps, first in Mauthausen and then in Dachau, where the Americans found him.

The Arrow Crossmen now occupied all public buildings, and Horthy's followers offered only feeble resistance. Only his elite guard took up the struggle, at the castle. During the night, the city echoed with shots as the Hungarian guards fought against superior forces. On the morning of October 11, all resistance was crushed.

Eichmann and his henchmen returned, and for Wallenberg a hectic and dangerous period now began. But he never gave up, no matter how hopeless things looked.

I remember the day he hopped on a bicycle and traveled to his various offices to encourage and hearten his Jewish colleagues, a trip he undertook at great personal risk.

Soon the persecution of the Jews reached a pitch that defies description. At night, we could hear the shots of the Arrow Crossmen's submachine guns when Jews, after being robbed of everything including their clothes, were shot down naked and thrown into the Danube.

It was at this point that the so-called international ghetto came into being, as decided by the Szálasi government. Negotiations for this had already begun under the previous government by the neutral legations, negotiations in which Wallenberg played a leading role. The buildings comprising the ghetto were furnished with Jewish stars and were under the protection of the legations. Jews who had protective passports lived there. Thus the Swedish houses mentioned earlier became part of this ghetto, and some thirty buildings now received Swedish protection.

Meanwhile, two Russian armies were rapidly approaching, one from the south under Marshal Tolbukhin, and one from the east under Marshal Malinovsky. Soon only the way to the west was open from Budapest. The roads to Poland were blocked, and only Austria remained possible as a destination for the continued deportation of Jews. When the railroad was taken over for military transport and the Nazis wanted to liquidate as many Jews as possible in the time remaining, they switched to a method that broke all previous records for cruelty and mercilessness.

Thousands of people were seized where they walked, where they stood. Women in high-heeled shoes and men without overcoats were forced to walk 125 miles to Hegyeshalom, at the Hungarian-Austrian border. That is how they solved the difficult transportation problem! It took over a week to walk that distance in the winter cold and snow, without food and without the possibility of resting under shelter. Unfortunately, we had no opportunity to intervene and save these people. Only if by chance one of those deported held a Swedish protective passport was there any prospect of getting him or her conveyed back to Budapest.

On one of the first days of December 1944, Wallenberg and I set out by car along the route the Jews were being marched. We passed those masses of unfortunates, more dead than alive. Ashen-faced, they staggered forward under prodding and blows from the soldiers' rifle butts. The road was edged with bodies. We had the car full of food, which we succeeded in passing out despite such help being prohibited, but it did not go very far. At Hegyeshalom we saw how those who arrived were turned over to an SS unit under Eichmann, who counted them like cattle. "Four hundred eighty-nine — check!" [Vierhundert-neunundachtzig — stimmt gut!] The Hungarian officer received a receipt that said everything was in proper order.

Before the transfer took place, we succeeded in rescuing about a hundred Jews. Some of them had the Swedish protective passport. Others we got released through sheer bluff. Wallenberg would not back down. He made repeated trips, succeeding in much the same way in bringing back still more to Budapest.

In collaboration with the International Red Cross, truck convoys were organized to pass out food to the deported. Further, at Wallenberg's initiative, checkpoints were set up at the roads exiting Budapest and at the border station to hinder the deportation of Jews holding the protective passport. In this way, an estimated 1,500 Jews were saved and returned to Budapest.

Now the legation staff found it harder and harder to continue its activities. Every day armed Arrow Crossmen burst into places that were under the legation's protection, plundering food and trying to carry off the personnel. We remained on full alert day and night, often having to rush out en masse to try and avert an attack of the Arrow Crossmen. Bluff and threats were good ways of driving them off.

The legation's continuing rescue operation became a race against time. Would we be able to hold out until the Russians came? It was a question we often asked ourselves. After long and trying negotiations with the Arrow Cross leadership, in which Wallenberg most often played the decisive role, we achieved a modus vivendi according to which those on the Hungarian side promised to respect our five thousand Swedish protective passports. The bait we held out was the prospect of Swedish recognition for the Nazi regime in Hungary through accepting a Nazi representative in Stockholm. True, Minister Danielsson had already received a message from the foreign office saying that the Swedish government obviously had no intention of recognizing the Szálasi regime, but we felt that for the sake of the Jews we should let the Arrow Crossmen keep alive their earlier illusions. The foreign minister, the fanatical and half-mad Baron Kemény, rubbed his hands together in glee at the thought that soon he would be able to appoint himself the Arrow Cross's first emissary to Stockholm. Meanwhile, the Russians were swiftly approaching the city. Kemény began to get upset over not getting the promised message about the question of recognition. Danielsson attempted to gain time through various declarations that the decision could be expected any day now, etc., but Kemény was close to losing his patience.

Thus our relations with the Hungarian government became

more strained every day. The mission's refusal to come along with the Hungarian foreign ministry staff to their evacuation refuge, Szombathely, in western Hungary, was regarded as an unfriendly act. On several occasions, critical statements about the legation and its staff came from the government. At the same time, a rumor began to go around Budapest that the Arrow Crossmen intended to stage a riot at the neutral legations to pillage and search for Jews.

Since the Russian armies were getting nearer every day, Danielsson decided, with our unanimous support, that the legation ought to avoid an open break with the Hungarian government just now, and consequently we should remain in Budapest. Instructions had been received from the Swedish foreign office in mid-December to the effect that the minister could decide whether the mission or some part of it should travel home or remain. We did not hesitate to stay.

Our greatest worry was Wallenberg's safety. The Arrow Crossmen hated him openly and intensely. He learned several times that they intended to murder him. In conversation with one of the staff of the Swedish Red Cross, Eichmann communicated his intention to have the "Jew-dog" Wallenberg shot. Eichmann's statement *could* be simply an empty threat, meant to put a scare into the legation staff, but it was not something to leave unchallenged.

Thus we sent a telegram home to the foreign office, asking that the legation in Berlin be instructed to take up the matter with the Germans, pointing out at the same time that theirs was the blame for the increased outrages against the Jews and against Wallenberg's Jewish staff. From an SS source we had learned that Heinrich Himmler was against these excesses and set a great deal of store by Swedish-German relations.

Consequently, the Berlin legation complained of the threat against Wallenberg and asked that the SS command in Budapest be ordered to respect mission members and other employees.

Veesenmayer's reply to the reprimand from Berlin seems to have been that Eichmann had good reason to criticize the Swedish legation's activities on the Jews' behalf, and especially those of Wallenberg, who behaved in a "far too unconventional [!] and unacceptable way." Eichmann may well have expressed the threat referred to, Veesenmayer continued, and in such a case it should not be taken literally, but more as a warning for the future.

By this point, the Russian armies had reached the outskirts of Budapest from two directions. The only connection still remaining open was the highway to Vienna, but it was now being raked with almost uninterrupted Russian artillery fire.

Feverish attempts were made to defend the city. Each one of the bridges was mined, strategic points were fortified, and tank traps and barbed-wire barriers were built in the central parts of the city. There were many indications that the Germans intended to evacuate at the last minute and turn the city's defenses over to the Hungarian troops. These were not considered to be worth much in combat, so there was hope that the city might surrender without a struggle. However, we expected there to be a transition period of a few days between the evacuation of the German troops and the entry of the Russians into the city, a period when the Nazi rabble would have a free hand! So with Danielsson's approval, I asked the Hungarian resistance movement — with whom the legation had been in touch on previous occasions — about helping us, should the legation and its offices be subjected to the rabble's violence. They promised to put a force at our disposal. I felt that we could now face the future with something like assurance. We also obtained our own weapons, buying two Russian-made submachine guns on the black market. One of the members of the resistance and I tried the weapons out on his father's hunting preserve early one morning, with the panicked game leaping away in all directions.

The members of our mission held a council of war and decided first of all to try and retrieve the legation building from the Arrow Crossmen.

Wallenberg was the ingenious one. Through his good connections in the Ministry of the Interior, he succeeded in getting one of the higher officials to put ten gendarmes at our disposal, and they were given orders to take over the guarding of the legation. While we remained discreetly in the background, the gendarmes arrived and announced to the disappointed Arrow Crossmen that the government had reassigned them. The Arrow Crossmen left, and the gendarmes installed themselves as legation guards.

We realized that the legation could no longer continue its earlier activities, partly because the Arrow Crossmen were after us, and partly because heavy bombardment of the city had begun both from the air and from Russian artillery that had now surrounded the city. So it was necessary to go underground, in both senses.

In this connection, it did not seem advisable for all of us to stay in the same place. We judged the Swiss legation the safest refuge, since it was still respected by the Arrow Crossmen. It lay on Castle Hill and had a good air-raid shelter. The minister, Ekmark, and the women settled there. I stayed in my apartment on Uri Street not far away, to be near the minister and to be able, when necessary, to get in touch with the German and Hungarian military leadership, who now kept to that part of the city. Wallenberg chose to stay on the Pest side, where his department had most of its offices.

The last time I saw Wallenberg was the tenth of January, 1945. He paid me a brief visit, and I remember how I pleaded with him to suspend his operation and stay with us on the Buda side. The Arrow Crossmen were especially on the lookout for him, and he ran great risks by continuing his aid work. But Wallenberg would not listen to me.

While the bombs rained down around us, we sallied out to visit the headquarters of the German SS. There, among other matters, I was going to try and work out some sort of protection for members of the mission. Again and again we had to hit the brakes of the car, for the streets were blocked by dead bodies, horses, toppled trees, and shattered buildings. But Wallenberg never hesitated at the danger. I asked him if he were not frightened. "Of course it gets a little scary, sometimes," he said, "but for me there's no choice."

During our visit to the SS general, Wallenberg was trying, among other things, to obtain guarantees that the Jews in the Swedish houses would not be liquidated at the last minute. As usual, Wallenberg stated his business skillfully and with intelligence. The SS general listened skeptically but found it hard to conceal that he was at the same time impressed by Wallenberg.

Wallenberg's words, the last time we saw each other, were typical of the seriousness with which he took his assignment. "I'd never be able to go back to Stockholm without knowing that I'd done all a man could do to save as many Jews as possible." And he did all that a man could, to the very last. He was tireless in his efforts to save Jews from deportation. Many are the stories of how he could pop up on the most unexpected occasions and succeed in preventing the removal of Jews with protective passports, or how he could stop the Arrow Crossmen from forcing their way into the Swedish houses. He swamped the Arrow Cross authorities with written petitions for relief for his charges. It was often he who was the prime mover in the neutral legations' protests, through joint memorandums to the Arrow Cross regime, against the inhuman treatment of the Jews.

Even if the mass deportations to Auschwitz by rail had stopped, the Germans made sporadic attempts to ship groups of Jews off by train.

Wallenberg always employed lookouts to warn him about a train's departure. On one occasion, he arrived at the station with several long lists of the holders of protective passports and demanded in an authoritative tone to check whether any such persons had by mistake been taken aboard. The Germans were taken by surprise, and right under their noses, Wallenberg pulled out a large number of Jews. Many of them had no passport at all, only various papers in the Hungarian language — drivers licenses, vaccination records, or tax receipts — that the Germans did not understand. The bluff succeeded.

Wallenberg sometimes arranged for special expeditions in which Jews who looked Aryan dressed in Arrow Cross uniforms, raided camps and prisons, and on several occasions succeeded in freeing a large number of other Jews on the pretext that they were being taken away to deportation.

How many people did Wallenberg save? To that question, a clear-cut answer can hardly be given.

I witnessed his stopping the deportation of a total of several thousand Jews at train stations, from the Swedish houses, and during the death march to the Austrian border.

It was through these acts that the rumor was spread of his almost superhuman ability, in seemingly hopeless situations, to snatch victims from the Nazi executioners. He became the Budapest Jews' hope of rescue from the final liquidation.

Yet it was not through the kind of personal intervention just described that he made his greatest contribution. It was as a negotiator that he achieved his greatest results. He was the driving force behind the agreements with the Arrow Cross regime that compelled them to respect not only the five thousand Swedish protective passports but also corresponding documents of the other neutral legations.

Wallenberg was always aware that saving as *many* people as possible was what mattered. "You yourself know," he remarked on one occasion, "how we're besieged every day by people who plead for a job at the legation, for asylum, or for a protective passport for themselves and their relations. When they can't come themselves, they send their Aryan friends to ask me for help. All of them want to meet me personally. I've got to be firm. Time doesn't allow me to devote myself to single cases when it's a question of life or death for Budapest's entire Jewish population."

Wallenberg held to this line rigorously.

To accomplish his ends, he applied every means he had. He bribed Arrow Cross officials. Sometimes he threatened execution. Other times he promised pardon after the arrival of the Russians. He used Foreign Minister Kemény's wife (who was of Jewish descent and greatly admired him) to influence her husband to approve the protective passports and so on.

As I mentioned earlier, after the war had ended, it was established that 50,000 Jews who lived in the foreign houses, the international ghetto, had survived. They were generally equipped with protective passports or similar documents issued by the neutral legations and the International Red Cross. Of these, Wallenberg had protected nearly half, from 20,000 to 25,000.

But Wallenberg's contribution extended even further. Besides his efforts for the international ghetto, toward the end he also worked to protect the inhabitants of Budapest's general or so-called sealed ghetto, where about 70,000 had been forced together. He could sometimes arrange for food deliveries to the starving, and he managed on several occasions to forestall the Arrow Crossmen's rampages in the ghetto.

But the Arrow Crossmen had, in their fanatical hatred of the Jews, decided to commit mass murder in the ghetto at the last minute. When Wallenberg got wind of this, he demanded that the German commander, General Schmidthuber, prevent the killing. Otherwise, Wallenberg would make sure that Schmidthuber would swing on the gallows when the Russians came.

Schmidthuber was shaken by Wallenberg's words and stopped the planned operation against the ghetto.

Thus Wallenberg contributed to saving still another 70,000 lives.

Jenö Lévai, in his book *Raoul Wallenberg — Hero of Budapest [1948]*, praises Wallenberg's efforts for the Jews in the sealed ghetto and concludes: "Wallenberg was the 'world's observing eye,' the one who continually called the criminals to account. That is the great importance of Wallenberg's struggle in Budapest."

Per Anger

[Translated from the Swedish by David Mel Paul and Margerta Paul]

[Additional note by the Honorable Per Anger to the dispatches in this volume]

These dispatches from Raoul Wallenberg to the minister for foreign affairs in Stockholm were sent by diplomatic mail from the Swedish legation in Budapest, where I was serving as a diplomat, between July and December 1944. They illustrate Wallenberg's efficiency in his work to save lives, his inventiveness, and his organizational skills.

Wallenberg arrived in Budapest on July 9, 1944, and as early as the 18th of the same month the first dispatch, accurately describing the desperate situation of the Hungarian Jews, was sent to Sweden.

Wallenberg writes in a matter-of-fact style, but between the lines you feel his compassion for and engagement in the fate of these people. These dispatches and the excerpt from my book, *With Raoul Wallenberg in Budapest,* will, I trust, help complete the picture of a man who became one of the greatest humanitarians in modern times.

Per Anger

June 19, 1944
Under-Secretary of State for Foreign Affairs Boheman
Stockholm

In reference to our private conversation, permit me to thank
you for the confidence you have shown in me.

I have presented the matter we discussed to the board of
directors of my company, who have given their consent to my
placing myself at the disposal of the Ministry for Foreign Affairs.

I have received similar approval from the Pacific Trading
Company AB and from Jacob Wallenberg, and have notified
both companies that I will not be available to conduct any
business during the period in question.

If necessary, I would be willing to relinquish my position on
the board of directors for the duration.

As soon as a final decision has been reached, I would be
grateful to hear from you, so that I may take the necessary steps
with regard to my business activities.

Sincerely yours,

---

*[Telegram from the Swedish Ministry for Foreign Affairs to the
Swedish embassy, Budapest, dated June 21, 1944]*

In view of interest here desirable Jewish question followed
utmost attention continuous special coverage including
suggestions appropriate realizable humanitarian efforts and
required relief efforts after war. Great interest in issue American
embassy here. Realizing present staff insufficient special task
consideration given seconding Raoul Wallenberg to legation
well suited good connections knowledge of Hungary. Any
objections please wire by return.

Cabinet

RW in the Swedish Home Guard, 1940. *(Courtesy of Birgitte Wallenberg)*

Passport photo, June 1944. *(Courtesy of the Raoul Wallenberg Foundation, Stockholm)*

SCHUTZ-PASS

Nr. 1/55

Name: Ladislaus Gold
Név:

Wohnort: Budapest
Lakás:

Geburtsdatum: 28. August 1910.
Születési ideje:

Geburtsort: Budapest
Születési helye:

Körperlänge: 163 cm.
Magasság:

Haarfarbe: braun Augenfarbe: blau
Hajszín: Szemszín:

Unterschrift:
Aláírás:

SCHWEDEN   SVÉDORSZÁG

Die Kgl. Schwedische Gesandtschaft in Budapest bestätigt, dass der Obengenannte im Rahmen der — von dem Kgl. Schwedischen Aussenministerium autorisierten — Repatriierung nach Schweden reisen wird. Der Betreffende ist auch in einen Kollektivpass eingetragen.

Bis Abreise steht der Obengenannte und seine Wohnung unter dem Schutz der Kgl. Schwedischen Gesandtschaft in Budapest.

Gültigkeit: erlischt 14 Tage nach Einreise nach Schweden.

A budapesti Svéd Kir. Követség igazolja, hogy fentnevezett — a Svéd Kir. Külügyminisztérium által jóváhagyott — repatriálás keretében Svédországba utazik.

Nevezett a kollektiv útlevélben is szerepel.

Elutazásáig fentnevezett és lakása a budapesti Svéd Kir. Követség oltalma alatt áll.

Érvényét veszti a Svédországba való megérkezéstől számított tizennegyedik napon.

Reiseberechtigung nur gemeinsam mit dem Kollektivpass. Einreisevisum wird nur in dem Kollektivpass eingetragen.

Budapest, den   28. September 1944

KÖNIGLICH SCHWEDISCHE GESANDTSCHAFT
SVÉD KIRÁLYI KÖVETSÉG

Kgl. Schwedischer Gesandter.

Schutzpass issued in September 1944, and signed by Minister Ivan Danielsson. Text in German and Hungarian reads as follows: "The Royal Swedish Legation in Budapest certifies that the above-signed will be traveling to Sweden with the Royal Swedish Foreign Ministry's authorization. His name has also been registered on the Collective Passport. Until departure, he and his living quarters fall under the protection of the Royal Swedish Legation in Budapest."
(Courtesy of The Raoul Wallenberg Committee of the United States)

V e r z e i c h n i s

der Angestellten (und deren Angehörigen mit Ausnahme der
Ehefrauen, Ehemsenner und Kinder) die in der Üllői Strasse
arbeiten und wohnen.

Name des Angestell-ten:	Familienmit-glieder:	Name des Angestell-ten:	Familienmit-glieder:
Bach Marianne	Bach Jenő	Glück Béla	
	Bach Jenőné		
		Glück Lajos	
Balabán Éva Mária	Balabán György		
	Balabán Györgyné	Glücksthal Pál	
Bartha László	Bartha József	Glücksthal Pálné	
	dr.Bartha Ferencz		
		dr.Gonda Henrik	
Bartha Lászlóné			
		dr.Gráf Tibor	Gráf Ignácz
Bárd Lipót			Gráf I.-né
Bihari Nándor		Gráner Ignácz	
...ros Lilla	boros Sámuel	Gráner Ignáczné	
	boros Sámuelné		
	boros Katalin	Hauser Lipót	ö.Nenény F.-né
	Kelemen Ferencné		
	Feld Kálmán	Havas Dezső	
		Havas Dezsőné	
Erschfeld Ervinné	Fehér Andor	Havas Livia	
	Fehér Andorné		
		dr.Havas Károly	
Buchbinder Endre	Buchbinder Henrik	Fejér Ernő	
	Buchbinder Henrikné		
Buchbinder Endréné	özv.Frank Lajosné	Herskovits Rozália	
	Frank Ilona		
		Horvát István	
Czeisler György			
...DénesIstvánné		dr.Horváth István né	
Ernster Lászlóné		Jakobovits Jenő	dr.Balog Mária
...nster László		Jánosi Engel Marianne	
dr. Falvi János	dr.Fleischmann L.	Kadelburger Gusztáv	
	Dr.Fleischmann L.-né	Kelecsényi Bdek	
Fenyő Béla	Fenyő Andrásné	Kelemen László	ö.Kelemen Gy.-n
dr.Fleischmann Ottó			dr.Kardos Lajo:
			dr.Kardos L.-né
Forgács Gábor		dr. Kendo Béla	
Forgács Pál			
Forgács Vilmos	Feitl Ignácz	Kenedi Andor	
	Braun Sándor		
	Braun Sándorné	Kertes Vilmos	Bandel Hilda
		Kláber László	
dr. Gergely Éva			
		Kláber Lászlóné	
Gergely Vincze			

Partial list of Jewish employees working for Wallenberg at the
Swedish legation in Budapest. Employees were exempt from wear-
ing the Star of David and hence not subject to laws governing Jews.
At one point their number reached nearly 400. (*Courtesy of The Raoul
Wallenberg Committee of the United States*)

Deportation lines of Hungarian Jews being sent to the concentration
camps, 1944. This and other photos of Hungarian Jews were taken by
RW's photographer and chauffeur, Thomas Veres, who concealed his
camera beneath a scarf. *(Photograph by Thomas Veres. Used by permission)*

OPPOSITE RW at his desk with members of his staff, November 1944.
(Photograph by Thomas Veres. Used by permission)

RW at his desk at the Swedish legation. The date the photo was taken, November 26, 1944, is indicated by the calendar, which served to conceal a wall safe. This was among the last photos taken of RW. *(Photograph by Thomas Veres. Used by permission)*

Maj and Fredrik von Dardel, RW's mother and stepfather, in
Stockholm, 1976. (Courtesy of Birgitte Wallenberg)

Portrait of RW done in Budapest in 1944, currently on display at the
United States Holocaust Memorial Museum in Washington, D.C.
(Courtesy of the Raoul Wallenberg Foundation, Stockholm)

Memorandum Concerning the Persecution of Jews in Hungary

Enclosed please find a summary of the current situation compiled by a well-informed source. For reasons of safety, the identity of our informant will not be revealed until later. I further enclose Report No. 2 from a source already used in the past. The contents of both appendixes confirm information received from other sources.

Where any of the information presented below has been obtained from an individual, the name of the informant will appear in a subsequent dispatch. The numerals indicated in the margin below will serve as future identification.

Conditions in Collection Centers

The parents of one of my informants were sent away in the direction of Poland on July 1. For some reason, the train was returned to the infamous camp at Békásmegyer — as the result, it was thought, of Archbishop Serédi's intervention at the time. My informant received a message smuggled from his parents, which indicated that they were lacking food and water. He then went there and managed to receive permission, through bribes, to hand over a parcel with food and water. According to his statement, his parents and the other prisoners were then half-dead. They were later taken to Poland.

Another informant visited the departure point at Kassa on May 25 and was shown around by the person in charge, a Baron Fiedler, to whom he had been introduced by a friend that very same day. According to Baron Fiedler, the camp, which covered an area of about 1.5 acres, had originally housed 16,000–17,000 individuals. The camp had been filled on or around May 12. On May 15, the inmates were taken to the newly created ghetto in Kassa. After three days, they were returned to the camp, and the deportations began sometime around May 19. When my informant visited the camp, about 8,000 persons in weakened condition remained. The

temperature was about 50 degrees Fahrenheit and the weather
rainy and windy. The prisoners were housed beneath narrow
covers held up by wooden supports. As their names were
called, they were loaded aboard the trains following an
extremely invasive body search by the SS, for which both men
and women were forced to disrobe. One woman tried
surreptitiously to hide her infant under the railroad car,
whereupon the child was seized by the leg and hurled
headlong into the car. The car was packed so full that the
passengers were forced to stand.

According to my informant, Baron Fiedler reported that
following an escape by several Jews he had ordered their
relatives hung by their feet and beaten around the crotch as a
warning to those following behind.

The Deportations
    A civil servant in a position to provide an overall view of the
transports describes them as horrible and unspeakably brutal.
Food often consists of one loaf of bread per car, sometimes of a
pound of bread and 8 ounces of marmalade. One bucket of
water is allotted to each car. The journey generally takes five
days. There are many deaths.

Treatment in Auschwitz, Birkenau, and Waldsee
    The enclosed reports, which state that everybody, with the
exception of able-bodied men and young women, has been put
to death, is confirmed by the fact that postcards have been
received here from these two categories of deportees, but none
from older people. A journalist assigned to the Hungarian air
force is alleged to have returned recently from the Katowice
area with information confirming this. I have, however, not yet
managed to speak to him.

The Reaction of the Hungarians
    Most people you speak to are ashamed of what is happening
and maintain that these brutalities are not being committed by
Hungarians but only by Germans. However this is not true.
Hungarian anti-Semitism is deeply rooted. Positive intervention
is usually limited to helping friends by providing food and
hiding places. Many deplore the persecution of the Jews,

pointing out that it is costing the Hungarians sympathy abroad, and that they risk being treated more harshly than Romania in the event of peace, since Romania's policy toward its Jewish population is known to have become more lenient of late. It would appear, however, that this awareness is limited to the leaders of industry. There is a certain amount of speculation regarding the punishment awaiting those who have taken an active part in these criminal actions.

I might mention, in this connection, that the presence of Jews is sometimes thought to constitute protection against bombing raids. Those who hold this view appear to believe that the scattering of the Jews into about 2,600 Jewish houses all over Budapest, instead of concentrating them in ghettos, is a deliberate act, and that this is also the reason why the Jewish workforce has been forbidden to seek shelter during air raids.

Escape Possibilities

The need for ration cards, baptismal certificates, identity papers; the requirement to wear the Star of David; the curfew for Jews during most of the day; the strict control of the streets at night; the lack of cash among Jews; the lukewarm sympathy of the Christian population; and the open and easily surveyable topography of the countryside all combine to make it difficult for the Jews to elude their fate by escaping.

Somewhere in the vicinity of 20,000 to 50,000 Jews are thought to have been hidden in Budapest by Christian friends. Of those who remain in the Jewish houses, it is likely that most are children, women, and old people. The men have been conscripted for work. During the week ending on July 7, a large number of baptisms were performed by Catholic priests. Greater restrictiveness now prevails, however, and three months' instruction is now required for baptism. Many priests have been arrested. By being baptized, Jews hope to take advantage of the rumored new regulations exempting those baptized from having to wear the Star of David. The number of baptized Jews in Hungary is reported not to exceed 70,000.

Some slight possibility evidently exists of acquiring Aryan papers belonging to people who have either been bombed out or killed. These command a very high price. I do not know of any cases of false identity papers, however, and the printing establishments are under such strict control that it is, at this point, virtually impossible to escape by this method.

The Jews of Budapest are completely apathetic and do virtually nothing to save themselves.

The Social Democratic Party is in theory pro-Jewish, but is virtually paralyzed and in all likelihood prevented from helping.

I am not familiar with the position and activities of the Communist Party.

Bribes and Corruption

A train with 1,200 Jews destined for Spain en route to Palestine departed quite some time ago, but is presently being held in Hanover. An agreement was allegedly reached between the Jewish Council and the Gestapo, unbeknownst to the Hungarian government, which was told by the Gestapo that the Jews in question would be deported as usual, i.e., put to death. The price paid supposedly amounted to F 30,000 per person, although I have not been able to verify this. Several individual escapes are alleged to have been effected by the Gestapo as a result of blackmail, but rumor has it that the victims were eventually killed in every instance.

I am not aware of a single case in which someone has managed to escape from a detention camp, except for the one mentioned in a previous report. The embassy has also received an anonymous report of an alleged escape from the camp at Békásmegyer. Bribes are apparently much less frequent than one might assume, partly because the entire rounding-up and deportation process is so mechanized, swift, and impersonal that outsiders wishing to intervene have not been able to get in touch with the camp commander in question.

Rescue of the Owners of the Manfred Weiss Concern

The entire family — some thirty-nine persons — was permitted to leave Hungary, staying for a month in Purkersdorf near Vienna, and then continuing on to Lisbon, where their arrival has been confirmed. President Chorin is presently in London, where he is engaged in anti-Hungarian propaganda, according to SS circles here. According to the agreement, Baron Alfons Weiss, Director Frans Mautner, and Baron Georg

Kornfeld — the latter voluntarily joined by his wife and son — are being held hostage in Germany, the former in Gmunden and the latter two in Vienna. They are being treated well, and each gentleman is supposedly allowed to go abroad for up to two weeks, one at a time. The Weiss Concern has been leased to a Hungarian company, which has been handed over to the Gestapo for a period of twenty-five years, against advance payment of RM 1,000,000 and $400,000. The company has thus been turned over to the Gestapo-Waffen SS Group and not to the Göringwerke.

Budapest, July 18, 1944

Memorandum Concerning the Treatment of Jews in Hungary

Deportations on a large scale have not resumed since the memorandum of July 18. Smaller contingents, some in third-class carriages, however, have reportedly crossed the border at Kassa after July 10, the date large-scale deportations ceased. In the meantime, the camp at Sarvar has been emptied and the prisoners sent across the border. Every effort is apparently being made to preserve secrecy: the Jews are for instance being transported with the Star of David removed — as for instance from the Ostbahnhof at 8:50 P.M. on July 26. On July 19, 1,650 persons, including Aryans — mainly intellectuals — were transported from Kistarcsa via Hegyeshalom to Germany.

Reliable eyewitnesses report that the houses in the city listed below were surrounded on the 20th, 24th, and 25th of this month, and that the inhabitants of all ages were taken away, some to forced labor service in the outskirts of the city. Treatment in the forced labor service is generally good. The organization now comes under General Lazar, who is considered humane. Actions like this continue on a daily basis.

The General Mood

Opposition among the general population has clearly been mounting during this period, both with regard to the Jewish question and other issues. This has not resulted in any kind of action, however.

The Position of the Head of State on the Jewish Question

His position is illustrated by the very real fact that the deportations were canceled per his order, but also by a number of smaller interventions. Among them, two verified instances of trains loaded with prisoners being ordered to turn back just before reaching the border.

That Horthy's power is a factor to be reckoned with is shown by the fact that while the above-mentioned trainload of intellectuals was sent across the border, the entire Jewish Council was detained by the Gestapo, so that they would not be able to report the matter to the head of state, who was judged to have enough power to order the train to turn back.

It has now been confirmed that the telegram from the king to the head of state was directly responsible for stopping the deportations.

Treatment in the Carriages

An extremely reliable eyewitness account now exists of the conditions that prevail during the train journey to the point of destination. My witness, an internationally famous scientist, was loaded into the carriage with blows and physical violence. He still displays an open wound on his cheek. The passengers were allowed to keep food and drink. The car remained sealed for four and a half days, and during this time no food was distributed. Those who had had the misfortune to neglect to bring something were offered food and drink by the others. The car was so crowded that everybody had to sit on their luggage throughout the journey. The heat was terrible. One person died before Hegyeshalom and was thrown out there, and the seal was temporarily broken. The passengers were given water each day through the intervention of kind people — otherwise, my informant told me, more would certainly have died. For a reason unknown to him, he was taken off the train in Vienna and sent back. The others were sent on. By that time two persons had evidently gone mad.

Sündermann's Speech

According to a report from the press department of the local Ministry for Foreign Affairs, a draft was composed within the ministry some time ago, defending the persecution of the Jews and denying what is happening at Auschwitz. It was sent to Berlin for approval. Berlin never approved it, however, but instead used the draft as the basis of the above-mentioned speech, the main thrust of which is, as you know, that the Jews themselves are responsible for their fate and that their treatment in Poland and in Germany was "fürsorglich" [welfare]. The tenor of Sündermann's speech was echoed yesterday in a statement by Legation Counselor Krell, in which he maintained, among other things, that mail delivery from the deported Jews was largely uninterrupted.

I checked on this immediately and found that only 14,000 postcards had been received from deported Jews from May 15 to July 12, i.e., representing at most 3 percent of the deportees. If you agree with the official German claim that most of the Jews are still alive, the statement that mail delivery is uninterrupted is patently absurd.

FOOD RATIONS

	NON-JEWS	JEWS
Wheat flour, per month	2,100 g	2,100 g
Rye flour, per month	700 g	700 g
Bread, per day	250 g	250 g
Lard, per month	600 g	0 g
Oil, per month	0 g	300 g
Meat, per week	100 g	100 g
Pork, per week	100 g	0 g
Sugar, per month	1,400 g	300 g
Butter	only for non-Jews	
Poppyseed	"	
Rice	"	
Paprika	"	
Eggs	"	

Names of informants referred to in July 19 [sic] memorandum:

1. Jewish Council
2. Local representative of Jewish Agency
3. Mr. Biro
4. Kelemen Lajos
5. Magyary-Kossa
6. Sos
7. Kertes
8. Koranyi

Number of Jews Deported

The figure representing the number of boxcars dispatched, as of my previous report (July 19) [sic], and left blank, is not available. The number of deportees as of July 1, however, was approximately 333,000. A later report will indicate the number of people deported since that date. The figure that is circulating here — 680,000 as of July 12 — appears inflated.

Budapest, July 29, 1944

Secretary to the Legation

Memorandum Concerning Aid to Hungarian Jews

Different Forms of Aid

Aid could be provided either within the framework of an agreement with the governments of Hungary and Germany, through private channels, or through local propaganda activity designed to induce the Jews to help themselves and to get others to help them, as well as making the rest of the world aware of their situation.

Objectives and Means

Because of the continually changing situation it is impossible to establish a final goal for relief efforts in the above respects. The important thing is to possess the financial and organizational means to respond to the demands of the situation at hand, preferably without having to seek prior approval.

Action Taken

Based on this assumption, some twenty persons have been engaged — mainly as volunteers, and most of them of Jewish origin although exempted from the requirement to wear the Star of David. The Swiss legation has made a similar arrangement, and moreover, Christian labor is difficult to come by. Even the Gestapo has had to employ Jews. Without this arrangement, it would have been impossible to cope with the · existing workload since the regular legation staff was severely overworked already when I arrived. A telephone with three extensions has been installed in the building of the B section. Several thousand stenciled forms have been produced at various times. Approximately P.1,000 [pengö, the Hungarian currency] has been spent on new office supplies, and half a dozen typewriters, desks, chairs, etc., have been borrowed from elsewhere.

A bill for costs incurred will be presented provided permission is granted the embassy to defray the same.

Indirect contact has been established with certain authorities
to ensure accuracy with respect to figures concerning
deportation and mail from deportees.

For my private residence I have rented a very beautiful house
on the castle hill suitable for representation when required. In
addition, an individual who came highly recommended has
joined me to help probe the highest German circles for future
developments.

The Route of Official Negotiation

Negotiations with the foreign ministry here have, as
previously reported, resulted in Hungary's agreeing for its part
to repatriation. It has declared that it is prepared to secure
special high-quality housing for our Jews, and several
individuals who have been able to show provisional passports
have been exempted from forced labor service and detention
centers, and from wearing the Star of David — the latter a
significant step on the way to rescue, since curfew and the risks
associated with it no longer apply.

Limited German approval is apparently tied to whether
Hungary agrees to send the remaining Jews abroad as "labor."
This means that the question of transfer to Sweden may have to
be shelved for the time being. I nevertheless request that efforts
be made to obtain partial clearance from Berlin.

I further request clarification of whether the embassy is
permitted to issue provisional passports to e.g., a brother, sister,
father, mother, husband, or wife of a Swedish citizen, or to a
person who has been deemed of vital importance to trade
between Sweden and Hungary or of comparable cultural
importance.

Private Aid

Relief activity has been initiated on a very limited scale.
Money has been requested — but not obtained — from a
religious organization that has been very active in aiding the
Jews, as well as from the newly formed Jewish Council for
Christian Jews. It would obviously be desirable to pursue this
avenue further, whether in the form of support to a camp
through the Red Cross, or in the form of support to individuals,
or organizations and individuals who have proved useful. I can

only regret that those who were most eager to send me here have not seemed to understand that funds are essential. There is endless suffering to try to ease in this place.

Informational Activity. Jewish Self-Help.

In my conversations with certain persons, two theories, probably rooted in the many rumors circulating in Budapest, are often proposed: that the postwar courts have already begun to operate, and that they have especially focused on those responsible for the persecution of the Jews. The Jewish policy of Hungary is feared to be seriously injurious to the country when peace is concluded, especially in comparison to Romania.

There must be some way of overcoming the apathy concerning their own fate, which still characterizes most of the Jewish population. The feeling of indifference among the general population has changed noticeably since my last report. We have to rid the Jews of the feeling that they have been forgotten. From this point of view, the king's message was very useful. Similar messages from other foreign institutions to corresponding institutions here would therefore be very important, apart from their role as an eye-opener for the recipient. I therefore return to my proposal that a telegram be sent from the archbishop to the bishops previously listed — a proposal now also made from the clerical quarters.

The mere fact that the Swiss and the Swedish embassies have received Jews, listened to them, and registered them has served to encourage both the Jews and those wanting to help. The greatest value of a successful repatriation effort, or the establishment of a Red Cross camp or financial aid, is that it would inspire hope in the breasts of a hundred thousand Jews and awaken their now paralyzed instincts of self-preservation.

In this connection, I would like to comment on the Allied propaganda. The Anglo-Saxon broadcasts have been roundly criticized for being filled with general threats of retribution, while offering little help, forgiveness, or suggestions of a practical political alternative. The Russian propaganda, which suggests magnanimity and love of peace, is generally thought to be better. If those now helping the Jews would at least be promised some future help, the propaganda would probably be more effective. It would also be important to the rescue of the Jews were the Russian proclamations in conjunction with the eventual invasion to be couched in such terms that the Jews are completely exonerated from any guilt.

Awareness of the Situation Abroad

There is no doubt that the attention of the foreign press has contributed considerably to easing the situation here. Continued publicity would therefore be desirable. In this connection, I refer to the enclosed report on the treatment of the Jewish population of Hungary.

Budapest, July 29, 1944

Secretary to the Legation

Memorandum Concerning the Jews in Hungary

Situation

Since my last report there has been virtually no change. Some small-scale deportations have taken place, but these are said to have comprised smaller numbers rather than whole railroad cars. This has made it difficult to verify my information.

Soldiers have continued to surround individual houses in Budapest this week, and Jews have been taken away without warning to labor service or to register for labor service. In some instances, they have then been permitted to return home.

On August 5, SS soldiers staged a coup against the camp at Sarvar during which the commander was forced to turn over 1,500 Jewish prisoners under threat of armored vehicles. As today is Sunday, I have been unable to verify whether they have passed Hegyeshalom. I refer to the enclosed eyewitness report, entitled "Bericht an die Königl. Schwedische Gesandtschaft" [Report of the Royal Swedish Legation].

For the past two days Budapest has been full of rumors, circulated by the Gestapo, that the great action against the Jews of Budapest is about to begin. I have not yet been able to confirm these rumors.

On the first of this month I had a conversation with His Excellency Miklós Horthy, in the course of which he asked me to provide him with some anonymous written suggestions for actions that might be taken. I submitted one that ended in the demand that individuals with collective passports should be exempted from wearing the Star of David, and that the clergy be given greater freedom to speak their mind. On the third of this month, I had a talk with the minister for the interior. He told me that he would welcome an even greater number of Jews leaving for Sweden and confirmed that they might be allowed to stay in special houses under Swedish protection before their departure. The general decision to deport the Jewish population of Budapest was unresolved, but they were now in the process of securing reassurances from Germany that no harm would befall them.

Both meetings were the result of private initiatives.

The Organization of the Rescue Operation

The staff of the B section now consists of forty individuals, organized into reception, registration, treasury, archives, and departments for correspondence, transportation, and housing, each under separate and competent leadership.

Another six-room apartment has been rented in an adjoining building.

About four thousand applications have been received. No more are being accepted until we have had time to go through and process these. Newly printed protective documents and passport affidavits will be sent out as soon as the applications have been approved.

Results Achieved

A number of individuals have avoided detention. Exact numbers will follow in a subsequent report.

Establishment of a Camp

This coming Wednesday or Thursday we will probably be able to empty the rental property Pozsony-utca 3, a Jewish house, of its present occupants and replace them with the same number of Jews under the embassy's protection. It would be most desirable if we could pay the moving costs and a small compensation to those Jews who are now suddenly vacating their homes in this way. The adjoining houses in the same street will eventually be transformed into Swedish collection centers. They should be able to hold an average of about a hundred people per house.

Budapest, August 6, 1944

Secretary to the Legation

Memorandum Concerning the Jews in Hungary

Situation

Rumors concerning the imminent deportation of the remaining Jews in Budapest continue to circulate, and August 28 is said to be the starting date for the operation. The Hungarian government is expected to take a position regarding the German proposals on the issue tomorrow. It is generally considered unlikely that the government would agree to cooperate in a deportation at this point.

The earlier guarantee that Jews holding foreign citizenship would not be interned before September 30 has been rescinded, and the foreign legations in Budapest have been alerted to the fact that internment is scheduled for the 26th of this month.

The state-run organ for the surveillance of foreign citizens here, KEOKH, had earlier guaranteed that registered Jews with Swedish connections would be exempted from wearing the Star of David, provided the embassy could certify that they were included in a collective passport. Since the number of such affidavits had proliferated, the KEOKH has announced that these affidavits should be designated *Schutzbrief* and contain a clause to the effect that the individual in question is under Swedish protection. Now that these protective documents have been issued, the KEOKH tells us that these privileges will only be granted if a *Schutzpass* is issued.

It should be noted that a holder of a protective passport is considered a foreign citizen by the local authorities. This means that according to the recent directives, these Jews must be interned on the 26th of this month, i.e., including those who were just exempted from detention by virtue of having acquired a protective passport. The Hungarian authorities maintain, however, that this new detention is protective in character, and the new camps will, according to the Ministry of the Interior, be differently appointed from the old ones.

The Organization of the Rescue Operation

Within the B section a special subsection for securing the release of detained persons has been organized. The section has also been organized more practically in other respects. New applications are again being accepted. I enclose a copy of the revised application form.

I am also enclosing a sample of the new protective passport. This is valid for travel only in combination with a collective passport. The validity of the latter can of course be changed to cover a shorter or a longer period. The protective passports are checked by a committee of four persons working within the section.

I would like to propose that provisional passports only be issued to individuals with close family ties to people living in Sweden and to their spouse and dependent children, as well as to individuals of long-standing and important business connections with Sweden and to their wives and minor children. Issuing provisional passports to extended families or to individuals whose activities have not been of importance to Sweden has proved to set an extremely awkward precedent. The embassy has been flooded with hundreds of requests.

The B section is presently working on inquiries and requests for information on various individuals from the foreign office. I will return to these in my next report.

The Establishment of Internment Centers

The new directives outlined above and the release of a large number of detainees, once completed, will require a large number of housing units to serve as internment centers. The authorities themselves seem to have done nothing to make good on their promise of providing improved facilities. To make certain that Jews holding protective passports will not be referred to Kistarcsa or some other camp of similar reputation on the 26th, the section intends to present the authorities with a fait acccompli in the matter of housing. To find suitable houses and apartment houses in such a short time will, however, be extremely difficult.

Results Achieved

Those already in possession of protective passports have
been released. A list of names is enclosed.

Budapest, August 15, 1944

Memorandum Concerning the Jews of Hungary

Since my last report, the situation has changed a number of times, without becoming substantially clearer.

Detention of all so-called foreign Jews — i.e., including those with Swedish protective passports — which was to have gone into effect on August 26, has entailed huge amounts of work for the section for Jewish Affairs. The authorities issued what amounted to an ultimatum, ordering the section, along with the Jewish Council, to organize the transfer of the Jews, estimated at 3,500. We were given seventy-two hours. The order was later rescinded, and the transfer never took place, in spite of the fact that the organizational work was finished. No new date was set. The official decision is thus still that all Jews regarded as aliens are to be interned.

Negotiations between Hungary and Germany have continued and have resulted in a pledge by the Hungarians to remove the Jewish population from Budapest. It is, however, far from certain that the Hungarian authorities concerned have any intention of carrying out this plan.

In accordance with this plan it was decided a few days ago that all able-bodied Jews have to submit to a medical examination and will be detailed to labor service in the countryside, at the front, or in the Budapest war industry. It has not been possible to get an exemption for Jews with protective passports.

The curfew for the Jewish population has been increased, and they are only allowed to leave their homes between noon and 5 P.M.

The so-called Finance Direction today dispatched patrols to confiscate valuables from apartments belonging to those Jews who have been removed to the ghetto, and which have been closed for a long time.

The day before yesterday it was announced that all Jews with protective passports would be exempted from having to wear a Star of David. This did not mean, however, that they would be free to live where they wanted or get their belongings back.

About 250 Jews under the protection of the embassy have been released from detention camps to date. An additional and substantial number will be freed, beginning today.

It would greatly help the Swedish Jewish operation if the Swedish press would report on the privileges granted those Jews who have been issued Swedish protective passports. The desire of the Hungarian authorities to demonstrate their goodwill to the rest of the world has clearly been the decisive factor behind the above-mentioned privileges.

A board has been formed for the purpose of resolving Jewish questions. This board is mainly made up of persons friendly to the Swedish embassy.

Collaboration with the Red Cross

There is collaboration with the Red Cross to the extent that the Red Cross is selecting people who ought to be issued protective passports and referring them to the Embassy's Jewish section. We have also collaborated on finding houses and other space.

Purchase of Food

The Section is currently purchasing food — initially, for 65,000 pengö. Food is expected to be in increasingly short supply.

Staff

Work has been divided into day shifts and night shifts. All employees and their families are exempted from having to wear the Star and have been issued identification papers by the Ministry for Foreign Affairs and the Ministry of the Interior. They have been told by the political police that they may keep their apartments even though they are not officially entitled to this.

The number of aid seekers is enormous. Thousands of applications are being processed. To illustrate how great the need is for an operation of this scale, I may add that most of the staff has had to work around the clock without a break on several occasions.

Another reason why the staff is so large is that every new order or ultimatum by local authorities means enormous amounts of work that has to be completed in only a few days or even hours. Because of the way the section has grown, it has had to move again, which naturally has entailed some problems. The reception is still located in the building at Minerva Utca 1A, i.e., next to the legation. However, all internal administration is being handled from Tigris Utca 8A, which belongs to the section. The house contains ten rooms and a basement.

The Phasing-out of the Jewish Section

As a result of the political situation, current plans call for the reception to be phased out beginning Sunday, the 17th of this month, and for the staff to be let go as work dimishes. Protective passports will still be issued, however, since there is some risk of pogroms in conjunction with the German withdrawal from Budapest.

September 12, 1994
[UNSIGNED]

Report on the Hungarian Jews

Since my last report the situation has improved somewhat.

The German detention center at Kistarcsa and the camp in Kolumbus-utca have been turned over to the Hungarian authorities. The embassy managed to effect the release of some of the detainees at Kolumbus-utca already before this.

Around 500 or 600 Jews — many of them holding protective passports — have been released from the detention centers. Currently only 450 remain in detention. Add to this an unknown number of people interned or imprisoned by the Germans. Next report will list the names of all Jews under Swedish protection still held by the Hungarians. All others may be assumed to have been freed.

The Hungarian authorities now limit their camps to the punishment of habitual Jewish criminals and to those who have been interned during the past month. The latter category does not include those jailed for a minor infraction, such as not wearing the Star of David, and, in accordance with the local laws, transferred for short-term internment.

Five thousand Jews, to be followed possibly by another 10,000, are currently being selected from among the Jewish population of Budapest for excavation work around the capital and to clear the sites after air raids. The first contingents were dispatched to surrounding towns today. These Jews are very poorly equipped in every sense — the problem of suitable accommodations, for one thing, will probably prove impossible to solve. The authorities in charge of these problems appear, however, to have the best intentions.

The agreement between the Hungarians and the Germans that Budapest was to be emptied of its Jewish population and that they should be concentrated in the countryside outside Budapest has hitherto been totally sabotaged by the Hungarian authorities. Not a single Jew has left the capital under the terms of this agreement. Because of this, the Germans have again threatened to take the matter into their own hands and assembled in Budapest those SS divisions that were in charge of the deportations in Hungary and Slovakia. Whether the German intent is also deportation abroad in this instance is unclear. The general opinion is that the plan is not likely to be put into effect unless the Germans use force against the government.

This week a bomb went off at a German military camp. The inhabitants of two Jewish houses located across the street were forcibly removed by German troops and imprisoned in a German police jail and a Hungarian detention camp. A few have already been let go, including two individuals holding Portuguese provisional passports. As far as I know, there was nobody under Swedish protection among those arrested.

This week nine former employees of Manfred Weiss were also arrested under the pretext that they were recruiting people for Swedish protective passports. They were released after only 48 hours partly as the result of the embassy intercedance.

Organization

The air raids have made our work much more difficult at times. Our staff has had to be increased again following the introduction of internal censorship, which has resulted in considerable delays for the section's daily outgoing mail. At its peak, it comprised about 115 persons. We have subsequently let some people go as a result of the decision to phase out the section gradually. We now have some one hundred employees. About forty of these will have to turn in their identification documents to the embassy within the next ten days. The staff IDs issued by the local Ministry of the Interior may be kept, however, since they exempt the bearer from having to wear the Star of David and from forced labor.

After September 16 no new applications will be accepted. The section may now close down as soon as the present applications for protective passports — around 8,000 — have been decided. Our plans are to issue a total of 4,500 protective passports, of which 2,700 have already been distributed.

It goes without saying that it is very difficult to distribute the remaining number fairly.

We have been told that people have sometimes made financial sacrifices to secure a protective or a provisional passport. We have discovered that certain individuals not employed by the section — among them some unscrupulous lawyers — have taken advantage of the precarious situation of the Jewish population and exacted large fees to handle the application for a protective passport. They have claimed to have connections among the staff.

Whenever possible, these outsiders have been reported to the police. One arrest was made, but the person in question was immediately released, since this way of doing business is not illegal according to Hungarian law. In cutting back on our staff, two individuals were mentioned as under suspicion. There was no proof, however, and neither was in any position to influence the decisions on protective passports.

Relief Work
The following sums have been distributed to date:

To the Jewish Council for soup kitchens	P.200,000
" clothing	300,000
To the Jewish Orphanage at Vilma-Kiraly-ut, which has been bombed out	35,000
Section for Relief Work for cash contributions to applicants lacking funds	30,000
Section for Purchasing for food purchases, to be distributed when situation deteriorates further	200,000
	P.765,000

(Three cases of sardines have been forwarded through the Red Cross to the Russian prisoner-of-war camp.)

The above total has been covered mainly through the following transfers:

PAID TO		RECEIVED FROM	
AB Cloetta	Kr.8,000	Stühmer Co	P.92,000
Troedsson & Co.	35,000	Dr. Johann Ertl	1,010,000
	Kr.43,000		P.1,102,000

Permission is requested to transfer funds as required.
(Letter to Troedsson & Co. from Dr. Johann Ertl enclosed.)

Results Achieved

The entire staff and their families, around 300 individuals, have been exempted from having to wear the Star of David and from forced labor.

Those in possession of Swedish protective passports presently in the Labor Service will be recalled to Budapest from their respective labor battalions as of tomorrow morning. It is likely that some will not be found or will be unable to find transportation, however.

Credit for the general release of the detainees is largely due the section. The official who ordered their release has been under constant pressure from the section.

The total number of individuals exempted from having to wear the Star of David as a result of the section's efforts is today about 1,100 out of the agreed-on total of 4,500.

Budapest, September 29, 1944

Report Concerning the Jews in Hungary

Since the last report the situation has improved somewhat. The release of those who had been detained has been completed. Only those Jews who are considered criminals remain in Hungarian detention. The list of all Hungarian detainees promised by the Hungarian Ministry of the Interior was unfortunately not completed in time for this report. Protective passports cannot be used to secure the release of Jews still remaining in Hungarian or German detention.

Jews are now being carted off to work on the fortifications. They are not inhumanely treated, as far as we are able to tell. The recall from forced labor of Jewish holders of Swedish protective passports is proceeding.

With the advance of the Russian troops hope is on the rise among the Jewish population that they will no longer be singled out. Many are said to have stopped wearing the Star of David. Their fears that the Germans will conduct a pogrom at the last minute remain unchanged, even though there are no concrete signs that one is imminent.

Mr. Grell, the counselor at the German legation, has voiced the opinion that even if the Germans were to intensify their efforts, we might still be able to count on preferential treatment for the Jewish holders of protective passports.

The Deportation Commando, which was stationed outside Budapest, has departed for Berlin.

The Organization

Due to the increase in the workload brought about by recent events, the phase-out has not been completed. Local mail still has to be sent by messenger, as mentioned in an earlier report. The size of the staff working with matters pertaining to those who have been drafted into the Labor Service has tripled. A special section has been organized to facilitate moving Jewish holders of protective passports into Aryan houses. This section includes two bankers from Credit bank, Makai and Lanyi, the

Swedish citizen Mr. Sixten von Bayer, and some society ladies. The section has an office of four rooms at its disposal.

Preparatory work on the opening of a hospital is now being conducted in cooperation with the Red Cross.

A purchasing department headed by Mr. Ekmark, the Swedish consul in Zagreb, has been installed on the premises of the Finnish embassy. The department has received and disbursed P.300,000 and 300 pairs of shoes to date.

A working committee has been formed with the Swedish Red Cross, the International Red Cross, the Zionist Organization, and the Jewish Council for the purpose of sending *Liebesgaben* [charity] packages to Hungarian Jews in Germany. To date, P.50,000 have been allocated for this.

In a telegram of the 7th of this month, the embassy requested that the Ministry for Foreign Affairs order and send paper, coats, and used clothing in the amount of 35,000 Swedish kronor for the section's use. We are unable to be more specific as to the clothing. Because of the urgency of the situation and the need among the Jews, which is becoming more visible with every day, we request that whatever clothing can be found be dispatched as soon as possible and that the shipping instructions outlined in the telegram be followed.

The suspicions mentioned in the last report that some passports were falling into the hands of the population were explained when it was discovered that a murderer with a previous prison record — obviously in no way associated with the embassy — had manufactured about forty protective passports — very poorly done, in fact — and sold them for 3–4,000 pengö apiece. Clippings from *Hetföi Hirlap* of October 1 and from *Pester Lloyd* of October 3 have been sent under separate cover along with a brief summary in German of the former.

Budapest, October 12, 1944

Report on the Situation of the Hungarian Jews

Since my last report the situation regarding the Hungarian Jews has deteriorated considerably.

The new government intends to draft the Jewish population to work in the countryside and on the defense of Budapest, and then expel them after the end of the war. The first few have already been taken away.

They have not been able to leave their houses for almost a whole week now, which obviously has been a great hardship. All Jews previously exempted were given six hours to move into a Jewish house. This regulation was partially rescinded shortly after going into effect. Many of these same Jews have been trying to hide in basements, empty shops, or with Christian friends this week, as well as in houses belonging to the Red Cross and the section located outside the embassy building. Also the death penalty has been introduced for minor infractions.

During the first night of the putsch, several individual arrests were made and there were several pogrom acts, in the course of which some 100–200 persons are estimated to have been killed. Several Jewish houses were also emptied by Arrow Cross troops and the occupants taken away to detention centers. These have largely been allowed to return, but a couple of hundred appear to be still missing.

The houses are now being systematically searched, and all men between the ages of 16 and 60 are taken away for labor service. A column of them was sighted by an eyewitness on the road to Gödöllö. The marchers were ill-treated, and a 60-year-old Jew lay dead and visibly beaten by the roadside, covered with newspapers. Beginning tomorrow, all the remaining men and all women between 16 and 60 are to be put to work on the fortifications. In some instances, people with protective passports have been attacked by armed bandits and their protective passports torn up. No holders of protective passports have as yet been reported killed. One has been condemned to death but given a reprieve. The premises of the Red Cross have been violated on two occasions. Negotiations are under way.

Two thousand Jews in the Labor Service were killed by the SS before the putsch, as reported in a telegram. They were walking on foot from the copper mines in Bor in Serbia to Hungary; also, 200 Labor Service Jews in Riskunhalas.

The Organization

The bookkeeping accounts as of the 14th of this month are enclosed, in addition to my special account with the Stockholm Enskilda Bank AB. I request that these be placed at the disposal of Mr. Olsen.

The events of the 17th were disastrous for the section. We lost the entire staff, plus a car which had been placed at our disposal free of charge, as well as some keys to locked rooms, cupboards, etc. I spent the whole of the first day in streets filled with bandits, on a lady's bicycle, trying to straighten everything out. Day two was spent moving staff members in imminent danger by car to safer hiding places and hauling food to them in a sack. Today only about ten staff members are missing, while some thirty have not yet come to work. One of the section's larger areas has been co-opted by the embassy to house the Swedish colony.

The minister for foreign affairs has asked me to see to it that the staff and their families are housed in special houses. We are working on this.

Results Achieved

A status quo has been achieved with regard to the staff situation.

The minister for foreign affairs has announced that 4,500 Jews under our protection will be allowed to leave the country. The German legation has announced that all obstacles to transit have been removed for 400–500 persons. The German legation has had no instructions from Berlin concerning the remaining 4,000, and did not know whether there were any negotiations on this issue with the Swedish embassy there.

Cancellation of the regulation referred to in the third paragraph of page 1 is the work of the section.

The protective passports have largely been respected with

regard to forced labor, detention, etc., depending on the individual official in question.

When the putsch broke out, some 40 individuals under Swedish protection were waiting with the Swedish group along with another 150 persons. Eighty of the latter were taken away. The 40 are officially under the embassy's protection for the time being and have been granted a reprieve until the 24th of this month.

Budapest, October 22, 1944

Secretary to the Legation

Memorandum concerning the Situation of the Hungarian Jews

Since the last report the situation of the Hungarian Jews has further deteriorated.

Probably in the vicinity of 40,000 Jews, of whom 15,000 men from the Labor Service and 25,000 of both sexes seized in their homes or in the street, have been forced to march on foot to Germany. It is a distance of 240 kilometers. The weather has been cold and rainy ever since these death marches began. They have had to sleep under rain shelters and in the open. Most have only been given something to eat and drink three or four times. Many have died. I learned in Mosonmagyarovar that 7 persons had died that day, and 7 persons the day before. The Portuguese secretary to the legation had observed 42 dead persons along the route, and Deputy Prime Minister Szálasi admitted to me that he had seen 2 dead. Those who were too tired to walk were shot. On the border, they were received with kicks and blows by the Eichmann Special SS Command and were taken away to hard labor on the border fortifications.

Photos are enclosed of civilians departing on a march of this kind (1 and 2), of departing military laborers (3), and of two girls, before and after the journey Budapest-Hegyeshalom-Budapest (4).

Twenty thousand military laborers have been taken to the border by rail. They work mainly on Hungarian soil. Photos are enclosed (5) documenting the work of the Swedish Rescue Commission.

Fortification work, mentioned in an earlier report, has been discontinued.

The Jews are collected in a central ghetto intended to house 69,000 Jews, but which will probably house more than this number, as well as in a ghetto for foreigners for 17,000, already containing 35,000 of whom 7,000 in Swedish houses, 2,000 in houses belonging to the Red Cross, and 23,000 in Swiss houses.

Thousands of people under Swiss and Vatican protection are taken away from here to the central ghetto or to deportation areas. The Jews live 4–12 to a room in the ghettos, the Swedish houses having the best conditions.

An epidemic of the Ruhr disease, as yet contained, has broken out among the Jewish population. Health conditions in the Swedish houses are still good, with only five dead so far. The section is now having all Jews under its protection vaccinated against typhoid, paratyphus, and cholera. The staff will also be vaccinated for their own protection.

The Jews are mostly very poor, as they are only allowed to take with them what they are able to carry during their repeated moves. Supplies will soon be disastrously low.

The Arrow Cross drag large numbers of them into their places and torture and torment them, only to take them away to the deportation centers.

There are rumors that the death brigade close to Minister Kovacs will begin a pogrom against the Jewish population. I do not believe that this pogrom will be widespread, since the SS organizations have reputedly been given orders not to engage in the wholesale slaughter of Jews.

The Organization

After the deadly blow dealt it in October, the section has again grown rapidly. The staff now numbers 335, in addition to some 40 doctors, house governors, etc. All these people and about the same number of family members are living in the section's buildings. There are ten offices and dwellings, of which one in the foreign ghetto.

Two hospitals have been established and improvised, respectively, with a total of 150 beds.

A soup kitchen has been started.

The Jews in the Swedish houses turn their ration cards over to the section, which redeems them and distributes the provisions.

A large part of the section's correspondence has been destroyed.

The Department for Provisions has made purchases totaling about 2 million pengö.

Results Achieved

The Section managed to extract an open command from the Honved Cabinet that all Labor Service Jews holding foreign documents would be returned to Budapest. After a military person sent out in one of the section cars distributed the order, about 15,000 Jews returned.

For a short time the columns marching toward the border were given food and medicine until the procedure was forbidden.

The sick have been picked up in rescue cars from the deportation staging points, about 200 persons in all.

By intervening in some way when the Jews were boarding the trains or being taken away, about 2,000 persons have been returned, of whom 500 from Hegyeshalom. This practice has unfortunately had to cease after the Germans in the Eichmann Command threatened violent action.

The Jewish holders of Swedish protective passports have managed better, relatively speaking, than those under the protection of other countries. No more than 8–10 appear to have been shot in Budapest and the surroundings to date.

Budapest, Decmber 12, 1944

848/ICO/MET

American Legation
Stockholm, Sweden
June 15, 1945

Brigadier General William O'Dwyer
    Executive Director
        War Refugee Board
            Washington, D.C.

Subject: Final Report of Activities of War Refugee Board from Sweden

Dear General O'Dwyer:

In accordance with your instructions, the following is the concluding report covering operations from Sweden of the War Refugee Board. It is intended to supplement and bring up to date my basic report submitted as of November 22, 1944, as well as to provide a final accounting of the funds placed at my disposal.

Since this report covers the period of operations from the date of my return from Washington in January, it is in effect simply a summary of 1945 activities. The scope of operations during the period had, of course, considerably contracted. The Baltic countries had ceased as an area of operations in September 1944. Hungarian operations came to a close in January 1945. Consequently, the greatest possible attention was focused on the fate of Jews and other civilian prisoners in Germany, as well as in pressing active rescue and relief operations in Norway. Certain limited activities were continued in Denmark.

A. Operations in Hungary.

Sufficient facts now appear at hand to support the conclusion that Hungarian rescue and relief actions initiated by the War Refugee Board from Sweden were the keystones of the most productive steps taken in that area, and paved the way for saving the lives of perhaps 100,000 Jews. The work of Raoul Wallenberg, actively supported by Minister Danielsson and his staff of the Swedish legation in Budapest, was nothing short of brilliant — to say nothing of being highly courageous. This group pioneered the program of constant and relentlessly increasing pressure on the Hungarian Government in behalf of the Jews, at the cost of seriously jeopardizing their own personal safety. Minister Danielsson informed Minister Johnson and myself that during their last weeks as officials in Budapest, Raoul Wallenberg had to hide in a different house every night, he was so hotly hunted by the Hungarian Fascists and the Germans. The program of issuing Swedish protective passports, of sheltering Jews in Swedish protective dwellings, and similar other activities in itself brought approximately 20,000 Jews under the safety of Swedish protection. At the height of this program, over 350 persons had been recruited to carry out this enormous task. This program set a pattern which soon was followed by the Swiss, Portuguese, and the International Red Cross, and in the end produced a combined program which probably afforded the greatest relief and protection to Jews in any European country.

Not until Wallenberg's records become available will the complete story of this program become known. We are informed that he kept extremely complete and documented records of a highly interesting nature, and that these records were still in the Swedish legation when the staff was forced to leave Budapest. . . .

With the submission of this final report, and in view of my new assignment at The Hague, I should like to express to you the real satisfaction and pleasure I have experienced in my association with the War Refugee Board. It has been most interesting and a real challenge. The entire program was very much worthwhile, and the only regrettable thing is that the War Refugee Board was not established a year or two earlier. I know that I could do much better had I this activity to undertake now, on the basis of experience gained, but the time element in this program afforded no opportunity to profit from experience or to learn from mistakes already made. To anyone here in Europe, however, it is extremely clear that the War Refugee Board accomplished an enormous amount of good.

Sincerely yours,

Iver C. Olsen
Special Attaché for
War Refugee Board

FINAL LETTERS

[All letters are written in German.]

Dear Mother!

We are incredibly busy and have been working day and night. At the moment it looks as if our first venture within the framework of humanitarian work will be successful. Great difficulties still lie ahead, however, and I cannot yet believe that this first project will eventually succeed.

Please be so kind and invite Dr. Lauer and his wife. I have learned that his in-laws and evidently also a small child belonging to the family are already dead, i.e., that they have been shipped abroad from Kecskemet — and there they won't stay alive for long.

Best wishes,
R. Wallenberg

Dear Mother!

I have lived here through what are probably the 3–4 most interesting weeks of my life, even though we are surrounded by a tragedy of immeasurable proportions, and even though our days and nights are so filled with work that you are only able to react every now and then.

I have set up a large office of 40 employees. We have rented two houses, on either side of the embassy, and the organization is growing day by day. It is obviously extremely uncertain whether it will be possible to achieve a positive outcome, given that everything ultimately depends on the general situation.

Many have disappeared, and no one is left in the countryside. Budapest, which used to be so gay, has changed completely. Most of the ladies from the better families have left the city, and the men are all at the front. Business is utterly paralyzed. It is becoming almost completely politicized.

My birthday was fun, inasmuch as I had discovered the date by accident the same afternoon and had mentioned it to my very capable secretary, Countess Nako. Two hours later I found on my desk a very beautiful set, briefcase, calendar, ink well, etc., along with a bottle of champagne and flowers.

I have rented a very beautiful 18th-century house on the castle hill with gorgeous furniture, and a lovely little garden and marvelous view, and I occasionally entertain there officially.

Please give my best to Nina, Father, and Guy.

Many regards,
R. Wallenberg

Royal Swedish Embassy
Budapest
September 29, 1944

Dear Mother,

I am keeping quite well and am very busy. Until a week ago we had lots of air raids, often forcing us to sit in the air-raid shelter for three or four hours on end. This past week we have been spared that kind of unpleasantness.

Despite this, everything is moving along very well. I gave some nice dinner parties for various officials who are important to my work. A few days ago I had invited some very interesting big game, namely Himmler's representative [Adolf Eichmann]. Unfortunately, something came up at work at the last minute and prevented him from coming. He is quite a nice man who, according to what he himself says, will soon shoot himself.

Otherwise, I have unfortunately had little time for any kind of social life. And there is actually very little of it around. Most people are in the country, and the general mood is not one to inspire much joy.

Our operation has been very effective so far. I have a staff of about 115 people, all of whom are working very hard. My own day consists mainly of seeing people who work here and who need to be given various instructions. Also people who bring me news, and finally a small stream of particularly unpleasant people, mostly of high social status, who elbow their way into my office.

I also travel around in my DKW and visit various officials. I enjoy these negotiations very much. They are often extremely dramatic.

About a week ago, I took my official car, a rented Studebaker, and went to a detainment camp on the Austrian border. The commandant refused to receive me at first, then he allotted me five minutes, and finally, after negotiating for four hours, I managed to have eighty people released the very same day and sent to Budapest. It was quite a moving sight.

I had hoped to come home right after closing down the section, as they said. Unfortunately, my trip home seems to have been quite delayed, since the closing of the section is also taking a long time. At least, I'm going to try to go home via Germany and hope it won't take so long as if the trip had gone via Moscow-Haifa.

Many regards to everyone and kisses to Nina. When's the day?

R. Wallenberg

[Nina had married Gunnar Lagergren, who worked at the foreign office of the Swedish Embassy in Berlin, in 1943. Nane Lagergren, with whom Nina was pregnant when RW visited the Lagergrens in Berlin on his way to Budapest, was born in October 1944.]

ROYAL SWEDISH EMBASSY
BUDAPEST
OCTOBER 22, 1944

Dear Mother,

Today you only get these lines written in haste. I can reassure you that I am fine. The times are extraordinarily exciting and nerve-racking. We keep working and struggling on, and that is the main thing, however.

Right now we are sitting by candlelight trying to ready the diplomatic pouch. There is a power outage — that is all we need in this great mess. Dozens of people are standing around me, everyone with pressing questions, so that I don't know to whom to reply and advise first.

I hope all is well with you, and I swear solemnly that you will get a more detailed account next time.

I will stop for today and send my best wishes and kisses to all of you.

Your
R. Wallenberg

ROYAL SWEDISH EMBASSY
BUDAPEST
DECEMBER 8, 1944

Dearest Mother,

I really don't know when I'll be able to make it up to you for my silence. Another diplomatic pouch leaves today, and once again all you get from me are a few lines written in haste.

The situation is risky and tense, and my workload almost superhuman. Thugs are roaming around the city, beating, torturing, and shooting people. Among my staff alone there have been forty cases of kidnapping and beatings. On the whole we are in good spirits, however, and enjoying the fight.

I sent a telegram in which I said that I was agreeable to taking over the Lagergrens' apartment. The conditions were as follows. My own apartment must be let through a rental agency, something to which Mr. Eriksson must first give his consent. I also ask that you let Frey Express handle the whole move. I don't want anyone to have any bother, so turn the whole thing over to Frey Express.

We can hear the gunfire of the approaching Russians here day and night. Since Szálasi came to power, diplomatic activity has become very lively. I myself am almost the sole representative of our embassy in all government departments. So far, I've been to see the foreign minister about ten times, the deputy premier twice, the minister for the interior twice, the minister of supply once, the minister of finance once, etc.

The wife of the foreign minister was a pretty close acquaintance of mine. Unfortunately, she has now left for Merano.

Food is very scarce in Budapest. We managed to stockpile a fair amount ahead of time, however. I have a feeling that it will be difficult to leave after the [Russian] occupation, so I doubt I will get to Stockholm until around Easter. But all this is idle speculation. No one knows what the occupation will be like. At any rate, I will try to return home as soon as possible.

It is simply not possible to make plans at the moment. I really thought I would be with you for Christmas. Now I must send you my best wishes for Christmas by this means, along with my wishes for the New Year. I hope the peace so longed for is no longer so far away.

Dearest Mother, I am also enclosing two photos that were just developed. You see me at my desk surrounded by my colleagues and staff.

The enormous amount of work makes the time pass quickly, and I am often invited to late-night feasts of roast suckling pig and other Hungarian specialties.

Dearest Mother, I will say good-bye for today. The pouch must be readied. Greetings, tender and heartfelt kisses to you and the whole family.

Your

R. Wallenberg

encl. 2 photos

Lots of kisses to Nina and the little girl.

[The Soviet Army's siege of Budapest began on December 8, 1944, the day this letter was written. Soviet authorities took RW into their "protective custody" and sent him to Lubyanka Prison in Moscow on January 17, 1945. He was never heard from again. The Soviets denied any knowledge of his whereabouts until 1957, when Andrei Gromyko, then foreign minister, announced that RW had died of a heart attack in 1947, in Lubyanka. There is ample but inconclusive evidence that this was not the case, and efforts to determine his fate continue.]

AFTERWORD

I have been involved with The Raoul Wallenberg Committee of the United States for a number of years. I have gotten to know Wallenberg's family, written about him, given lectures on him, been caught up on a day-to-day basis with thinking about his heroism, as well as with the angst and mystery that still surround his arrest and imprisonment. Yet *Letters and Dispatches* has provided me with the first opportunity to assess Raoul Wallenberg in his own words. Neither reading nor speaking Swedish, I have been limited to second- or thirdhand sources, and to memories that have been colored by time or edited by the very human inability of the soul to contemplate for long certain experiences. Through this collection of Raoul Wallenberg's personal and diplomatic writings, in other words, I have finally been able to meet Raoul face-to-face.

Each of us who reads *Letters and Dispatches* will perceive Raoul Wallenberg differently. He is a lightning rod for powerful emotions; he and the causes associated with him attract people of enormous diversity. For many, he is the ultimate role model, certainly of the Holocaust, and perhaps even of the twentieth century. United as we are by his name, our vision of him must necessarily be colored by individual perception of the myth.

For me, reading Wallenberg has proven more exciting than I could have imagined, in part because some ideas I have developed over the years about his character are strengthened by being able to compare the letters and the dispatches. For example, I have always thought there must be a strong connection between Wallenberg's training as an architect and the precision behind the planning of his rescue mission in Budapest. And indeed, what strikes me most forcefully about both the letters and the dispatches is the always incisive, blueprint clarity of Wallenberg's thinking, and the way in which it is applied to a larger vision of things.

However different they are in form and content, the letters can be found in the dispatches, and the dispatches in the letters. In the summer of 1929, during a climbing trip in the French Alps, Raoul tells his grandfather he was the only one of the group to sleep peacefully through a night spent on wooden benches in a cold mountain hut. His remarkable gift to adapt and survive, whether in Ann Arbor or Mexico City or Cape Town or Haifa, would stand Wallenberg in good stead in Budapest, where he was sometimes forced to change houses nightly to escape Adolf Eichmann's attempts against his life. From that same early letter we can already discern Wallenberg's approach to problem solving. He tells his grandfather that he needs to expand his French vocabulary (his pronunciation and grasp of grammar were both excellent). Rather than rely only on his daily lesson, young Raoul finds a French edition of a Swedish book with which he is already familiar and studies the translation. His love of challenges both physical and mental was matched by an ability to cut through extraneous details and to locate the most direct route to resolution. How invaluable this would prove when he was faced with the struggle between life and death in Hungary, the greatest challenge to body and spirit he would ever face.

We celebrate Wallenberg's uniqueness, his being one of a handful of people who helped to save lives that the rest of the world had given up for lost. Yet these letters introduce us to someone whom we instantly recognize as one of us. They give human scale to his monumental achievement. They also introduce us to Gustaf — dominating, domineering, imposing himself upon Raoul's life and urging him on to great things. His worldly influence on Raoul was crucial. Yet worldly or not, Gustaf had his Victorian, patriarchal prejudices. How difficult it is, for example, not to groan at his attitude toward women, set out in that extraordinary letter in which he attempts to save Raoul from the pitfalls of romance. As it turned out, at least in this regard, Raoul set his own course (as was, after all, his grandfather's ultimate wish). In Budapest, Wallenberg depended heavily upon women to help with his mission. One was his brilliant and elegant translator for all his high-level negotiations, Elizabeth Kasser; another was the influential and cultivated wife of the Hungarian Arrow Cross foreign minister, Baroness Elizabeth Kemény Fuchs, whom Wallenberg mentions in his final letter to his mother. And then there was his mother, Maj, with whom Gustaf worked closely to shape Raoul. From his grandfather he learned to engage an unusually good and incisive mind; from his mother he learned tenderness and compassion.

What Raoul did absorb were Gustaf's careful lessons in practical diplomacy, as we can see in that 1934 letter where the grandfather instructs his charge in how ever so gracefully to sidestep an offer without giving a definitive answer and without offending. In Raoul, Gustaf also found a talented disciple in his design to revolutionize Swedish trade. Gustaf's internationalism and vast diplomatic experience, coupled with Raoul's own travels as a student and "volunteer," did prepare him, as his grandfather had anticipated, for a place of prominence in world affairs. That place turned out to be far different than either would have ever imagined.

The education of Raoul Wallenberg was always part of a "program." Travel and language skills were crucial, and the lessons were well learned. He wrote to Gustaf in French and in English; his final letters to his mother were written in German, the language he was using on a daily basis in Budapest. It was not until I read these letters that I learned that he had even studied Russian. (For me, this provided a small measure of hope that knowing Russian may have eased his way after his arrest and deportation to Moscow in 1945.) All the letters stress practical application. To apply oneself, to make oneself useful, these were nearly moral responsibilities. Raoul was never discouraged from pursuing his artistic inclinations, but he was encouraged to develop them in a practical manner, hence the study of architecture in Ann Arbor rather than painting in Paris. Gustaf had no greater worry than that Raoul would follow the frivolous fate of wealthy young men in world capitals, including Stockholm, and give up the good fight. Or, worse, turn out like Raoul's cousin Gustave Wally, who ended up in Hollywood as a movie actor and dancer (by all accounts he was charming and great fun). Raoul had some acting skills of his own, and they were displayed magnificently in Budapest.

However, it was Gustaf's influence, his program, rather than

Gustave Wally's, that won out. Raoul always felt that there should be a design to one's energies, an organization for one's actions. There is a direct line from the fourteen-year-old Raoul's grade-improvement chart to his design of the famous "Schutzpass," which Per Anger discusses in his introduction to the dispatches. Between them was Gustaf's encouragement to develop business acumen in a variety of settings, so that his grandson was constantly forced to assess new problems and to develop skills that could be adapted quickly to the needs of the moment. Raoul chafed at some of his grandfather's directives, but eventually he put them to full and very practical use.

As the Budapest dispatches show, Raoul wasted little time in setting up his own program. The large, multifaceted rescue operation required of him almost superhuman energy and diplomatic skill if he was to deal with the persecutors, their victims, the other foreign legations that had agreed to help save Jewish lives, and even his own government. At one point he had over four hundred Jewish volunteers working in his special section of the Swedish legation. He also had to use tact in dealing with his Swedish coworkers. He was, after all, a "volunteer" diplomat, and not part of the old-boy network that dominates most diplomatic services. Wallenberg's early banking experiences — unhappy though they were — were also helpful. The records of his financial transactions, which are filed among the Swedish Foreign Ministry's documents, indicate a sound head for using hard currency. He was not afraid of money and he knew how to place it quietly and judiciously so that it might do the most good.

We begin to see how Wallenberg was uniquely, almost miraculously, prepared for Budapest. Even his architecture projects at the University of Michigan, such as the assignment to design affordable housing, are premonitory. In Budapest, one of his greatest challenges was to find a way to place 35,000 people in buildings designed for fewer than 5,000. Again, he was prepared for the responsibility.

In the dispatches we find a worldly and sophisticated Wallenberg, a man who understands the impact of newly emerging technology and how it can be manipulated. He is not only aware of the power of the press but correctly gauges the impact of radio as an immediate and useful tool for propaganda. His pragmatic appraisals of radio and the press suggest someone who would have felt equally at ease on the Internet highway. He would certainly have found a way to exploit the media to protect "his Jews," or "his Bosnians" or "his Rwandans."

In the end, it was Wallenberg's great enthusiasm for life, for the grand drama of life, that enabled him to offer the Jewish community of Budapest the greatest gift of all: hope. I knew as much before I'd read these letters and dispatches, of course, even though now I understand better its source. I learned it from stories such as that of Susan Serena Tabor. Susan and her mother were rounded up by the Arrow Cross, locked up in a brick factory for a number of days, then forced to march on foot toward the Austrian border. Susan told me that after days with no food or supplies, and only handfuls of snow for sustenance, she and those with whom she was being herded toward death had begun to believe that they deserved the fate that awaited them. "We were too despondent even to weep, our eyes never met, we only stared downward as we awaited our fate. All hope had departed, and when we lost hope we also lost the courage and the will to live." They were shoved by the Nazi guards into a dirty stable to pass the night.

> Then suddenly the stable doors were opened and several well-dressed men in civilian clothes walked into our midst, surrounded by guards with bayonets. One of them, the one holding a large book, moved quietly among us. He gently touched old women on the shoulder, looked into their eyes, and said a few words of kindness. He apologized for not being able to help us all. He said, "I have come to save a nation. I must save the young ones first." He then asked all of us who had the Swedish safe pass to give him their names. My mother and I had no Schutzpass, but because of Raoul Wallenberg's compassion and concern, hope returned to my soul. With hope came courage. I grabbed my mother's hand and pulled her from the stable floor. As those few women with the safe pass walked out with Raoul Wallenberg, we joined them. When they climbed onto the back of the Swede's truck, we ran into the woods and returned to Budapest on foot.

Before her death, Susan Tabor spoke all over the world about how she had been saved by Raoul Wallenberg. What he gave her was hope. He gave many people hope. The American government representative for the War Refugee Board, Iver Olsen, who had recruited Wallenberg to go to Budapest, and who was in charge of a number of Jewish refugee efforts in the Baltic and in Scandinavia, wrote in his final report that Raoul Wallenberg was responsible for saving the lives of 100,000 Jews.

It was a colossal achievement, but if the dispatches in this book give us the measure of it, we have to read between the lines. Rather than triumph, we find Wallenberg's frustration. In the sentence, "Money has been requested — but not obtained," we can read the inaction of others too far away, or too uncaring, to contribute to the cause. I find it one of the saddest sentences ever written. Another is, "Those who were most eager to send me here have not seemed to understand that funds are essential. There is endless suffering to try to ease."

And there is an endless amount to remember in this anniversary year. The Raoul Wallenberg Committee of the United States has initiated a multicultural, academically interdisciplinary study of nonviolent heroes for children in grades kindergarten through eight, called *Raoul Wallenberg: A Study of Heroes*. There are excellent Holocaust programs throughout the United States and Canada. The United States Holocaust Memorial Museum in Washington, located at 100 Raoul Wallenberg Place, and the Simon Wiesenthal Center in Los Angeles are both superb sources for information. Across the United States and throughout the world there are Raoul Wallenberg committees and individuals who work tirelessly to educate the public about this compassionate and nonviolent hero, and to assist in solving the mystery of his fate.

By introducing the man behind the cause, *Letters and Dispatches* will help us all remember.

Rachel Oestreicher Haspel
President
The Raoul Wallenberg Committee
of the United States

SELECTED BIBLIOGRAPHY

Adachi, Agnes. *Child of the Winds*. Chicago: Adams Press, 1989.

Alexander, Lynn. *Safe Houses*. New York: Atheneum, 1985.

Anger, Per. *With Raoul Wallenberg in Budapest*. New York: Holocaust Library, 1981.

Berg, Lars. *What Happened in Budapest*. Stockholm: Forsners Förlag, 1949.

Bierman, John. *Righteous Gentile*. New York: Bantam Books, 1983.

Bjorkman-Goldschmidt, Elsa. *Ur den Varld Jagmott*. Stockholm, 1967.

Dardel, Fredrik von. *Raoul Wallenberg: Facts Around a Fate*. Stockholm: Proprius Förlag, 1970.

Derogy, Jacques. *Le Cas Wallenberg*. Paris: Editions Ramsay, 1980. *Le juste de Budapest,* revised version, 1994.

Fant, Kenne. *R*. Stockholm: Norstedts Förlag, 1988.

Forbes, Malcolm, Jr. "Raoul Wallenberg." In *They Went That-a-Way*. New York: Simon and Schuster, 1988.

Freed, G. B. "Humanitarianism vs. Totalitarianism: The Strange Case of Raoul Wallenberg." *Papers of the Michigan Academy of Sciences, Arts and Letters* 46 (1961): 503–28.

Ginzburg, Eugenia. *Journey into the Whirlwind*. Translated by Paul Sevenson and Max Hayward. New York, 1967; reprinted 1975.

Haspel, Rachel Oestreicher. *Raoul Wallenberg: A Hero for Our Time*. New York: Raoul Wallenberg Committee of the United States, 1981; revised, 1985.

Hinshaw, David. "Sweden's Neutral Policy in Two Wars." In *Sweden: Champion of Peace*. New York: 1949.

Isaksson, Borje. *Omojligt uppdrag: Raoul Wallenberg kamp i Budapest*. Stockholm, 1975.

Joseph, Gilbert. *Mission sans retour*. Paris, 1982.

Karelin, Victor. *Das Buch von Raoul Wallenberg*. Freiburg, Germany, 1982.

Kung, Andres. *Raoul Wallenberg Yesterday, Today*. Stockholm, 1985.

Lester, Elenore. *Wallenberg: The Man in the Iron Web*. New York: Prentice Hall, 1982.

Levai, Jeno. *Black Book on the Martyrdom of Hungarian Jewry*. Zurich: Central European Times, 1948.

——— *Raoul Wallenberg*. Translated by Frank Vajda. Melbourne, 1988.

Lichtenstein, H. *Raoul Wallenberg — Retter von Hunderttausend Juden*. Cologne, 1982.

Linnea, Sharon. *The Man Who Stopped Death*. Philadelphia, 1993.

Marton, Kati. *Wallenberg*. New York: Random House, 1982; reprinted, Arcade Publishing, New York, 1995.

Moshinsky, Elfim. *Raoul Wallenberg Is Alive*. Jerusalem: 1987.

Philipp, Rudolf. *Raoul Wallenberg: Fighter for Humanity*. Stockholm: Fredborgs Förlag, 1946; revised edition, 1980.

Raoul Wallenberg Committee of the United States. *Raoul Wallenberg's Children*. New York: Raoul Wallenberg Committee of the United States, 1991 (December).

Rosenfeld, Harvey. *Raoul Wallenberg — Angel of Rescue*. Buffalo: Prometheus Books, 1982.

Shifrin, Avraham. *The First Guidebook to Prisons and Concentration Camps*. Berne: Stephanus Edition Verlags AG, 1980.

Sjoquist, Eric. *Affgren Raoul Wallenberg*. Stockholm: Bonniers Förlag, 1966; revised, 1974.

Smith, Danny. *Lost Hero*. Springfield: Templegate, 1987.

Strobinger, R. *Das Ratsel Wallenberg*. Düsseldorf, 1982.

Swedish Institute, *Raoul Wallenberg*. Translated by Victor Kayfetz. Stockholm, 1988.

Szel, Elisabeth. *Operacion Noche y Niebla*. Madrid, 1961.

Terelya, Josyp. *Witness*. Milford, Ohio: Faith Publishing Company, 1991.

Trepper, Leopold. *The Great Game: Memoirs of the Spy Hitler Couldn't Silence*. New York: 1977.

Villius, E., and H. Villius. *Fallet Raoul Wallenberg*. Stockholm, 1966.

Werbell, Fredrick E., and Thurston Clark. *Lost Hero: The Mystery of Raoul Wallenberg*. New York: McGraw-Hill, 1982.

Wulf, Joseph. *Raoul Wallenberg*. Berlin: Colloquium Verlag, 1958.